*Early Morning*

Also by Kim Stafford

# Early Morning:

## REMEMBERING MY FATHER, WILLIAM STAFFORD

Kim Stafford

*Graywolf Press*
SAINT PAUL, MINNESOTA

Publication of this volume is made possible in part by a grant provided by the Minnesota State Arts Board, through an appropriation by the Minnesota State Legislature, a grant from the Wells Fargo Foundation Minnesota, and a grant from the National Endowment for the Arts. Significant support has also been provided by the Bush Foundation; Target, Marshall Field's and Mervyn's with support from the Target Foundation; the McKnight Foundation; and other generous contributions from foundations, corporations, and individuals. To these organizations and individuals we offer our heartfelt thanks.

MINNESOTA
STATE ARTS BOARD

NATIONAL
ENDOWMENT
FOR THE ARTS

Published by Graywolf Press
2402 University Avenue, Suite 203
Saint Paul, Minnesota 55114
All rights reserved.

www.graywolfpress.org

Published in the United States of America
Printed in Canada

ISBN 1-55597-372-8 (cloth)
ISBN 1-55597-389-2 (paperback)

2  4  6  8  9  7  5  3  1

Library of Congress Control Number: 2002102959

Cover design: Christa Schoenbrodt, Studio Haus

Cover photograph of William Stafford: Christopher Ritter

Fontispiece photograph: Mike Markee

# *Contents*

# *Prologue*

IT'S MORNING, BEFORE FIRST LIGHT, 1965. I'm with my brother Bret at the tailgate of the family station wagon on the gravel shoulder of a road. We grope by dark in the back of the car where our bikes lie tangled in a heap, the pedals and handlebars locked together. We drag them out, work them free, then stand them side by side.

"Ready?" Our father's voice from the dark.

"I guess so." My brother.

"You lucky kids." Our father puts one hand on my shoulder and another on my brother's. I'm shivering, partly with joy. Daddy has given up his writing time before dawn and brought us to the top of Chehalem Mountain, so we can start our bike ride to the Pacific with a long coast downhill. The real work, the climb over the mountains and the thickening traffic, will come later, but he has given us this easy beginning. Then he is in the car, turning back across the road, heading east, and we watch his taillights dwindle toward home.

My brother is older, so he goes first, clambering onto his bike and gliding west down the dark road. He disappears into the gloom. Then it's me in a rush—cold wind in my face, knuckles clamped, damp smell of the forest, gravel popping from the wheels. In time, the sun rises behind us, touching everything green with gold—fields and trees, a blur of mailboxes, the dashed centerline of the road. Then sweat. Fire in my lungs. My brother a speck at the top of the road's long climb. No water. That tight passage called the Van Duzer Corridor where giant trees crowd the twisting highway. Cars on a curve ripping past within inches, and my wheels skidding in gravel toward the ditch.

How long can you feel a hand, steady on your shoulder, after that hand pulls away?

ৡ

# The Way It Is

There's a thread you follow. It goes among
things that change. But it doesn't change.
People wonder about what you are pursuing.
You have to explain about the thread.
But it is hard for others to see.
While you hold it you can't get lost.
Tragedies happen; people get hurt
or die; and you suffer and get old.
Nothing you do can stop time's unfolding.
You don't ever let go of the thread.

WILLIAM STAFFORD
1914–1993

*I.*

*You Follow*

# My Father's Place

A FEW DAYS AFTER MY FATHER DIED, I needed to sleep alone at the home place, to go back to the room I shared with my brother when we were young. Mother was away. I came to the house after dark, found the hidden key. In the home labyrinth, your feet know the way. Down the hall in the old garage, I turned into the study my father had built, where I stood a moment: dark walls, dim rows of books, papers on the desk, the making place. Then up two steps to the kitchen, a turn down the hall, and into the room of childhood.

For the first time in years, I slept deeply from the moment I lay down—until I woke at around 4 A.M. Mother had told me that since his death she, too, had been wakened at my father's customary writing time. As I opened my eyes, the moon was shining through the bedroom window. The house was still, the neighborhood quiet. Something beckoned me to rise, a soft tug. Nothing mystical, just a habit to the place. Lines from a poem of his came to mind:

> When you wake to the dream of now
> from night and its other dream,
> you carry day out of the dark
> like a flame.

This beckoning before first light brought a hint from my father's life, and I accepted it:

> . . . . . . . . . . . . . . . . . . . . .
> Your life you live by the light you find
> and follow it on as well as you can,
> carrying through darkness wherever you go
> your one little fire that will start again.
> —*from* "THE DREAM OF NOW"

3

I dressed and shuffled down the hall. In the kitchen, I remembered how my father would make a cup of instant coffee and some toast. Following his custom, I put the kettle on, sliced bread my mother had made, and marveled at how sharp my father had kept the knife. The plink of the spoon stirring coffee was the only sound, then the scrape of a butter knife. My father's ritual pulled me on: I was to go to the couch and lie down with paper. I took the green mohair blanket from the closet, turned on a lamp, and settled in the horizontal place on the couch where my father had greeted ten thousand early mornings with his pen and paper. I put my head on the pillow just where his head had worn through the silk lining and propped my notebook against my knees.

What should I write? There was no sign, only a feeling of generosity in the room. A streetlight brightened the curtain beside me, but the rest of the room was dark. I let my gaze rove the walls—the fireplace, the dim rectangle of a painting, the hooded box of the television cabinet, a table with magazines. It was all ordinary, at rest. In the dark of the house my father's death had become an empty bowl that filled from below, the stone cavern of a spring. I felt grief, and also abundance. Many people had written us, "Words cannot begin to express how we feel without Bill. . . ." I, too, was sometimes mute with grief. But if my father had taught me one thing about writing, it was that words *can* begin to express how it is in hard times, especially if the words are relaxed, direct in their own plain ways.

I looked for a long time at the bouquet of sunflowers on the coffee table. I remembered sunflowers are the state flower of Kansas. I remembered my father's poem about yellow cars. I remembered how we had eaten the last of his summer plantings of green beans.

I thought back to my father's last poem, the one he wrote the day he died. He had begun with a line from an ordinary experience—a stray call from an insurance agent trying to track down what turned out to be a different William Stafford. The call had amused him, the agent's words had stayed with him. And that morning, 28 August 1993, he had begun to write:

"Are you Mr. William Stafford?"
"Yes, but. . . ."

As he often did, he started his last poem with recent news from his own life before coming to deeper things. But I wasn't delving into his writing now. I was in the cell of his writing time, alive earlier than anyone, more alert in welcome, listening.

The house was so quiet I heard the tap of my heart, felt the sweetness of each breath and the easy exhalation. It seemed my eyes, as in one of my father's poems, had been "tapered for braille." The edge of the coffee table held a soft gleam from the streetlight. The stack of magazines was jostled where he had touched them. Then I saw how each sunflower had dropped a little constellation of pollen on the table. The pollen seemed to burn. The soft tug that had wakened me, the tug I still felt, wanted me awake to ordinary things, to sip my bitter coffee, to gaze about, and to wait. Another of his poems came to mind:

> How still earth stayed that night at first
> when you didn't breathe. I couldn't believe
> how carefully moonlight came.
>                     —*from* "Letting You Go"

The way moonlight touched the curtain seemed to be instructing me how to breathe, to think, to wonder. My father had said once that time alone would allow anyone to go inward, in order to go outward. You had to go into yourself to find patterns bigger than your life.

I started to write ordinary things. Then I came to the sunflowers. This could be told wrong if I tried too hard. My father's way is not about trying, not about writing poems, not about achievement, certainly not fame. His way is being private before first light, with your breath, the scratch of the pen. His way is something like worn silk, a blanket, and that dusting of pollen from the sunflowers.

My head fit his dent in the pillow. My hand moved easily with the pen:

> pause at the gate to take off the one big shoe
> of his body, step forward light as wind.

In the uninterrupted abundance of my own time, I finished a page, closed my notebook, and rose for the day. As my father would say at such a time, there was much to do but I had done the big thing already.

Who will take my father's place in the world of poetry? No one. Who will take his place in this daily practice of the language of the tribe?

Anyone who wishes. He said once the field of writing will never be crowded—not because people can't do important work, but because they don't *think* they can. This way of writing is available to anyone who wishes to rise and listen, to put words together without fear of either failure or achievement. You wake. You find a stove where you make something warm. You have a light that leaves much of the room dark. You settle in a place you have worn with the friendly shape of your body. You receive your own breath, recollection, the blessings of your casual gaze. You address the wall, the table, and whatever stands this day for Kansas pollen.

"There's a thread you follow," my father wrote. Deep night, and early morning, my page of writing, pollen on the table—these were the filaments I would need in the work he left me.

# Executor

THAT MORNING BACK HOME was my first experience in a strange role for which my father had been preparing me all my life. By the time our father died in 1993, my older brother Bret had been dead five years. I sensed that my sisters, Kit and Barbara, had each been close to our father in their own ways, but he had not asked them to take charge of his literary work. Our mother, Dorothy, was spared. I was the writer, the teacher, the one who worked at Lewis & Clark College as my father had before me. Three months before his sudden death by heart attack, he had summoned me to go over a copy of his will. When I arrived from the house where I lived alone, a mile away, my parents had official papers stacked on the dining-room table. From among them, my father picked up the will. As usual with such formal things, he was cavalier. "It's only money," he said. But then he put his finger on a sentence that riveted me: "My literary executor will be my son Kim."

"Daddy," I said, "that sounds like a lot of work."

"You'll be great at it."

My whole instruction was this one sentence for the mysteries that reside in the poems, notes, daily writings, letters, manuscripts, photographs, audiotapes, and other documents that constitute the William Stafford Archive—some sixty cartons—and in my memory. I'm still trying to decipher the code.

After my initial shock, I accepted the idea that someday far in the future I would be his literary executor. He had published over fifty books and thousands of poems in magazines. I supposed I would ship my father's papers to some library and let the experts put it in order. My job, really, was my own writing. Then came August 28.

By all accounts, my father's last day had been his version of a perfect one, perhaps even in the way it ended. Twenty-five years before, he had written a note to himself, "Let me die at the right time" (Daily Writing, 27 August 1968).

He rose early, settled on the couch before dawn to write a great poem, shared breakfast with my mother, went to his desk to "do the hard things first"—in this case a book review challenging Carolyn Forché's anthology *Against Forgetting* for the *Hungry Mind Review*—took a glorious nap after lunch, and responded to a flurry of letters. (One friend received not one but two letters my father wrote that day.) Then my mother called him to the kitchen. She had been making a cream pie when the blender exploded, scattering lime pie-filling everywhere. She called, and in a moment he came in from the study. In good spirits, he went to work cleaning up the mess and turned to her.

"Better get another spatula," he said. Then, without another word, he fell backward to the floor. When my mother heard how hard his head hit, she knew he was gone.

Mother called my youngest sister Barb, who rushed over. The paramedics came. They covered him with a sheet and asked my mother to fill out the paperwork. They took him away.

Once we had all gathered at home, we survivors sat at the kitchen table. We talked and we cried. Mother, hurt and beautiful, sat where she always sat—the side of the table nearest the kitchen work. Kit and Barbara were holding each other close. I found myself at the foot of the table, opposite my father's empty chair. In our small circle the conversation swelled, but then faltered to the kind of silence where my father would have turned us outward abruptly, almost heartlessly toward the events of now.

"How about some tea?" he might have said. Or, "Dorothy, I'd better go water the beans. They don't know Bill died." His mind would not obey proper grief. With a start, I realized my own mind was wandering: "His shoes," I thought, "are too small for me."

We were numb, but knew he would have made a sorry invalid. He liked to be in charge—not of others, but of himself. He had begun to write poems about turning eighty, his birthday just a few months away; they were not inviting views. My mother had told me once that the way he described his own father sounded like a good description of himself: "Quiet, but unquestionably dominant." When we were learning to drive, at an intersection he urged us to "be decisive—no dithering around." That is exactly how he had crossed to the other side. As one friend put it, "When Bill would die, his spirit would go out in one burst of light."

The next day, when we could go into the study, we saw all the busy clutter of his desk—letters coming and going, his low-grade computer, photographs, books, his camera bag, and his hat. One of his letters caught my eye: "I'll send flight info later." Another: "Keep us alerted . . . Adios." But beside the keyboard was one page with only four big words:

And all my love. Stunned by those last words, I turned over the page—the letter was from a friend in Wisconsin, reporting hard news:

> I mourn the death of my father on July 31. He was eighty-three and lived a good life, though I wish his last years had been happier. . . .

We passed his last page hand to hand. When it came a second time to my mother, she opened a window into the past.

"Oh, Billy," she said. She looked at me, at Kit, at Barbara. "When we were living in Elgin at the beginning, and having a hard time, I left. I was pregnant and feeling bad. For some reason Bill couldn't help me, couldn't care for me, be kind. I went back to California to be with my mother. We were so poor, and things were tough. I just didn't know if I could do the kind of life we had. Bill wrote me a letter saying it was cold in Illinois and would be cold; he was poor, and probably would always be poor. He said he didn't want to live with a baby. He said I should decide. I got on a train for Elgin."

She looked down at the page—the shaky letters, but four clear words. "One time I got discouraged and went for a walk by myself. When I came back, and went into the bleak little apartment we had there, Bill was gone to work, but on the table was a knife, and half an apple, and a note with those same four words—'and all my love.'"

"So he remembered," I said. "How long ago?"

"Almost fifty years," she said. "He must have felt. . . ."

"Felt something coming."

"Yes. But he remembered. Isn't that just like Bill?" We held the page to the light of the window.

"Love" wasn't a word my father used. He signed his letters "Adios." He often said, as a rule for life, "no praise, no blame." He would shake his head to indicate a slant kind of approval, and when we gave him a really good present for his birthday—a ten-speed bike—he was uncomfortable. The unspoken deep affection he lived by was like the idea in his poem about the Eskimos—their disdain for "People who talk about God." In his world, a fact so pervasive as love need never be named. But at that moment he broke with his custom when secret pain told him it was time.

The thin box of paper that always held my father's most recent writing was there on the desk, and together we opened it. Although his correspondence that day was filled with plans for future projects, journeys, and gatherings, the words he wrote in the privacy of his last waking seemed to announce an end:

28 August 1993

"Are you Mr. William Stafford?"
"Yes, but. . . ."

Well, it was yesterday.
Sunlight used to follow my hand.
And that's when the strange siren-like sound flooded
over the horizon and rushed through the streets of our town.
That's when sunlight came from behind
a rock and began to follow my hand.

"It's for the best," my mother said—"Nothing can
ever be wrong for anyone truly good."
So later the sun settled back and the sound
faded and was gone. All along the streets every
house waited, white, blue, gray; trees
were still trying to arch as far as they could.

You can't tell when strange things with meaning
will happen. I'm [still] here writing it down
just the way it was. "You don't have to
prove anything," my mother said. "Just be ready
for what God sends." I listened and put my hand
out in the sun again. It was all easy.

Well, it was yesterday. And the sun came,
Why
It came.

"I'm [still] here writing it down. . . ." I knew he used brackets sometimes
for words he might omit in revision, but hadn't quite let go. This time,
though, the word "still" is of another dimension. He is still; he is still here;
he is here in a way more quiet and implicit than any careful use of the com-
mon language might convey. He is still here writing it down, just the way it
was—and is, and will be.

My father's last poem has helped me to imagine this book. When I look
at his poem's sense of overlapping time, I recognize that it provides a way to
shape this story—a story that develops not chronologically, but by accumu-
lation. As Jean-Luc Goddard said of his approach to creation: "Every film
should have a beginning, a middle, and an end—but not necessarily in that
order." Working from memory with a complex subject, I have no other
choice. When my father wrote that last poem, was it an end, or a begin-
ning—or was it a middle, a hinge-point between before and after?

We didn't know it then, but we had begun what he called "that slow
dance over the fields" with his departed spirit. We would find things from
him, remember things about him, learn from one another, dream, and cre-
ate new ways to know him that had not been possible when he was alive.
For my mother, this new partnership began with a dream several nights
later, in which my father announced firmly to everyone, "Don't silence

Dorothy. Dorothy's meant for living." This dream was a gift to her, and she began to shoulder the hard work, with help from friends, of responding to the bushels of letters and cards that came to her.

My sisters and I planned a gathering at Lewis & Clark College, where many shared recollections of William Stafford the teacher, the writer, the friend. Shortly after this, I began to lose track of the rest of the family and felt myself pulled into my father's ongoing career. As I slid down this solitary path, I thought back to my father's own withdrawal from the family after my brother died. But his withdrawal from us had been isolation by grief; mine was frenzy for work: setting up the literary estate, trying to interact with a family lawyer, the Social Security ritual, the Death Certificate, biographical facts for writers of obituaries, and not least the ongoing rush of publishing imperatives for poems and projects my father had in process. I called on my friends, and they helped me set up procedures for the most crucial deadlines. Everyone was working hard, and I couldn't help thinking it took half a dozen of us to keep up with the output my father had habitually conducted alone.

In a hundred phone calls I learned the rhythm of revelation.

"Kim! How nice to hear from you. . . ."

"And good to hear your voice. I have some hard news. . . ."

The closer the friend, the less they could say: "How's Dorothy? Okay. Good-bye."

Each night at my own house I would fall into bed, sleepless, stunned. Once my girlfriend called at 2 A.M. I wasn't responsive to her needs, she said. She was in grief. Hadn't she loved Bill, too?

❧

# Slow Dance over the Fields

W̲HEN LETTERS AND CARDS BEGAN to flood the house from his friends—notes from Robert Bly, Naomi Shihab Nye, Eugene McCarthy, and Jimmy Carter among the hundreds—we decided to make copies of a William Stafford poem to send out in response. We urged mother not to write a personal note to everyone, but of course she felt she had to. Hadn't Bill answered everything? She had a heritage to maintain. With her notes we sent one of many consolatory messages my father had written over the years. His poem "Assurance" seemed to be a way we could raise our faces and talk back to the darkness around us:

> You will never be alone, you hear so deep
> a sound when autumn comes. Yellow
> pulls across the hills and thrums,
> or the silence after lightning before it says
> its names—and then the clouds' wide-mouthed
> apologies. You were aimed from birth:
> you will never be alone. Rain
> will come, a gutter filled, an Amazon,
> long aisles—you never heard so deep a sound,
> moss on rock, and years. You turn your head—
> that's what the silence meant: *you're not alone.*
> The whole wide world pours down.

After several weeks, I was wearing thin, and I needed to spend some time with my daughter Rosie. Eleven, she cried when I first told her about her grandfather's death. But then she cheered up. In some ways she was more like him in her grief than anyone: you did what the world needed and licked your wounds alone.

On a visit she burst through the door and said to her grandmother,

"Greek Mama, want to see my new Barbie?" (She had adopted the terms "Greek Mama" and "Greek Papa" at an early age, when she could not master Grandma and Grandpa.) My mother tried to develop enthusiasm for the Fashion Barbie but made a poor showing. Undeterred, Rosie went through the house showing others how the little shoes fit, the coat, the veil, the purse in hand.

My own grief had been volatile. I was distant and tender by turns. Not so Rosemary. She was confident, with all the swagger of age eleven. When I grew silent, she demanded, "Dad, what's wrong?"

"I'm just thinking about my daddy, I guess."

"Bill lives in his house," she said. "He's just there reading. He doesn't read books. He's listening to us. He doesn't say anything. He doesn't need to."

After a few weeks, I took Rosie camping at the beach. We set up the old family umbrella tent at the edge of the dunes, built a fire, made our meal, and then went by moonlight toward the beach. It was a lucky Oregon night—no rain, and the drama of high clouds crossing the full moon. We climbed the highest dune, tumbled down its open flank, climbed and tumbled again and again in the dark, laughing in spite of sand down our shirts, and all that had happened. Then we rested at the crest, where moonlight made the dune grass shine.

"Rosie," I said, "you haven't cried, except that one time. You seem pretty happy."

"Dad," she said, "I have my feelings. I just don't show them the way others do." We looked out across the horizons of the dunes, and then the waves.

"I don't have to hold on to Bill," she said, "and I don't have to let him go. He's part of me." A breeze rustled the dune grass. Distant, the breakers smacked down like a drum.

"There was something in his face," she said, "no camera ever got—it was his calm. I have his calm." She leaned toward me. "And nobody really dies. There are just five people: Sad, Shy, Curious, Angry, and Happy. Everybody comes out of those five, and then goes back. I'm not even a girl, really—I'm just kind of a mind-ship. . . ."

Suddenly, I missed my father, wanting him to hear that. She was teaching what he taught—to listen everywhere.

We climbed and tumbled down the next dune, then walked to the edge of the waves, turned south, came back north, and staggered to camp.

As I drifted off toward sleep in the canvas smell of our old tent, sand in my toes, her words in my head, I felt the slow return of my father. Rosie's words recalled his delicious freedom—surrendering to writing without a plan, to the self you are.

Back in town, I would pick up a poem or a letter or a page of thoughts my father had typed for himself just to keep track of his daily response to what he called "the emergency of being alive." As I read I sensed his company, heard his voice, entered into what he was thinking and feeling.

Eventually I went to my father's collected poems of 1977, *Stories That Could Be True,* to find what my journey with Rosie had recalled.

### With Kit, Age 7, at the Beach

We would climb the highest dune,
from there to gaze and come down:
the ocean was performing;
we contributed our climb.

Waves leapfrogged and came
straight out of the storm.
What should our gaze mean?
Kit waited for me to decide.

Standing on a hill,
what would you tell your child?
That was an absolute vista.
Those waves raced far, and cold.

"How far could you swim, Daddy,
in such a storm?"
"As far as was needed," I said,
and as I talked, I swam.

I love that. Robert Bly calls it the most important poem by a parent for a child in the twentieth century. The poem was clearly important to my father, too, since he kept revising it all his life, often reading a different version in public performance than the one published in his book. The first draft from June 1959 includes some tantalizing phrases useful to me in grief:

Out there the waves revised and revised their world. . . .

Waves of change were revising mine; the deaths of my brother and then my father had left me as the man in the family. I had to revise my life. What was the new horizon of my responsibility? Farther down:

You waited for me to decide
whatever the day should mean.
There was no way except [for me] to seem steady,
gazing where we turned: a father is to read well.

As he revised those lines, our father grew stronger. He would not "seem" steady, he would be so. He would not "read" well, he would say what he believed: "As far as was needed. . . ."

For me it was otherwise. I needed my *child* to tell me how it was. On the dune by moonlight, when I asked her to tell me about her grief—asked for her story by name—I heard her most amazing self appear.

In his last year, my father had taken me aside. "Rosemary keeps to herself when she visits us," he said. "She goes her own way when she is around us, and that's good. She needs to be independent."

Now I wonder. In his poem he needed to be steady for Kit. Most expressive in his poetry, he could be reticent in life. Was he only pretending Rosie's independence didn't hurt him? Was he protecting me by adopting an attitude of ready distance, or protecting her, or himself? Was he really talking about how he had learned to let me go, into my own busy life? What did he think when he was not in the presence of witnesses like us?

In the archive of his writings, where I had found my father's successive versions of his poem about Kit, I also found a copy of a letter he had written to Rosie. He had enclosed two of his photographs—one of Rosie looking wild-eyed as she blew out the candles on her tenth-birthday cake, with her young cousin Marah in the background. He identified their faces, with his unique humor, as "the manic child," and "a certain vicious child." The other was a photograph of himself. With his hair comically brushed forward and a sad clown's scowl, he looked like Moe of the Three Stooges. He identified this as "the Indian man." Even knowing my father's reckless affection, I find this a very unusual communication to a ten-year-old granddaughter. This is how he taught her to love:

Dear Rosemary,

 With the enclosed pictures I introduce you to some regrettable branches of the family. I believe it is time that you learn and beware of certain parts of your background.

 The manic girl with the big eyes and mouth is a relative of yours. You may even be able to detect in yourself some of her characteristics—for instance, letting your true self appear in a wild state at birthday parties. The little face beside that wild girl is another relative; I think she grew up and took the part of a certain vicious child selling Bibles in a movie called "Paper Moon." Don't ever go see it.

 The Indian man is an uncle of mine, part of our tribal background. He is not a very nice man, as you can see. Don't ever talk to him or go for a ride with him in his car or on his horse.

Your saintly grandfather—
Holy Willie

"Holy Willie's" greatest wish for those he loved was this: we would let our true selves appear in a wild state. And not be saints.

ॐ

# *Dear Folks*

O N THE DAY MY FATHER WOULD DIE, I woke by starlight outside
our family's handmade country house north from the town of Sis-
ters, Oregon, a hundred miles from home. In the dark, I listened to coyotes
yapping and wailing in the meadow before me. I looked up at the stars, just
beginning to dim, and remembered my dream: a man lay dead in a gutter,
with a rope around his head, and I was lost and alone. I knew he was a
father, though he did not look like mine. With a flashlight, I wrote that
dream into my pocket notebook and then rose to greet the day. I needed a
big day to finish the novel I called "Affinities: Voices from the House of
Travelers."

The day before, when I first sat down to work, I had felt the urge to
write my parents a note of gratitude, to recognize what they had given me.
When I returned from mailing it, I plowed through a day of glory at the
desk. That night I slept deeply under the stars, and waked to the dream of
a father lost, and went to work. The altitude there makes summer morn-
ings cool, and afternoons hot as the sun swings west, but then wind comes
softly through the pines.

To start the prologue to "Affinities," my fifty little stories set in Paris,
I searched through fragments in my notebooks—inklings, glimpses,
hints:

love turns to grief, and grief to stories.

how you see your own life from far away—and suddenly it is later.

All stories in "Affinities" are told to a woman in a coma—Asia—in
an effort to invite her back. "You traveled so many roads, maybe I
will cross the thread of your memory—that crossroads of the heart
you touched so often."

With these and other bits before me, I sat down to write the prologue addressed to my main character, Asia. I had written her story, but now she was silenced and I needed to speak to her soul.

In the morning, I was wrapped in a blanket. By noon, I didn't notice anything but the pages before me. By afternoon, I had my prologue.

> Asia, can you hear me? . . . They say you can't. That no matter what I say, your sleep will go on. They say I can speak anything into your silence, and it won't matter. They say I can't say anything to hurt you, that I can sit here by your bed as long and as often as I like, for you have gone so deep you hear no one. . . .

I sat back, looked out at the meadow. Everything was calm, still, easy. The sun shone behind gold aspen leaves. I stepped outside to listen to the wind, to feel the low sun on my face and hands with a sense of a whole book in me and stillness all around. Time moving steady like a river. I was witness to the long journey of Asia, who slept and perhaps would not wake, while a devoted voice told stories into her silence. . . .

The phone. It was Mother.

"Kim, I have some bad news. Bill had a heart attack and died."

I got in the car and started east to tell my sister Kit at her house ten miles distant. I flowed past the pioneer barn at Camp Polk, the old school at Cloverdale, then through that stretch of empty juniper land. When I turned into her drive, Kit's horse looked up, her dog came bounding forth, and then she came through the gate, happy to see me. I told her the news. We sat in the dry grass and cried. Then we started west over the mountains, where at the top of the pass she rolled down her window to shout, "We love you, Daddy! Hear us!"

Several days later I went alone to my father's study to sit in his swivel chair, turn slowly and feel—his absence, or his presence? I gazed at his shelves of books, the scale for postage, the worn black leather camera bag, the window facing south into the yard. I turned over things I found, but carefully, so I could return them to exactly the position he had left them. Among the papers spread wide on his desk, the scatter of his last day's work, and the note of four words, I found my letter from Sisters, open where he had left it:

27 August 1993

Dear folks,

   Before plunging into my writing here at Sisters, I pause to write
you both this note of gratitude. It's hard to say exactly for what.
This place, this time, my life, my curiosity. . . .

I put the letter down. It would not lie flat, but stood up from the creases I
had made in folding it to fit the envelope. My last words to my father had
reached him.

   I looked up at his favorite books, worn to tatters. On the shelf, the cam-
era he held so often his hands had worn through chrome to the body of
brass. His old hat, punished by rain and sun. And then I turned to the wall
of his own books. I crossed the room and read the titles: *West of Your City,
Traveling through the Dark, Allegiances, The Rescued Year, Stories That Could
Be True,* and on through the fifty titles arrayed there on the north wall,
spines blue and purple, gray and brown. But my hand went out to the thin
green one—that odd pale green so popular at mid-century—his first book,
*Down in My Heart.* This was my father's 1947 master's thesis describing his
experience as a conscientious objector during World War II. Long closed,
it opened only stubbornly.

   From my childhood forward, my father had been so productive a writer
that when asked about the release of his next book, his answer was often,
"Which one?" But this, the first, the one co-authored by World War II,
was bedrock. It was an artifact from deep in his life, a book he called a
"peace relic." Now I was the literary executor, and this book was in my care.
I opened it to the prologue where the narrator, my father, talks to one of
the characters, George. I remembered George was loosely based on my
father's pacifist friend, Chuck Worley. In the book, George has refused
all cooperation with the U.S. government, gone to prison, enacted self-
starvation, and finally drifted into a coma. As I read the opening lines, I
heard my father speaking softly in the room:

   I'll just sit here by your bed, George, and talk to you quietly
   tonight, maybe for a long time, because I don't know when I'll get
   a chance again. I don't know whether you can hear me or not, but
   I'll talk along anyway, in hope. . . .

The hair on the back of my neck stood up. I couldn't breathe. I stared at the words, so similar to the words I'd written in my novel on the day my father died: "Asia, can you hear me . . . ?" Then my father's voice spoke to me:

> It's getting dark outside; you can hardly see the trees along the drive now, and the lamps near the gate are on. There were a few flakes of snow when I came out from town, but I can't tell now whether it is snowing. The whole hospital is quiet, and the man in charge of this floor said I could stay as long as I wanted to. It's unusual, he said, but they don't know what to make of your case. . . .
>
> I want to talk through to you, George, a collection of stories I made of what happened to us in the war years. I don't know whether you can hear it, or whether anyone ever will; but I want to say these things, because we are a lost people—you and I and some others—and we saw an event that few others could experience, a big event that made us silent and engulfed us quietly. . . .

I closed the book and fit it with shaking hands back to its place on the shelf. Hard things in my father's life were rhyming with hard things in mine. I felt his words teaching me that all of life and writing come to this: you speak to a silence while time engulfs you.

In time, I might find clues to my father's isolation, and to my own. Divorced five years, I lived alone, often at odds with myself. In my writing, I tried to bring a woman back to life with stories. If my father spoke to his mute friend George, and I to Asia, what was our need? And what was our chance of being heard?

The office where I stood was a hive for thousands of busy words, quietly waiting. Surely, my father was on the road and would be home soon. Or he was alone in the desert, exploring back roads. Or he was at a meeting with some eager stranger who had called, out of the blue, and asked for his help. I could call out to him any time. Wasn't he in the next room, the workshop, fetching the right tool for our work together? Or was he in this room with me, trying to tell me something I couldn't quite hear?

*II.*

*Among Things That Change*

# Stories from Kansas

O NE EVENING ON THE ROAD I was talking with William Kloeft-corn, the Poet Laureate of Nebraska, and I realized this was my chance.

"Bill," I said, "what can you tell me about the town of Beatrice? That's where my mother's people lived."

"Oh, God," he said, "that's the most conservative town in America. You could come back to Beatrice after twenty years away, and everything would be exactly the same. Comforting in some ways. Or suffocating." He thought a moment. "Beatrice . . . ," he said. "Kim, there's only one town like it, and that's Hutchinson, Kansas."

"Hutchinson!" I said. "That's where my father's from! I got that conservative slant in stereo?"

"Makes you wonder," he said, "doesn't it?"

If my destiny has been Midwest heritage, West Coast upbringing, what can that combination mean? If Beatrice and Hutchinson are so alike, maybe that's what made my mother and my father, meeting in California during World War II, recognize each other's homesick Midwest ways. Maybe the twin anchor of our family heritage in the Midwest had a moderating effect on our childhoods, as we moved eight times, zigzagging across the country in search of something that felt like home. Was it moderation? Training in silence?

For my father, the prone memory of Kansas was a kind of magnificent flat mountain, a quiet paragon. Plain, it was the source of abundance. Distant, it was the standard for comparison in all dimensions. I was watching my father when a family friend, asking about our experience on a recent journey, spoke of a landscape we had enjoyed. "Was it pretty or was it flat?" she said. My father winced. For him, flat country was the definition of defenseless beauty.

I have since learned the Kansas motto, *Ad Astra Per Aspera,* "To the stars through difficulty," or "After struggle, heaven." And I have heard a Kansan report, "We are a state unused to literary affection." But my father poured lavish praise on every feature of that endless horizon. It wasn't just a good place that laced through our childhood like a thread of gold; it was the one and only good life. If you dropped a plate while setting the table, he would say with delight, "Woops!" Then, as he helped sweep up the shards he would explain that "Woops!" was the Kansas word for "Excuse me." What a joy that outlook was for a child! Why apologize for a "mistake" when you could celebrate the unpredictable? Or he would tell how the boy at the Kansas picnic, when asked whether he was full, replied, "Oh no, I ain't full—I'm just down to where it don't taste good no more." My father never got enough of Kansas. The ecologist's observation on the biota of tall-grass prairie mirrors my father's reverence for deep life there: "Prairie life is 80 percent below the surface." From the roots of Big Bluestem grass to the stars above, for my father Kansas was *it*.

Once when my parents were passing through the Midwest, they stopped in a vacant little town all alone on the prairie. Even my father reported there was nothing there. It was 5 A.M., and a young fellow came out from the service station to see what they needed. But first he looked up at the big sky, took a deep breath, and exclaimed, "Smell that air!"

"He was a rich man," my father said.

It wasn't all sunshine in those stories our father told us when we were young. But even the darker Kansas tales were told with verve. He remembered going as a young child with his parents to sit in their Model T Ford and watch the Ku Klux Klan march across a field in their robes of slit sheeting in the early 1920s. His mother would gesture toward the marchers, guessing the names: "Isn't that so-and-so?" Gossiping for pure pleasure about the subversive foolishness of their friends and neighbors was the Stafford family's recreation.

> Our mother knew our worth—
> not much. To her, success
> was not being noticed at all.
> "If we can stay out of jail,"
> she said, "God will be proud of us."
>                     —*from* "OUR KIND"

He remembered his family, in one version of their truth, as intimate and supportive kin. But there were other remembered versions as well:

*A Catechism*

Who challenged my soldier mother?
  Nobody.
Who kept house for her and fended off the world?
  My father.
Who suffered most from her oppressions?
  My sister.
Who went out into the world to right its wrongs?
  My sister.
Who became bitter when the world didn't listen?
  My sister.
Who challenged my soldier sister?
  Nobody.
Who grew up and saw all this and recorded it and
kept wondering how to solve it but couldn't?
  Guess who.

In such a landscape, where did my father get his fierce sense of inclusion, his world-citizen view? Was it from his parents? Or from the character of the prairie, the "quiet of the land"? In many ways, the Kansas of his childhood was a rough place. Within his own family, his aunt Madge was verbally devastating in her toxic assessments of the people lined up as in a shooting gallery just for her. Years later, in a letter my father reported some of Madge's classic remarks as she surveyed the hometown—Hutchinson—from a moving car:

This old car runs too fast. I can't drive in funeral processions.

There's the Shears'—she had an eye out last week.

There's the Golberg place—paid $25,000. Cancer.

It must have been Madge and the kinfolk who gave my father his pleasure in "talking recklessly." It was always a lucky time when he would announce, "Since we're talking recklessly. . . ." And then we could say anything.

> Mine was a Midwest home—you can keep your world.
> —*from* "ONE HOME"

Titles of my father's poems hint at his affection: "Stories from Kansas," "Prairie Town," "Tornado," "Earth Dweller," "What I Heard Whispered at the Edge of Liberal, Kansas." His poem "The Rescued Year" reads like the first draft of a novel, nubby with the texture of felt life: " . . . empty silos . . . all along the Santa Fe . . . the creed . . . my sight is a river . . . the greatest ownership / of all is to glance around and understand." When I pour my reading self into a Kansas poem of my father's, it's like entering a photograph by Walker Evans or Wright Morris, stepping into wise sensation.

> Which of the horses
> we passed yesterday whinnied
> all night in my dreams?
>> I want that one.
>> —*from* "STORIES FROM KANSAS"

When he sent his first book of poems home to his brother's family, he wrote on the flyleaf the last line from "One Home": "Wherever we looked the land would hold us up." Certainty in the past tense—that was my father's Kansas.

His Kansas patriotism saturated our childhoods. Any topic that arose in family conversation would—like water seeking the sea—arrive eventually at some comparison with Kansas. "In *Kansas*," my father would say with emphasis, and then the authority of perfection—good or bad—would be revealed: the best kind of evening, the most pungent smell, the most unusual gossip, the strangest character. My father's Kansas legends were behind all we did as a family, the places we went, the people we met. His private writings show how Kansas informed his experience. On one family trip, for example, he reported what came to him as he stepped outside our motel in Canada.

> I remembered something, a part of my life so pervasive and important that I hadn't missed it when it ended: the slow ritual of summer night—all quiet and distant, all dimensions wide, all sounds blended, all colors mild, time held still. . . . Religions have tried for

this. Cathedrals claim to achieve this. Kansas, every summer night, had this.

—DAILY WRITING, 13 JULY 1960

Wherever we went, he was accompanied, and so were we.

He must have begun telling Kansas stories to me early in my childhood, for at the periphery of my own memories I find Cow Creek (ridiculous name, but the glory of his boyhood in Hutchinson), the Ninescah, the Smoky Hill, the Cimarron. I felt I was there when Billy held the end of the trotline for catching channel catfish as his father hurled the baited hooks into the deep. And my father's stories of traveling to Colorado in a $25 car, or of hiking cross-country as a boy, eating a robin, drinking rain from pools in the rock, sleeping in a cave—all that heritage gave us a biblical origin for adventure, morality, and joy.

In his daily writing one morning in the 1950s, my father reported that "Shakespeare carried all his past with him, twisting it any old way to meet the present. Like a gypsy in a wagon, he had it all with him." For my father, Kansas was that wagon where he could rummage for whatever he needed.

His mother was Ruby, his father, Earl. We viewed the grandparents we never really knew as royal heroes of threadbare perfection: "Poverty plus confidence equals / pioneers. We never doubted" ("American Gothic"). His sister was Peg and his brother Bob. There was the tribe of nine cousins Bob had with Mar. With Peg, there was uncle Bill Kelly and their two boys. Our visits with them all were mythic quests into the golden land—the long delirium of the drive from Oregon, the short, sweetly chaotic affection of the visit, and then the coming away.

> My family slept those level miles
> but like a bell rung deep till dawn
> I drove down an aisle of sound,
> nothing real but in the bell,
> past the town where I was born.
> —*from* "ACROSS KANSAS"

My father reached back all his life for what he had as a child, or almost had. He yearned toward Kansas, and the poems made this yearning visible, audible, strangely eternal. I didn't know until after he died why we never lived

there, never moved back. Like so many questions, this one had the enig-
matic answer that rings like a refrain in my father's life in the aftermath of
World War II: Why did my father come west? The war. How did he meet
my mother? The war. What set him on his path as outsider, pacifist, soli-
tary? The war. And why not move back to Kansas? Because his pacifism in
the war cut him off from home. He couldn't go back, he could only go on.
And yet, perhaps because his exile from home was lifelong, my father's love
for Kansas was pure. In a short, unpublished account of his life he wrote in
the mid-1960s, he tells about his beginnings there:

> All of my life has been accompanied by certain mild, persistent
> presences. In the little towns where our family lived we used hand-
> me-down furniture—Grandpa's old humidor, Grandmother's
> marble-topped dresser. For a while we lived in one of Aunt Mabel's
> houses; from that town her Hay, Grain, Feed, and Seed Store seeks
> me out, a constant beautiful smell like all the Kansas fields at once.
> Aunt Madge would chug up the alley, past the hollyhocks, in her
> Model T, delivering margarine wrapped in newspaper. Mother
> would be in the kitchen or sometimes would be ironing in the
> dining room all a long afternoon. At a certain sound today I hear
> Father turn onto the gravel drive at supper time, home through
> those regular blocks laid out by the compass. We always knew
> where north was.
>
> All was leisurely, to the tempo of the porch swing, those slow
> years growing up. Every day seemed endless. And the nights—I
> never did understand them because they were always there and
> gone, somewhere. I never could stay awake through one. . . .
>
> These days I must look back to my father, my mother, now even
> a brother too, gone. Far, far longer than they might have guessed I
> have lived; but I reach for them, easily. As I write, it occurs to me
> that I am accompanied by a perpetual sense of chosen austerities:
> for all those people I hold a certain poise in my might; whatever
> comes, their presence has already given me great bonuses. Gently
> their presence accompanies my life, on and on.

Gently, persistently, inescapably, this Kansas heritage was to be ours as well.
My brother inherited a quest that sent him repeatedly away toward an

older path, toward smaller, more primitive places than our home in Portland. I believe he was seeking the little towns and old ways that our father fed us from the start.

When we stopped at Coronado Heights in western Kansas on one of our early odysseys, I ran away from everyone to be an Indian for an hour. I forced my way through a thicket of poison oak and climbed a bluff, where I stood up breathless on the gritty eminence. Before me the long grass was ocean, the wind low music crawling toward me. What I saw I could not possess, but would never forget. My gaze across that wide land became my recollecting vision for the long week after, as I writhed itching in a Colorado motel, smeared pink with Calamine while the others hiked the Rockies. For that week I lived a sample of my father's life, gone from the good, remembering. I remembered the prairie pond, the eager, intimate willows, the suspended zone in the water where jewel-like bluegills shimmered in the sun.

I remembered a lazy river leading a green ribbon of the wild through civilized farms on the plain, the arching cottonwood shade forming a house for a free child. I remembered the thrill when my Kansas girl cousins, big and beautiful, spotted a cute guy on the street outside, ducked for cover behind the parlor couch, and shrieked in a husky whisper, "Grody!" The wide prairie and exuberant love.

I had my own physical taste of Midwest glory on a few indelible occasions. Although our family never lived in Kansas, we spent a year in farm country, Indiana. On my uncle Oscar's farm when I was still small enough to get lost in a field of young corn, I first came upon the wonders of an artesian well. At the center of the open tank before me, water pearled over the throat of a pipe rising from deep in the earth and trailed splashing into the tank that brimmed and let the water run away down a ditch between the corn rows. The sun was low in the morning, and gold was everywhere—the tassels of the corn, the dust of the road, and the happy lip and lip of water spilling and spilling without cease.

That's how Kansas lived in our lives when we were young and far away in Oregon—always rising, always golden, tireless with untouchable glory. After my father died, I paid a pilgrim's visit to the Flint Hills north from his hometown in Kansas. I saw how the flat land formed his mind: the slightest tilt of topography would send a prairie stream wandering, obeying every nuance of imperceptible slope to turn this way and that like the supple variety of his mind—just the kind of thread of free thought and self-contained right action my father followed all his life. I watched a wolfish spider carry a lizard's tail into a turtle's track in mud—just the kind of compact natural emblem I find in his poems again and again. I rubbed my thumb in the silk pod of milkweed—the sense of home in the local, the immediate universe of small glories where "God is not big; He is right." I felt in my own body the benevolence of his childhood, a sweetness he never forgot, even when World War II sent him into exile.

> Forgive me these shadows I cling to, good people,
> trying to hold quiet in my prologue.
> Hawks cling the barrens wherever I live.
> The world says, "Dog eat dog."
> —*from* "SOME SHADOWS"

Only after my father died I began to share his feeling: shadows clung to me from far away. They reached for me in dreams and memories and my father's poems. When I took up my father's writings about Kansas, the Great Depression, and World War II and beyond, I realized that for him to enter the solitude of writing was like a return there, a journey back to kinship with the dear departed, with his youth, his hard-won escape from time's cruelty. For a few moments he could jump off the train furious to depart the world he loved, fall through the dark, and roll safe in the deep grass prairie—just for a moment. Then he had a poem, his passport to a place outside time that would enable his poise in the present. All through our childhood, before first light, in his writing time our father lived far away.

# Radio Show Called the Thirties

PERHAPS THE 1930S WERE NOT A BETTER TIME. There were lynchings, prejudice, and hatred. No penicillin. The Great Depression made life hard. But it was a time with unusual gifts for some. And in that time, the young William Stafford received his basic allegiance to honest human life that I consider—along with my mother's similar sympathies— my own most mysterious inheritance.

What will a writer be without patriotism (except allegiance to all people), without materialism (except a love for objects resonant with story), without ambition (except to be utterly honest)? What my father did not have turned out to be his source of greatest power. And together with this power William Stafford got two assignments at the end of the 1930s: one was the writing of a thesis for a master's degree in English. That one he completed by writing *Down in My Heart*. The other assignment was World War II itself: survive it, question it, tell others. He labored at that assignment for the rest of his life. When he stood on the railroad platform to say good-bye to his father in the winter of 1942, they would never meet again. My father went off to Civilian Public Service camp (CPS), a university for outsiders.

During World War II, the country's climate shifted—shifted like a sudden ice age from which we have not recovered. My father believed reconciliation should be a basic approach in all dealings with what others might call an enemy. I need to get back there to glimpse the development of his belief. For I was raised—schooled by him and by my mother—in ways they learned in an isolating time during the war and after, a time where they each had to live by the conscience of an internal exile.

On the eve of World War I, Sir Edward Gray uttered a prophetic sentence: "The lamps are going out all over Europe; we shall not see them lit again in our lifetime." This sentence was paraphrased often in the letters my father's family wrote to one another during World War II: "Things will

33

get better when the lights go on again." I'm not sure for my father the lights ever did come on again. Not on a national scale.

The insight reaches back to Thucydides: "The strong do what they can and the weak suffer what they must." But the trick is to know who is really strong. As our parents taught us, the "victory" that ended the war—with a bomb that calls all biological existence into question—left America in the position of being the weak bully forced to rely again and again on armament rather than diplomacy. In the 1930s this strange predicament was developing; but at the same time, by contrast, so was the character of my pacifist father.

His was a life of constant, quiet witness. In his last year, friends asked him to take part in a panel on cultural differences as manifest in significant writers. My father chose to represent Gandhi by providing a series of questions that show a convergence—Gandhi's ideas, my father's phrasing, and the understanding he seemed to have acquired very early in his life:

> Can a good person be a good citizen in a bad country.
>     Is there such a thing?
> Can a good person be a good friend of a bad person?
> Can you speak truth to power?
> How loud do you have to say no to an evil command?
> How softly can you safely say yes?

I begin to hear Gandhi fall away, and my father speak through his own experience:

> They give you a flag and watch how hard you wave it.
> Should your effort be to overcome those who oppose the
>     good as you see it?—or should you try to redeem them?
> No matter who. . . .

In that closing ellipsis I hear a series of names, the "evil" men we have somehow created by pouring our trust into military power: Hitler, Tojo, Kaddhafi, Khoumeni, Saddam Hussein, Slobodan Milosevic, Osama bin Laden. . . . In my father's view, appeasement and military frenzy are two forms of human weakness. He lived the middle way by strength through conscientious witness for reconciliation, not through force.

Somewhere in my father's youth—the marvel of Kansas in the 1920s and 1930s (if you start life poor, the Crash of '29 is not a threat)—he gathered all his faith in humankind and held it to the end. It was a "radio show called the thirties" for him, because the famous were far away, but the just were near. At the end of his life, he remembered the beginning, a parade when he was a few years old during World War I:

### Learning

A piccolo played, then a drum.
Feet began to come—a part
of the music. Here came a horse,
clippety clop, away.

My mother said, "Don't run—
the army is after someone
other than us. If you stay
you'll learn our enemy."

Then he came, the speaker. He stood
in the square. He told us who
to hate. I watched my mother's face,
its quiet. "That's him," she said.

Home life for the Staffords in the 1920s and '30s had its poverty and its troubles, but I sense from my father's poems and from his character that his was a buoyant childhood. Evil may have seemed more like a distant parable than a local curse. In fact, much about life in that time was surreal. His father once sent him an article about the rampant sin of Wichita, where a carpenter turned Quaker preacher named "Mr. Nice" led the cops on a raid of a speakeasy and found two thousand pints of moonshine behind a hidden door.

Then there was the Red Cross golf tournament during World War II—reported in another letter my grandfather sent my father—where the cost of the bullets in the military salute was more than the income from the benefit. And everybody played golf to show their patriotism. This is the kind of contorted world described by my father's poem "Serving with Gideon":

And now I remember The Legion—gambling
in the back room, and no women but girls, old boys
who ran the town. They were generous,
to their sons or the sons of friends.
And of course I was almost one.

Was he—almost? I believe my father was so severely free of worldly ambi-
tion he would not have recognized prestige as a gift. Instead, he watched
the ways prestige could be cruel:

in our town the druggist
prescribed Coca-Cola mostly, in tapered
glasses to us, and to the elevator
man in a paper cup, so he could
drink it elsewhere because he was black.
     — *both stanzas from* "SERVING WITH GIDEON"

He watched, he pondered, and he read. At my father's boyhood house
in Hutchinson, I've seen the porch roof under the shade of a tree—the
little outdoor room under the eave where my father spent whole summers,
climbing up to be alone with books. I've wandered the prairie of the Flint
Hills, the Sand Hills, the fringes of unambitious Kansas rivers with their
Eden of trees and vines, fragrances, turtle and coon and catfish. And I find
in poem after poem he spun from that time a world of spiritual comfort.
The Great Depression could be rich for a poor family that loved to read
and talk. Without prosperity, they were free to revel in the local and the
everyday.

that year did not escape me: I rubbed
the wonderful old lamp of our dull town.
     —*from* "THE RESCUED YEAR"

If I have not found the right place,
teach me; for somewhere inside, the clods are
vaulted mansions, lines through the barn sing

for the saints forever, the shed and windmill
rear so glorious the sun shudders like a gong.
　　　　　　　—*from* "EARTH DWELLER"

Part of what he describes may be the nostalgia of any grown person for the treasures of youth, but my father was talking also about the strangely rich civilization of the Great Depression, the 1930s in the heartland. In the world today, our president has a certain prerogative, our army a certain power, money a certain swagger. But if you live in a world where the elevator man has to drink his Coca-Cola alone, in a paper cup because he is black, what will your own way be?

Look down, stars—I was almost
one of the boys. My mother was folding
her handkerchief; the library seethed and sparked;
right and wrong arced; and carefully
I walked with my cup toward the elevator man.
　　　　　　　—*from* "SERVING WITH GIDEON"

When my father read that poem aloud, he often added the word "paper" to emphasize how tender both solidarity and courage can be: "I walked with my paper cup toward the elevator man." For the Sioux warriors of the plains, I have been told, the greatest act of bravery, called "counting coup," was to disarm an enemy without injury to him. To snatch away a spear or club without so much as scratching or even touching your foe—this was true courage. Killing was easy, and the act of a coward. Counting coup was hard, the act of a truly confident man.

I think of my father now, wielding a paper cup, a question, a level look, a poem. He was brave in the only way he could be, for the world had changed. Kansas and his childhood receded. He had to take the intricate wisdom he had developed in that time and carry it forward. He reports in one poem that his father had taught him how the softness of snow "can freeze the tiger's foot" and wind "can finally teach the rock."

# *Objector*

WHEN I REACH BACK TO KNOW the roots of my own pacifism, a strange scene comes to mind—typical in my apprenticeship of wordless messages from my father.

Where were we going, my wife beside me, my father sleeping in the back? I can't remember. Why were we driving through the night? I have no idea. The background is a blur, but I do remember I was at the wheel when a tire failed on a dark curve, and I fought the car thumping and weaving to a stop. Behind me, my father sat up, alert.

"Atta boy! Just right. Let's hope the spare is good." And we were out of the car to rummage in the dark for jack, tire iron, a block of wood to place on the soft cinders of the road shoulder, and the spare.

My wife held the flashlight, and my father stood ready to wave any cars on past. He stepped back to let me "have the glory," as he would say, allowing me to be the hero of small things. As I crouched to work the jack, I heard the distant buzz, a swarm of motorcycles coming our way through the night—big ones. This was California backcountry at a time when such a meeting could be dangerous. I glanced at my wife, her body grown smaller with fear, and I clenched the tire iron in my hand.

As the gang swung around the curve toward us, I looked at my father. He was standing with a theatrical slouch, the most pronounced nonchalance I had ever seen. His baggy pants helped the effect, and the way he leaned back onto his left heel, face turned up in good humor. It was the quiet, the insistent, the unmistakable posture of a pacifist. *Nothing is going to happen. You can do what you will. You will not draw me into violence.*

Headlights caught us. The gang slowed, stared, swiveled their shaggy heads to exchange glances, then accelerated and swung on past, their departing black fringe and chrome leaving me quietly shivering as I worked in the dark.

That glimpse of my father confirmed a lifetime of conversation and puzzlement about the ways of the peacemaker. The pacifist knows, "It is in the minds of men that peace is won." This was quietly a topic in our house from the very beginning. My mother once introduced a public library program by saying, "The biases in my life have been toward children, nonviolence, the natural miracle of the earth. . . ." From childhood, she had only the use of her left hand, and her ways as a parent were all about invitation and welcome, never coercion or force. Her father, a minister in the Church of the Brethren, had been a believer in nonviolence, and in that spirit my parents had always agreed. I know this was a home topic from an account in my father's daily writing from 1959, when he had heard me talking with my brother before sleep about war, "arguing in the dark":

KIM: I don't want to kill anybody, even if someone takes over our country.

BRET: God is on the side of the good country; he guides Theodore Roosevelt and Abraham Lincoln and George Washington.

KIM: But he guides the people who don't want to kill, too.

BRET: But they aren't famous.

Somehow our father had become a pacifist in the cradle of his own family from very early on. There is a story that when he was first in school, he came home to report that two black children on the playground had been taunted by the others.

"And what did you do, Billy?" his mother asked.

"I went and stood by them."

He didn't taunt, he didn't turn away, but also he didn't fight. He stood by them. (I can imagine his childhood version of the brave slouch of the peacemaker.) As with many facets of my father's character, this story shows that his family—the grandparents I never knew—may have formed him as a man of conscience and forthright witness, too clear and confident in his approach to resort to violence. At several points in his writing he refers to his father, vaguely, as a pacifist. And in a poem from May 1960, he reports a moment from his childhood, titling the poem with a phrase from the standard formula for justifying conscientious-objector status ("Describe the nature of the religious training and belief that is the basis of your claim . . ."):

### Religious Training and Belief

"You shouldn't go to war," my mother said:
"My father was a Russian, my mother was a German—
  they're both dead."

"My folks were Bohunk-Limey-Indian-Dago—
  they're dead too.
Pass the potatoes," my father said—"you."

If our father had been a pacifist from the beginning, he wasn't prissy about it. When I turned out to be a slow reader in grade three, my father promised me a gun if I got into the top reading group. I succeeded right away, and the pump-action pellet gun was mine.

My father claimed he could strike a match "from across the street" with his .22 when he was a boy. (The most interesting part of this story now seems to be the location of the feat—in town?) When he went away to college in the 1930s, he was the only student in his boarding house who brought his gun along. A roommate picked it up and shot a hole in the parlor wall; my father, the pacifist, had to give everyone a lesson in gun safety. Hearing stories like these as a child, I reveled in his verve, even as I absorbed his clarity about aggression: it's never okay. Nor, if you are alert, should it be necessary. Violence signals a failure of imagination.

I remember a trip to Kansas when we stopped in the shade by a prairie river. Our father surprised us all by producing his .22 pistol from somewhere in the car and inviting us kids to line up, pick out a target on the opposite shore, and see if we could nail it. How I loved that little gun: the blue steel cylinder spinning neatly on its axis, the crosshatch pattern on the grip, the hammer set on safety, or cocked back ready to strike. It felt natural in my hand, and even safe—once he taught us how.

For a pacifist, for a poet referring constantly to the "little lives" of the wild—the humble claim of prairie dog or quail—my father's habits of speech revealed a man schooled as a hunter from an early age. In a poetry workshop, he spoke often of hoping to "scare up" an idea in the process of roving through recollection. To my ear, that is a rabbit or pheasant flushed from the stubble of a Kansas field. The day before he was drafted, according to one prose fragment among his papers, he went hunting with a friend, who quizzed him:

"Do you think they'll put you in prison?"

"Yes. . . ."

"Does it scare you to think of all they might do?"

"I've got an imagination."

This little scene haunts me now, for "all they might do"—the glance of a nation at war aimed at the puny life of a pacifist, a "conscientious objector," a CO—in 1942 was severe. Yet despite his vulnerability, my father's ambition was boundless. A target of his own country's disdain, even hatred, he had begun his mission of universal reconciliation.

In a little town in Arkansas, a few months after that conversation with his friend, my father came close to being hanged when local hotheads learned he and his two friends were COs, "slackers," or in the mob's estimation "spies." The residents of the CO camp were already in trouble for helping an African American family, and for addressing their black neighbors as "Mr." and "Mrs.," against local custom. Then my father and two other COs went into town on a Sunday afternoon. My father's detailed account of their near-hanging in *Down in My Heart* is as riveting as anything I can imagine reading. Once the crowd got revved up, their patriotism turned to collective hostility, and things began to spiral out of control:

> "We ought to break that board over their heads," someone suggested. Several others repeated the idea; others revised the wording, expanded the concept, and passed the saying along. Some spoke of "stringing them up."

One of the COs with my father (the one who is, and isn't, the character George in the book) had written a poem that the crowd snatched from his hand and passed around, believing it to be some kind of code to guide the German army in their conquest of America. After my father died, I obtained a copy of that poem:

> McNeil . . . hmmh, some town McNeil
> Pronounce it Maac, like all the natives do
> Dilapidated, all run down, no civic pride
> Why should there be there's
> Nothing to be proud of here
> . . . . . . . . . . . . . . . . . . . . . . .
> And loaded freighters grumble thru at night.

"There!" shouted one among the mob as he brandished the poem in his hand, pointing to the last line. "That's information. That's them troop trains!" "It must be for a foreign power," another said. But even in the presence of this "subversive evidence" and the mob's hot mood, my father and his friends managed to stand, speak, reason—and stall—with enough quiet courage to mediate tempers until the sheriff arrived to save them.

A key moment in the drama was when one in the crowd demanded to know what my father was reading. It was Whitman's *Leaves of Grass*. Then the demand was what he had been writing. A letter. The demand to see the letter. Even in the face of this confrontation, when his life may have hung in the balance, my father refused to surrender the letter. He kept it in his pocket and quietly talked his accuser out of a chance to see it.

My father, even then, was utterly in possession of his life as a writer.

When I read the poem about McNeil that whipped the crowd's anger to a higher pitch, the poem strikes me as an act of aggression foreign to the pacifist cause. To be effective, the COs had to be more sensitive, kinder, and more aware than those around them. Reconciliation can't begin with either insult or judgment, both of which enact distance, but only with a recognition of affinity, which promotes connection. Prejudice is prejudice, and that incident in McNeil did not find its source among the local patriots alone.

Even at a distance, my father's position as a pacifist in that war casts a long shadow. His stance in wartime isolated him for life: "My country is No Man's Land" (Daily Writing, 13 May 1968). My cousin, running for class office in college at a little Kansas town, was taunted in the 1960s as "the nephew of that noted communist, William Stafford." My father told me once when he came home after World War II, his friends didn't want to talk to him anymore. His family was supportive, but his wider circle was broken. Again, it's mysterious how I sometimes learned the depths of my father's character only after his death, as when I found an interview that describes how his close friends in college abandoned him because of his views. They no longer wished to speak with him. He reported one of them saying, "I think you ought to be killed." He had departed from a sense of inclusion in the world of home into a life of often lonesome witness for tolerance in the world. As he says in the poem "Clash," which seems to describe a drama of domestic violence:

I hid in the yard.
Policemen would come for me.
It was dark; waiting was hard.
There was something I had to win.

He had to win a sense of his own destiny as separate from the hysteria
around him. A friend has pointed out to me that this is a poem about his
betrayal by "mother country."

. . . . . . . . . . . .

I did not have to kill.
Time had made me stronger.

I won before too late,
and—adult before she died—
I had traveled from love to hate
and partway back again.

The poem ends with the personal bargain that formed my father's life from
the war forward: "when I learned that great word—'Choose.'"

In *Down in My Heart* my father pointed out, "a war is a time of rest for
a pacifist; the war itself is an incident, a lost battle in itself; it is just a part of
those cheatings, bluffings, maneuverings, which we have got to stay out of
all the time." It was also a time, however, as evidenced by the book, for
fierce reflection on what brings aggression into play. He could learn from
fellow COs, as well as from the war-frenzied citizens who surrounded them,
that "anger is not conducive to perception" (from an interview in the 1990s).
My father believed "paying attention to the lens [of the mind] will help
you understand the image" (a separate interview, 1986). He tells in *Down in
My Heart* how easily available and yet often ignored are the common tools
for deeper understanding:

The face is what we use for getting acquainted. The face of Ken,
our camp mystic, was still and lined, with heavy brows and
steadfast dark eyes. In human affairs almost everyone shouts loud
enough, but few listen well enough. Ken listened.

In my own habits of mind I find a strange artifact of this family heritage. When I can be strong but humble in the face of a difficult task, I can begin without fear. Humility is power. To be common but right, to be ordinary but clear is to be difficult to defeat. My father would speak of this effect as a kind of jujitsu, where the aggressor's force becomes an advantage to the pliant but resilient resistor. Somehow I learned this from a father who called World War II the time when "I was in training to save us all" (Daily Writing, 1 August 1968).

I have been warned by COs from my father's generation that his experience, or rather his outlook on their common experience, was unusually positive. With the exception of certain contributions by COs in "detached service" (those who worked outside the camps in mental hospitals, for example, are said to have made lasting contributions toward a more humane treatment of the insane), many COs found themselves paralyzed at the sidelines of history. As one CO told me, "Bill regarded those years as rewarding but many did not." Another said that many COs in the camps felt they were simply "doing time." The camps, according to this peace veteran, were places to hide COs from a nation drunk on patriotism. Where my father reported a series of constructive experiences in peacemaking, others remembered years of disillusion. One CO said to me, "There wasn't a lot of discussion of pacifism among the men. I guess each man thought he knew what the others believed and there was no point in discussion." My father's account, as I remember from childhood and read in his writings, was quite different. For him, the war years were a time of intense inquiry into the world-citizen's daily work, and how to practice this in a nation that had toppled into patriotic violence.

My father was sustained throughout his life by a continuing thread of curiosity and witness. College continued his childhood fascination with reading; the years in camp continued his ethical inquiry from college; and his subsequent career as a writer continued the life of witness practiced at pacifist camps in wartime. Home never died, Kansas never receded, war was never resolved.

They were called "Conchies" by those who mocked them. Most who met my father and his fellow conscientious objectors defined them by what they would not do: they would not be soldiers, not kill on purpose. But the COs defined themselves by what they *would* do: they would actively seek alternatives to violence, and refuse to augment the killing. In their world apart during World War II, the COs in my father's account worked with great heart to envision a way to avoid the next war.

> It takes such an intricate succession of misfortunes and blunders to get mobbed by your own countrymen—and such a close balancing of good fortune to survive—that I consider myself a rarity, in this respect, in being able to tell the story from the subject's point of view; but just how we began to be mobbed and just where the blunders and misfortunes began, it is hard to say.

My father's book asks a series of questions, then answers with stories. "When are men dangerous?" "How can dangerous men, over time, become friends?" "When we are few, but right, how can we help each other?" And "What does victory—with Hiroshima—mean?"

In one incident in *Down in My Heart,* my father reports the arrival of the COs at a U. S. Forest Service camp in the mountains of California:

> At first some of the Forest Service men had talked largely, among themselves, when some of our men had happened to overhear, about their enmity for COs; and I myself had overheard one man, later our friend, say in the ranger station, 'I wish I was superintendent of that camp; I'd line 'em up and uh-uh-uh-uh'—he made the sound of a machine gun.

"One man, later our friend. . . ." No matter what an adversarial person says or does, for a pacifist, friendship is both future possibility and present approach. It is impossible to become an enemy without the consent of the victim—or as my father called the recipient of hatred, "the subject."

For my father, then in his twenties, this idealistic approach was the only way. In the words of one character in this book, "[an argument] isn't settled for us until everyone feels all right. I wish we could figure out a better way." The goal of the COs was not to win, but to include.

From the late 1930s, when he was a student at the University of Kansas, my father knew he was headed toward the isolating act of pacifism in wartime. His draft board in Hutchinson was headed by a retired military man who demanded where my father had come by his objection to war. Years later, my father relished repeating his reply to that interrogator: "You were my Sunday School teacher, sir, when I was a child. You taught me not to kill. I never forgot." Result: CO status.

Sunday School and war—it was a strange time. By my father's account, one of the ironies of a nation sliding toward war is how the threads that weave the fragile fabric of peace lie everywhere. German literature had been praised to my father since childhood. His great-grandfather had been a Civil War veteran, but his own father carried poetry folded into his wallet for solace, and had been nudged by World War I toward a pacifist temperament. A great tide of pacifism swept the country after the Great War, and the conscientious objectors of World War II were simply those who had failed to unlearn their belief in nonviolence.

By January 1942, my father was off to the CPS camp near Magnolia, Arkansas, where he joined several hundred young men who had come by many roads to their opposition to war. Amish farm boys, Mennonites, Quakers, and Brethren men all came from the traditional peace churches. Fundamentalists from Appalachia held the four words "Thou shalt not kill" sufficient cause. Intellectuals from Chicago and New York had been recruited to peace by the writings of Tolstoy and Pascal. One CO told me the most thoughtful men in camp were less interested in naysaying commandments, and more alert to a proactive vision, a search for a whole way of life informed by peace. He said one direct way of posing the question might be, "In war, what would Jesus do?" Nights by the stove in camp, though dead tired from a long day of doing "alternative service of national importance" with an axe or shovel, some of the men were yet wild with talk.

Separated from the militaristic fever of their contemporaries in uniform, but isolated also from domestic life on the home front, they were free to think bold thoughts, and they schooled one another in new ways to see history and practice human behavior. They pooled their books and made a library. They decided collectively to rise before first light and give their best energy each day to the life of the mind: classes, performances, debates, writing, reading, discussion. After the sun rose they would trudge off for the day shift, doing physical labor under the direction of the U.S. Forest Service, the Soil Conservation Service, and other agencies. There was a sense in the camps of time out of time. Daily life could be both radically restricted—the camp was a kind of prison—and also radically progressive. In that time, for example, military units were segregated, but the CPS camps were not.

In this camp school my father developed his lifelong habits of writing each day before dawn, of honoring fellow seekers of understanding from whatever background, of seeing in human cruelty episodes where we let "the fragile sequence break," but also might by heroic calm find our way back into community. Heroic calm: the courage to not agree when those around you capitulate by saying "All diplomatic alternatives to war have been exhausted."

Through his practice of writing evocative letters home, and poems, essays, thought-pieces of all kinds, my father gathered the manuscript for *Down in My Heart* and submitted it to the University of Kansas as his master's thesis in 1946. When the book was subsequently printed by the Brethren Publishing House in 1947, my father shipped a carton of copies home to his brother Bob, the bomber pilot, who proudly gave them away to friends and neighbors. The copy in the library at the University of Kansas is stamped "Gift of Bob Stafford, Fredonia, KS."

I try to imagine an antiwar protestor of my own generation passing along such a manifesto to a brother in uniform, a Vietnam veteran. In my father's family, the spirit of inclusion was manifest. "Bill," his brother said at the time, "we're both heroes, but your heroism is the harder kind."

In a letter home from the darkest days, my father reported that war "exploded our family apart." His brother was off to Texas in the air corps, his sister was married to a navy man stationed overseas, and my father was sent to Arkansas and then to an isolated camp in the California hills. Yet my father and his siblings remained very close. Shunned by most of his contemporaries outside the family, he continued to search for conciliatory links to the aggressive patriots around him.

In camp, the COs received $2.50 per month from various church resources. (A soldier my father met during the war said, "Two-fifty a month—that's not bad." "Two dollars and fifty cents," my father replied.) They cherished a typewriter here and there, a stash of paper, scraps of news, a new axe handle, a phonograph, sturdy work gloves, a book or a guitar or a lively song:

I got that opposition to conscription down in my heart,
    down in my heart, down in my heart.
I got that opposition to conscription down in my heart always.

They printed rugged magazines, wrote editorials, produced plays, per-formed CO versions of common college songs. They knew Amish people back home in Kansas, at a certain hour each day, would sing hymns for them. In camp, they might hold still at that hour and feel the hum. They knew many nearby despised them in dangerous ways. They could not stop the war or win the peace in a hurry. And yet, the most alert among them were as rich in spirit as anyone. As my father said, they were in this work for the long haul.

Having a pacifist father taught me that peace is a time not for rest, but for action. What we have called "peace" since 1945 was a time for quiet but sustained activism, and this is how my father lived his life. For over fifty years he and my mother were members of the Fellowship of Reconciliation, the international organization that undertakes a mission more intricate than the antiwar stance of some of my contemporaries. "If you want peace, work for justice," is one motto of the FOR. And my father, to the surprise of some during the period of the Vietnam War, questioned the demonstrators of the age. In October of 1968, he wrote in his daily writing:

> The people we found alien in the 1940s—pressing for victory, set-ting up the Cold War, developing the bomb, strengthening the West—have turned against the war in Viet Nam and have increased attempts to achieve 'social justice.' This change, too, is motivated and marked by much that still separates us: (1) aggression is a means of attaining ends, (2) the machinations of certain evil persons must be stopped, (3) distrust, punishment, stern behavior are essential.

When we watched high-decibel activism on television, my father would shake his head. The true pacifist, in his view, seeks peace in both the short- and the long-term, not stridency now for vague future ends. Many activists of my generation were fueled by fury, but the heroes of my childhood were another kind. CO visitors to our house were announced by a talismanic ut-terance from my father: "He was in CPS." I remember these visitors as lively, good-humored, both bold in thought and calm in manner. My fa-ther once told me when he was with someone from CPS camp, a "Saint from the Kingdom" as they used to say, he felt a golden light come into the room. It was an unusual thing for him to say, and memorable. "I don't know if others feel it," he said, "but I do."

My father once wrote, "Children of heroes have glory for breakfast" (Daily Writing, 22 August 1967), and that's what our house felt like when COs came around. Our father disagreed with almost everyone we knew most places we lived. We had humble fare but great resonance. It is hard for many to look back to World War II as anything but massive opposition to the bullies Hitler, Mussolini, and Tojo. To our father the bully had been war itself: "Of those atrocities used to justify the war—the atrocities proved and punished [at Nuremberg]—what proportion occurred before Germany was at war? War causes many of those evils used to justify it" (Daily Writing, 12 April 1967).

I sense that my father was lonely the rest of his life for the intensity of purpose he felt with others in camp. I have been told of the experience soldiers can have, no matter how horrific their combat: nothing at home can ever match the vitality of war, and this is the greatest secret they must keep from those they love at home. No one here, finally, can measure up to comrades in battle; no comfort here, finally, can outvalue the intensity there. How can soldiers tell their own young children details of the killing fields? But our father's stories from the war years were available, and connected directly to words and actions in present time. Still, I wonder if, after his heroic days as an outsider in war, my father found us kindly but tame. Our intentions were fine, but did we stake our lives on them?

Once you take the kind of stand he did—a pacifist in what some still call "the good war"—you may gain a lifelong habit of seeing connection where others see division. I remember an old professor in Kansas telling me after my father died, "Your father bridged two warring parties—the academic poets of the 1950s and '60s, and the younger poets like Bly and Wright. He had friends on both sides."

As the soldiers were sent home at the end of World War II—about seven hundred soldiers for each CO, my father noted in a letter to his brother—the CPS camps sent forth a generation of freethinkers in all directions. Perhaps the most visible but least important result of this diaspora is what has been called the "San Francisco Renaissance" of the 1950s and '60s. Before drugs turned it askew, this creative convergence began with an infusion of creativity from Brother Antoninus (William Everson), Glen Coffield, Adrian Wilson, Kermit Sheets, and others gathering in the Bay Area from pacifist centers like Camp Angel on the Oregon coast. Less visible but far more important, following their release in 1945 and after, were

the contributions by COs in higher education, the arts, the treatment of
the mentally ill, and international relations. The pacifist tribe had spent
the war years as artists and radical thinkers isolated together, seething with
ideas. Inside the camps the COs were broadening their conception of how
to make peace with foreign cultures and peace with the creative mind. New
ways to dismantle racial prejudice in the face of social inequality came
from reading the likes of Basho, Confucius, Walt Whitman, Gerald
Heard, Tolstoy, Ibsen, Goethe, and others (to mention only a few of the
book titles I remember seeing among my father's share of the camp li-
brary). Outside the camps, by contrast, citizens were swept up with fo-
cused ethnic hatred, reading magazine articles showing how to distinguish
a Chinese face (a good ally) from a Japanese face (a bad enemy).

Maybe real thought is the first casualty of war, a luxury to be aban-
doned like silk stockings. As my father wrote later, "It is the alternatives
that get lost when you / know you are right" (Daily Writing, 21 December
1968). Caught up in the frenzy of response to atrocity, it gets harder to
know what is true. In a poem called "History" (Daily Writing, 29 De-
cember 1957), my father points out that "every soldier / is justified (but for
fictions needed / to maintain discipline)." The objector who maintains
compassion for both sides, on the other hand, will suffer a more complex
predicament: "you have had an emotion, dreamed a thread / through time;
you feel the twinge of traveling, / the hurt that intelligence insists on
having."

"I have always felt that a raised voice was a mistake," my father said in
an interview the year he died, "in the sixties or anytime." After the Gulf
War, he published "Some Questions About Victory" in the *Hungry Mind
Review*:

> Is there a quiet way, a helpful way, to question what has been won
> in a war that the victors are still cheering? Can questions be asked
> without slighting that need to celebrate the relief of a war quickly
> ended. . . ?

After this opening, his questions become increasingly tough and searching:

> Maybe a successful performance that kills tens of thousands, that
> results in the greatest pollution in history, that devastates a nation,

that helps confirm governments in the reliance on weapons for security—maybe such an action deserves a cautious assessment? Maybe some people might be forgiven a few thoughtful moments amid the cheering?

I hear his voice here—quiet, intense, and intelligent. For a poet committed to the intuitive mind, he was a forthright thinker, private but political.

Does an outcome that surprised everyone confirm your faith in overwhelming armaments as the mode of security for your country? If so, do you think that other countries may reach a similar conclusion? Has establishing the superiority of your own terror made you feel secure against the terror that others have learned to be so effective?

As a child, I didn't often hear such directly challenging words from my father. I don't remember hearing him debate these issues in public or belabor them in private. But my parents' way of thinking was a consistent resource in our lives. I remember one example that can stand for many. Along about grade six Bobby Elliott wrestled my sweaty little body and pinned me hard to the ground. I remember the feeling in my arms I *must* overcome him, followed by the recognition I could not. Later, when I told my father, he said—in but one variation of the many enigmatic assurances that filled my childhood—"Wrestling is one way to win." He did not elaborate. It was up to me to figure out other ways by observing, pondering, practicing.

I remember playing war, leaping from behind a tree to fling dirt-clod "grenades" at my temporary foes—Pat, Bobby, Jimmy, my brother Bret. The clods were thrown high, in a long arc, and as they fell toward their targets we whistled the descending scale we had learned from TV replays of bombing runs over Japanese and German cities. Those games thrilled me for a time, but finally scared me, and then bored me. For eventually little warriors with dirt clods escalate to rocks, and then the game changes to real fear and hate. Or the game degenerates into a shouting match: "You're dead! I got you!" "Did not!" "Did too!" "I quit!"

Even in childhood, I was more interested in my father's tales of camp and the characters who walked the country barefoot and nibbled poison oak to gain immunity. Those who fought not men but forest fires. Those who quietly fought hate. Those who survived danger by the courage of their minds.

When I ponder how my father offered his CO heritage to his children, the story goes in many directions. For one, my sense of vocation. I teach at the college where my father taught. Campus to me is the Camp. I sometimes feel that my life is grafted to my father's life, that an old part of myself lived through the Great Depression, and my witness now might dissuade the pilot of the next Enola Gay. I know I am a believer beyond available evidence. This mythic focus keeps me blind, I am sure, to much of the cynicism that can creep into any institution that has a mission but is a corporation. Like my father, I keep to my destiny as I see it. A believer in reconciliation, I work at a college, but I work for a cause bigger and farther away—what my father called "the unknown good in our enemies." How did he offer this view to me, and to my siblings?

In 1966, our father addressed the parents of my peers in a Presbyterian conference on Vietnam. I have his notes before me. Again, his position is not combative, and his voice not strident, but his questions are unflinching:

> The strongest nation in the world, with no present danger to itself, acting without formal declaration of war, under firm military conscription, has burned, used gas, threatened atomic force, systematically invaded non-involved nations. Restraint must come from citizens. Hence our meeting. Coercion by violence has hardened much of the world; that feeling lasts. But moderating it is the patient, worthy job.
>
> We dominate the world; for the future it is essential that we reach community, not supremacy. The danger currently is to others. . . . Politicians need citizens who will permit them to behave reasonably. We must see in time that public opinion does enable rational leaders to moderate conflict. We can lose; we can pull back; we can seek not domination but conciliation.

This is what I was made to understand as a child in daily life: the "patient, worthy job" of the pacifist. I never heard my father or my mother shout. Neither ever spanked us. My brother and I didn't fight—physically or verbally. Our friends refused to believe this. How could it be? But to us the mystery was the opposite: Why would a sibling need to fight or a parent

shout? Even at a young age, we knew private action had larger conse-
quence. Anger was a world event: "That's how countries go to war." A
shout was a blow: "My friend, let's figure this out." Among the four kids,
there might be squabbles, subdued whining now and then, and episodes of
pouting when hopes faltered. But to fight was to fail. To raise your voice
meant you had forgotten. If you kept forgetting, you were sent to the
garage to sit alone on a cold step and "think about it."

Going back through my father's papers, I find conflicting sorrows that
schooled him to his steady ways. In 1943, while exiled in his remote
CO camp, he published a poem about his brother Bob called "Family
Statement":

> My brother, flying a plane in this war,
> > may come up that long ramp to the exit
> > and go into tomorrow.
> He may turn his face away from our small play by the
> > mulberry tree, and kill a man.

Yet there was no civil war in his family. Bob was a good soldier, my father a
good pacifist, and they relished news from each other. The objector does
not find fault, but seeks to understand another person's predicament. A na-
tion need not find fault in the people of another nation, but should seek
conditions of mutual benefit. When governments fail, individual people
must take charge. That is the hard, patient, worthy work.

My father's sense of distance from his country's swaggering ways went
forward from World War II all through his life. I remember him nodding
when Eugene McCarthy pointed out a subtle truth. The federal govern-
ment's change of name in the 1940s from the War Department to the
Department of Defense signaled a cynical consolidation of power by the
military. If a country is at peace, it can dissolve or at least diminish its War
Department. But if there is never any real peace, if the influence of a
country can only be maintained by military presence abroad and at home,
if a country's international bravado creates a succession of foreign tyrants
who worry us, then a continuous stream of revenue must sustain the De-
partment of Defense.

On his first trip to New York City in 1955, my father reports back to his
brother in Kansas about his walk all over the city—Greenwich Village,

Rockefeller Center, the United Nations. What he sees does not assure him:

> NYC impressed me as a strenuously *foreign* city; I hardly felt a part of those people's country. . . . The UN—big and impressive as it is—seemed feeble, helpless in the face of something big and organic seething all around it. My good wishes go to all efforts to organize and aid the society; my fears are that uncontrolled forces are really wagging the world. I even had a sense of being a bystander, and probably an innocent one—and perhaps an innocent victim—in my own country.

Is this simply the response of a Kansas country boy to the big city? From traveling with my father I know that such a contrast with home could exhilarate him. But his view was bigger than New York, bigger than the United Nations—for nations, after all, win and lose wars. But people always lose. As he wrote after the Gulf War, "In this war again humanity lost."

The philosophy of the CO position was part of our upbringing, but what about the practical decisions a young man makes in wartime? When I went to college in the fall of 1967, one of the most provocative images that greeted me was a poster on the wall behind the desk of my Spanish teacher, José Sobré—a black-and-white photograph of Joan Baez and two other happy *muchachas* with their legs crossed and their eyes full of invitation, a couch filled with triple promise below the words, *"Las muchachas dicen que sí a los muchachos que dicen que no."* (Girls say yes to boys who say no.) My good professor was trying to tutor me in the past perfect tense. But my heart raced. In the Vietnam era, for some, to be a pacifist could bring the embrace of the beautiful. Strange reversal. My father's poem, 1943:

> My brother is in the army that wins, swearing, proud of a flag.
> The movie stars are making him happy,
>> taking those long trips we read about and see pictures of.
> The common soldier is hero in this war:
>> my brother was one hundred yards away in the crowd
>> when a private, in a ceremony on a stage, kissed Tana Randis
>> (currently seen in "Land of Desire").

. . . . . . . . . . . . . . . .
My brother and I are both crying
     in this glittering chromium time
     in the saddest war.

—*from* "Family Statement"

Real ideas and quiet voices have long had a tough time in this country of ours.

In the spring of 1970, in Eugene, I was wakened by a call from Berkeley. A bail bondsman told me I had to come up with a thousand dollars to get my brother out of jail.

"My brother—Bret? That can't be. He lives right next door here in Eugene. He's not even *in* California."

"He's in jail, son. Trust me. The only way he's getting out is bail—very soon. I have to make a lot of calls. There are hundreds of them."

It was true. One day my brother was next door, a college student. Then he and his roommates decided to drive 700 miles through the night to Berkeley to see what was going on, and suddenly they were protesters. There was a romance to the troubles, and they didn't want to miss it. Not long before, he had shown me one of the questions on his sociology exam that in hindsight seemed a secret imperative to get out of the classroom and start learning from the world:

> To what extent can you explain individual student decisions
> whether or not to participate in the recent sleep-in in Johnson
> Hall by means of concepts contained in readings on socialization,
> group pressure, cognitive dissonance, or related material included
> in this course?

Could you best answer that question by thinking, or by research at the scene? Freshly arrived in Berkeley, they parked on a backstreet just as a demonstration surged from the campus to engulf them. The National Guard caught my brother and his friends in the throng, busted them, and herded them onto the sheriff's bus. They were booked, a Frisbee was confiscated, and they went to jail.

My first thought at the time: "Where am I going to get a thousand dollars?" And my next: "Why didn't Bret invite me to go along?" I scrambled for the cash and bailed him out, but now I wonder, "Why did my brother have the bail bondsman call me, not our parents?"

Bret had the privilege to be the first from the family to encounter our local draft board. Today when I read the board's mailing address, at a distance of three decades, the plain name of the street still gives me a thrill: Warner Milne Road. My brother went before them, and they worked him over. He had submitted documents from the family's Brethren past, including such direct language as "war is sin," and they had a field day with him. He was shaken, wouldn't talk about it. They granted him CO status, but he had earned it practically by hand-to-hand combat.

My way was easier, perhaps because he had cleared the path. My father was somewhere on the road when my appointment with the draft board was approaching, so I went to my pastor. He grilled me, attacked with skill and fervor every belief I had about the power of reconciliation. Then, unable to shake me, he wrote a glowing letter to my board, saying my family background was strong and consistently pacifist. "There is a warmth and compassion there," he wrote, "that grows out of a solid faith and takes shape in a nondestructive way." At my hearing, I looked up at a row of stern old men. They asked about the nature of my belief that was the basis of my claim for CO status. I gave a long speech they silently received. My testimonial included points from the CO application I had typed out the preceding night:

> The same religious training and belief which made me, as a child, opposed to the *idea* of war, now compels me to refuse the *act*. I cannot participate.

To my surprise, and strangely to my disappointment, they waved me through. I had imagined my part in our father's story, my own odyssey as a branded pacifist exiled to glory in the mountains. But instead my forms were stamped, and I was sent back to college to await the call.

I remember with surreal clarity the night of the Lottery, at the dark depth of the war in Vietnam. Anyone from those days will remember the Lottery, the official random chance by which each birth date was assigned a priority number for conscription. For me, it's one of those remembered scenes that is gut-strong in power but unreliable in detail. For my brother and for me, the mythic story of our father had come to bear on our own lives. I remember gathering in my brother's house with his roommates, the peace veterans of that Berkeley jail, to settle around the television and watch the national ritual on prime time. But there my grasp of detail softens. Was it really like a game show, a cage spinning with white balls, each stamped with a birthdate? Was there really a kind of celebrity emcee, and a token citizen onstage to take out one ball after another, line them up, and so establish which young men would be called to duty, and which would be spared? The heartless truth that night: life was a lottery, and war was television.

It's strange what such a time in history does. To some young men, young women said yes, and to others no. To some young men, the draft board said no, and to others yes. And then the lottery sifted through a generation. I wasn't chosen. I never quite mastered the past perfect in Spanish, but I kept living under my own spell from my father's past.

He had a song he learned from a Mexican on the fire-line, sometime in World War II. When we were too young to listen to the radio and music made at home was all we had, sometimes he would take down his old Stella guitar, the one he had traded a hatchet for during the war, and try to remember the words and the tune. He was a limited guitar player, and the guitar itself was a poor one. All I can remember of all he could remember is this one line: *Mas allá del sol.* "Beyond the sun"—what happens? For my father there was always that imagined place where people get along, where they have learned to be both congenial and direct with one another. How to get there? His path was a quiet one, insistent. From a poem he wrote during the war, I know the early version of his devotion to the way of the world patriot, the pacifist: "I won't walk another street until this one is worn out by the sun."

My father gently mocked me for my idealism on several occasions. I was such a dreamer, always making bold plans and suffering disappointment when institutions or other assumed allies—or my own abilities—did not sustain me.

He would look at me. "Kim. Oh Kim—the bitter habit of the forlorn cause."

I thought he was chiding my wasted effort. After his death, I found these very words in one of his poems. He wasn't mocking me after all. He recognized I had been infected by his own ways: "The bitter habit of the forlorn cause / is my addiction."

All his life, and throughout his witness in my life, my father sought the threshold where bitterness dissolves, where an exiled objector is welcomed home to a world that has learned inclusion, peace, and justice. In the last month of his life, as he wrote in the early morning of August 6, Hiroshima Day, he gave up his resistance and let himself believe:

### November

From the sky in the form of snow
comes the great forgiveness.
Rain grown soft, the flakes descend
and rest; they nestle close, each one
arrived, welcomed and then at home.

If the sky lets go some day and I'm
requested for such volunteering
toward so clean a message, I'll come.
The world goes on and while friends touch down
beside me, I too will come.

# Caesar Is with You

MY OWN ADDICTION NOW has become my father's company, how his voice comes back when I sit with his writings. As the days and weeks after his death have turned to months, to years, I spend time simply reading through the files. My experience in his archive can be volcanic.

I remember a story my brother told me long ago. The provincial government of British Columbia had decided to build a dam in the mountains in a big hurry—so fast they didn't fell the trees in the reservoir's canyon before the waters rose. There were claims about the recreational opportunities available to all, once the lake filled. But when the first citizens ventured onto the water in their pleasure craft, they found that—without warning—a great, buoyant tree in the deep might work loose from the earth and rocket to the surface. Soon, no one dared go there.

In the archive, a conversation, a scene, some isolated remark my father uttered deep in the past comes out of nowhere to seize my heart. Sometimes it is a silence I remember, or even a glance in my direction at a crucial moment. These arrivals can shock, or console. When I read, or simply sit in the presence of my father's papers, I witness memories striding into my mind like burly ghosts—"friendly but not tame." Since he is gone, my father can appear at any time.

After holding his papers in an office we rented above the Fat City Cafe in southwest Portland for several years, we had a scare. Going to work one day, I met firemen on the stair. There had been a grease blaze in the kitchen below, and the customary aromas of burgers and coffee were enriched by the dusky smell of burned paint. I asked if there was any danger.

"No problem," the fireman said. "It's under control." When I opened the door to the office, there was a hint of smoke, but everything was untouched: the wall of banker's boxes to my left, the door propped for a desk on double file cabinets, the old computer, the card table where we did our sorting, the bookshelves with first editions, and in the corner the box of tapes of my father's recorded voice. The jumbled tapes had not been indexed or copied: Studs Terkel interviews William Stafford . . . Stafford talks to Tom Averill's class in Kansas . . . Wm. Stafford reads "The Dream of Now" . . . Stafford talks to Henry Lyman . . . "The Animal That Drank Up Sound," read by the author . . . "New Letters on the Air" . . . and bootleg tapes of William Stafford giving readings all over. People had sent us their copies, and we didn't really know what we had. That would have to wait for another time.

I took out the tape of my father's last reading, at Portland State University, 13 August 1993, and put it in the player. In that shabby office, crowded with his papers and flavored by smoke, suddenly he was there in the room with me. It was from that poem again—"The Way It Is":

> There's a thread you follow. It goes among
> things that change. But it doesn't change.
> People wonder about what you are pursuing.
> You have to explain about the thread.
> But it is hard for others to see.

As often in his readings, his quiet voice electrified everything. The event of the poem began with my father's long, audible inhalation, like a syllable before the first word—commanding a silence his alert stance somehow enforced. And then the title enlarged syntax by embracing the first line:

> The way it is—there's a thread you follow. . . .

It struck me as a poem with incredible specific gravity. He read it through, there was a pause, and then he made a joke. Typical: "I felt like coming up here and making a bow, when Henry talked about my humility. . . ." Everyone laughed, released from the tough truth of his poem into the pleasure of his genial presence. This was the unique diplomacy of my father's public persona. A friendly messenger, he put us off guard, then stunned us with difficult treasure, then shrugged it off and stood before us like a grandfather fond of jokes.

I remember the scene. Henry Carlile, an old friend, had introduced my father that day. The packed room was windowless, getting warm. Several blind technicians from the public radio station were expertly fingering the controls of their recording equipment to one side. At the podium, Henry had told about arriving at my parents' house years before on his motorcycle for his first meeting with William Stafford, the quiet writer at home. My father's response—"my humility"—made us laugh because it was true, and not true. Yes, he was a humble man compared to some loud voices we knew. And above his desk, I knew he kept a quotation from Saint Catherine: "My visions make the soul more humble, as it gains a deeper and deeper knowledge of its own nothingness." Yet my father took on the role of a thoughtful Caesar when he gave a public reading—quietly in command. He knew how to make us laugh. "Do not be afraid," he would say, appropriating a notorious line from Latin class, "Caesar is with you."

I hunched over the tape player at our card table in the office, wanting to absorb every nuance of his voice. From that first poem, with the brief insulation of his joke and our laughter, he went directly into the next, a text we found later in his papers as a passage of prose, a farewell:

I haven't told this before. By our house on the plains before I was born my father planted a maple. At night after bedtime when others were asleep I would go out and stand beside it and know all the way north and all the way south. Air from the fields wandered in. Stars waited with me. All of us ached with a silence, needing the next thing, but quiet. . . .

I remember the breathless tone in the room, as we listened—no, as we *waited* through my father's words for that next thing:

A great surge came rushing from everywhere and wrapped all the land and sky. Where were we going? How soon would our house break loose and become a little speck lost in the vast night? My father and mother would die. The maple tree would stand right there. With my hand on that smooth bark we would watch it all. Then my feet would come loose from Earth and rise by the power of longing. I wouldn't let the others know about this, but I would be everywhere, as I am right now, a thin tone like the wind, a sip of blue light—no source, no end, no horizon.

After that declaration of departure, my father explained to us why he had read it. He said nothing about its message, his great distance from us already, how allegiance to his native place mattered more as mortality approached. No, he talked as if this evening were about poetry:

> Well, I felt a special need to scramble around for things I haven't
> showed to people or talked to people around here, because I was
> pretty sure a lot of people I know would be here, and that's true. So
> I looked for different things, things that haven't been published.
> The things that I have relied on too often, I put into another
> pocket, and I don't think I'm going to get them out.

This meant he would not read the strongest poems many of us knew from his work. He would make this occasion unique by surprising us with something more direct, more intimate than famous texts could accomplish. He went into one of his list poems, a "stunt," his "Sayings of the Blind." He announced the title, paused a moment to look toward the blind technicians at the recording monitor, let the richness of this exact convergence develop, and then began:

> Feeling is believing.
> . . . . . . . . . . . . . . . . . . . . . . . . . .
> All things, even the rocks, make a little noise.
> The silence back of all sound is called "the sky."
> . . . . . . . . . . . . . .
> Edison didn't invent much.

Who was this man, to read such proverbs directly to the blind? What was his form of humility, and how did he say good-bye? Come loose from Earth, he would "rise by the power of longing."

Today I take out his 1978 collection of poems, *Stories That Could Be True,* and turn it over to find the photograph that most looks like my father to me. Although the photo is attributed on the dust jacket to my sister Barbara, I know our father took it of himself. The evidence is clear: he stares the camera down, with the stern expression of a man alone, a seeker. (I don't remember him ever looking at me like that, but he *was* like that.) He is on the deck behind our house, his face framed by the sliding glass door where we had sawed a hole in the kitchen wall to let in light. You can see his left arm reaching to hold the camera toward himself. His hair is untamed, his face not quite in focus, the bushy gray of his eyebrows rangy, and his gaze both calm and fierce. In that image he is the quiet, poised, welcoming, hawkish, friendly-but-not-tame czar of my childhood.

One time, after my father had read a stunning poem to start a program, someone in the audience spoke up: "Do you want us to applaud," she said, "after you read a poem like that?"

"Applaud?" my father said. "I want you to get down on the floor and grovel!" Everyone laughed. Then things quieted down. He had us. But what was he saying?

One time my graduate advisor—an eminent professor—apologized for missing a reading my father had given at the University of Oregon.

"You can get away with that once, Stanley," my father replied, "but then you start to lose your chance." Caesar had spoken, not a humble poet one could ignore lightly. I watched my teacher not know how to take that. My father didn't explain.

At another program, after my father had read a poem that seemed like simple talk, a voice blurted from the audience.

"I could have written that."

"But you didn't," my father said, looking down at the upturned face. He waited one beat of silence. "But you *could* write your own."

That was it: there was an aristocracy of creation. Membership was absolute, but available. Forceful people were excluded, the proud, the pretenders—excluded because they declined "to be willingly fallible in order to find their way." But anyone who told their own puzzling story could be in the circle. Anyone who paid attention by writing or speaking their own truth could be Caesar of the vast, fragile empire of one life, and by that witness, join the tribe of seekers my father represented, and championed.

When my father would stand, after he had been lavishly introduced, and walk *empty-handed* toward the podium, he had a certain independent shuffle, an "I am out for a walk on the prairie alone" look. Then his left hand reached back, and by the time he turned to his audience he had unfolded a set of half-sheets of paper drawn smoothly out of his hip pocket. He would look at us and begin. No dithering, no extra moves, often no title—just the first thread of the experience itself.

This is the hand I dipped in the Missouri. . . .

A bomb photographed me on the stone. . . .

If you were exchanged in the cradle. . . .

Motorcycle, count my sins. . . .

He would put an arabesque in the air before us, a philosophic sculpture. There would be a beat of silence after the last line—and then my father would make what sounded like an apology, a turn from the substance of the poem to a friendly observation on the occasion of our gathering: "I just wanted to start with something that occurred to me recently. . . ." (Sometimes the friendly tone of this welcome would contrast starkly with the poem—designed to "give them a jolt," as he would say.) He would slip the poem into the fabric of our daily life. No matter how extreme the poem, it belonged to us all, because it came from a source available to anyone.

Once I accompanied my father on his circuit in Virginia. The journey had by his custom the easy rhythm of a seasoned traveler: a town, a motel, a nap, then a meeting "in good time" with the local host, dinner with a few local people my father eagerly interviewed (often deflecting their questions about him), the arrival at the hall where the reading would be, the friendly interchange with people as they came in, then the dimming of the lights, the host giving an introduction, and then my father rising to be our voice. I remember he had told me the poems in such a sequence should not all be good ones. "The temptation of the writer," he said, "to make each poem in a program stronger than the last is not a kindness to an audience. They need to have some rest." That evening, he gave them rest, but not in the form of a poem. He gave them a silence at exactly the right time. He had just read "Thinking for Berky," with its final challenge:

Sirens will hunt down Berky, you survivors in your beds
listening through the night, so far and good.

And then he paused, his face bent down, but his eyes looking at us. The room was still. Time abandoned us, went marching importantly away. Even that poem with its power and challenge receded into another realm.

By that silence we were gathered, held, deepened. The whole apparatus of travel, publicity, my father's career, individual decisions by members of the audience to attend that evening, the host's friendly welcome and introduction, the listing of my father's accomplishments, and even the poems themselves—these were all a prelude to the real treasure, that silence. . . .

Then my father spoke, and the tone in the room descended to poetry, to this place in Virginia, to his voice and our listening, and soon the program was over.

I remember thinking at the time he had conducted us to a hidden spring in the forest, the secret source of his words. In silence, in easy waiting, in the companionable alternative to haste—solitude—we might dwell. The magnitude of that place was there for all of us. A poem, a visitor was simply the guide for each life to find that place.

A few nights after my father's last reading in Portland, we held a program in his honor as part of the Portland Poetry Festival, a voluntary summer tradition that has since come to an end. In 1993 the festival was dedicated to my father. In addition to his reading, the festival included formal conversations about his work, readings by others at various locations around town, and an evening for him to receive our gratitude. A local actor, Keith Scales, scripted a passage from *Down in My Heart* to perform onstage; we hired a Mexican singer—a man named Candelario—to perform *canciones rancheras*. I remember standing onstage with both my sisters, as we took turns reading our father's poems back to him. He sat with our mother at a table below, and around the room were friends, wine, flowers. Barbara read "Assurance," Kit danced, and I read "Roll Call":

> Red Wolf came, and Passenger Pigeon,
> the Dodo Bird, all the gone or endangered
> came and crowded around in a circle,
> the Bison, the Irish Elk, waited
> silent, the Great White Bear, fluid and strong,
> sliding from the sea, streaming and creeping
> in the gathering darkness, nose down,
> bowing to earth its tapered head,
> where the Black-footed Ferret, paws folded,
> stood in the center surveying the multitude
> and spoke for us all: "Dearly beloved," it said.

I looked down at my father, his great hands folded, gazing toward us, or beyond us. Had his long life in poetry come to this?

I go back to the balance point, the moment after "Roll Call," after I said my father's words, "Dearly beloved. . . ." I looked down at my parents: my mother's winsome smile, my father's regal stillness, not quite knowing how to accept the homage of his children and his friends. If he was gazing far away, beyond us, so was I. For I remembered how "Roll Call" was written.

He was traveling—like his father who was by turns a traveling salesman, an oil company rep, a power company inspector—but for the work of poetry. He was coming down by train, he had told me, from New England into New York City, and he had been watching hills, farms, forest and field, and riverbanks with the mud prints of nocturnal creatures. As he got closer to the center of civilization, he started to see old refrigerators in those rivers, the bodies of rusted cars, the concrete debris of abandoned factories, and the thickening roads, bridges, wires. It was then he began to write "Roll Call." He had become the voice of the Ferret, prepared for travel of another kind. "Dearly beloved."

Long after my father died, I found a note he had written the year I left home:

Last night the kids in our living room stayed up to talk after
Dorothy & I came out to bed, and they were talking about us, or
about to do so—benevolently. I happened to think: this may be the
only, and is probably the best, memorial service I will ever get.
—DAILY WRITING, 27 MAY 1967

*III.*

*You Are Pursuing*

❦

# Obedient Crimes

I N  O U R  F A M I L Y  H O U S E, there were two unspoken rules: (1) don't do the wrong thing, and (2) don't live the wrong life. The wrong things could be itemized—little acts of selfishness that disregard the needs of others. But the wrong life was the absence of the right life, and this was a mystery. The right life had to do with generosity, I gathered, and friendship, celebration, art. But there was more, for the right life was beyond service to others. The source of that service—the seed of generosity and the source of creation—was internal, well hidden.

If both your parents are teachers, left-handed, Midwestern, frugal, soft-spoken, highly ethical, hard-working—and they expect you to serve the world wisely—what might you want to be when you grow up? What might be your source of power? In my case, sequentially over fifty years, I wanted to be a boy, with nature . . . and then a thief, with wealth . . . then a saint, with virtue . . . an Indian, with the wild . . . laborer . . . poet . . . seeker . . . partner . . . and father. It was only after my father died I realized the vocation "father" must include them all, the vocation where you: "Pull the bow: a gentle motion. / God will do the rest."

When I was a boy, beginning this journey, by some contradictory imperative I had to become a thief. In a household of good people, little crimes felt necessary. It was a way to grow taller fast. Or a way, strangely, to practice the good life by inventing it on your own. My criminal phase peaked in the second grade, but collapsed after the family left San Jose for Oregon and I turned eight. Some fine spunk fled out of me.

Maybe it started when I stood staring into the low treasure cave of Joaquín Murietta at the Alum Rock Park east from San Jose. Our father taught college, and our mother taught school, but as I stared into the cave and thought about Joaquín, hope shot through me of riches without labor, style without servile conformity. I wanted more than I could have. My brother pulled on my shoulder. A dove called. Quail skittered away. From the cave, my brother and I walked up the canyon to the little zoo where the coyote paced back and forth in the dust, where the raccoon slept with paws hung down from its branch of polished oak.

The coyote sat down, flung up its nose, and howled. My brother put his arm over my shoulder. We were pals. Somewhere way off in the hills a wild coyote answered with a distant wail that pierced my heart. Did my brother feel the thrill? I looked into his mild face. The raccoon opened its eyes a moment, looked at my brother, then at me. We had to go home then, my brother said. It was a school night.

Our father's poem "The Star in the Hills" was written about that place. Lines from that poem show my father's deft ways:

> A star hit in the hills behind our house
> up where the grass turns brown touching the sky.

Could this poem have been his response to the loyalty oath that faculty at California colleges had to sign?

> . . . . . . . . . . . . . . . . . . . . . . . . . . .
> A guard who took the oath of loyalty and denied
> any police record told me this:
> "If you don't have a police record yet
> you could take the oath and get a job
> if California should be hit by another star."

Our father knew how to make his greater loyalties clear:

> "I'd promise to be loyal to California
> and to guard any stars that hit it," I said,
> "or any place three miles out from shore,
> unless the star was bigger than the state—
> in which case, I'd be loyal to *it*."

My father could sign the real oath, write a poem about the imagined one, and feel right. But what was my star, my loyalty? Sometimes it takes a flirtation with crime to help a child learn a first, clumsy version of art's rebellion against complacency.

My private education in crime came with several spectacular failures. First, I stole a Bible on my own. Then I stole a pair of gloves with Gary, my shoplifting tutor. Finally, alone, I pulled off the perfect crime—I mean the perfect act of oblique obedience to my father's teaching.

One morning we had an earthquake lesson in school: if the roof crashed down we should dive under our plywood desks. And in the afternoon our teacher took us to church to pray. I felt tremors inside my body. When you are that small you arrive at an exaggerated sense of your own invisibility. In church, concealed by the smoky weave of the organ music, I hunched low in my solitary pew to reach for that little New Testament someone had left behind. I scuffed my feet to cover the soft tearing sound as I stripped the owner's name on the blue paper from inside the cover. If the name vanished, the book became mine. The blue paper made a wad that fit in the hymnal I closed.

Church laid out such a sleepy hush. The preacher talked adult words. I clutched my testament, carried it home, kept it under my pillow, safe. Later, the bedroom shelf. Then a shelf in the living room.

When my father found it, he tried to decipher the stray pencil strokes still visible on the blue flyleaf. He wrote what he thought he could read there: "180 Maro Drive." (But isn't "Maro" one of Virgil's names?) He drove me sternly in our old Dodge, cruising aimlessly. He looked over at me on the seat beside him—over, and down, for I was very small that day. "Never steal," he said. "Never."

I decided to run away. I made it four blocks, pulling my wagon. But I went back for my jacket as the evening chill touched my shoulder, and I arrived by chance at dinnertime. Then came bedtime, then morning, then spring.

In the spring came the gloves—new gray leather and just my size where they hung on the back wall in the variety store. My friend Gary and I planned the heist, drifting down the aisle past plastic soldiers, hobby beads, hickory bats, and goldfish burbling in the tank.

I slid my right hand into a glove and clenched till the leather rippled and squeaked. With the gloves on my hands, I knew I could conquer tetherball. I only needed two, and the chrome rack held dozens. Behind me Gary whispered, "When shall we go for it?" Then the clerk came toward us, straightening and bustling. I yanked off the glove, and we scooted away along the next aisle toward the parking lot.

I remember the day we passed together into the criminal fringe. Gary strutted, the little man of action, and I slunk after him. He slipped the gloves under his sweatshirt and waltzed out with swagger. His face turned away from the clerk peering at him with her glasses like little triangles. I watched it all through the fish tank. At my distance, between the slow gold shine of the fishes Gary was bubble-small as he disappeared through the swinging door. I followed, and out back by the Dumpster he gave me the gloves—*gave* them to me. He didn't want them, he said. When he ripped off the tag and handed me the gloves, I felt like a sparkler had been lit inside my body. I would never stop living like this . . . and I would never do this again.

When I got home, the family swirled busily about me. I opened the old plywood toolbox in the garage, and slid the gloves in under some rags. Then I played with my brother in the yard, but my heart wasn't in it. I kept drifting toward the garage. "Hey," my brother said, "let's dig the cave!" The magnetism of the gloves pulled too strong. Suddenly my father stood at the workbench. The timing felt right and I casually opened the box.

"Hey," I said, "look what I found!" I held up the gloves.

"Found?" my father said. "Found where?"

"Right here in this old box."

My father held the gloves to his nose, inhaled, and smiled. "Tell me where you really got them," he said.

"Well, actually, Gary and I . . . we . . . see, we were walking along minding our own business and this car drove by really fast and this lady rolled down the window and threw these gloves out on the street!" My father smiled, smelling the gloves again.

"What kind of car?" he said.

"It was fast," I said. "A fast car . . . and white, maybe a Dodge."

"Like our Dodge?" my brother said. Others had come into the garage. My mother looked puzzled. She glanced at my father. My sister reached for the gloves, but I pulled them away.

"And what did the woman look like?" my father said.

"Actually," I said, "Gary stole them from the store." My mother looked into my eyes.

"Then why do you have them?" she said.

"He gave them to me."

"Gave them. Hmmm." My father looked into me. "Then you have to take them back to the store," he said, "and apologize."

My father drove me there and waited in the car. The woman with the glasses listened to my confession, took the gloves, then called the manager, who asked my name, and banned me from the store—for a week. Exiled from paradise, I trudged toward the parking lot. My father spoke of other things as we drove away.

Even that agony didn't cure me of crime, only made me more sly. Why wasn't I more like my brother? No one had to voice that question. It hung in the air.

Once at the playground, I heard someone crying in the laurel hedge. I peered into the room kids had hollowed there. It was Bret. His face seemed far away. I crept inside and stood by him.

"I thought of another name they could call me," he whimpered. The kids had taunted him, he said. "Bret?" they would shout. "Hey, *Brat,* isn't that your real name—Brat?" Now he stood in the dusty room where the laurel branches had been splintered by generations of children hiding from their own kind.

"What did you think?" I said.

"They could call me *Hair Barrette,*" he said.

"They could?" I looked in his eyes. I heard the kids shouting at play, out there in the sun.

"Don't tell anyone," he whispered. "I just thought of it."

"Okay," I said, "don't worry." For some reason, it didn't occur to me to tell him how I had been told a hundred times, "*Ki-yum?* That's a *girl's* name." It didn't matter. I couldn't help it. But Bret was in pain, his imagination working overtime to hurt him.

That evening I stood by the crib and held the bottle for the baby. She looked into my eyes. My grandmother in the kitchen hummed. Somewhere my brother played gently with his turtle the size of a silver dollar. My little sister came to stand beside me. The baby stopped feeding and gazed at us without a sound.

Not long after the gloves, I found a small green purse in the scuffed grass of the tetherball court. I carried it to the laurel room and emptied its coins onto the ground. I buried $1.86 in silver and copper in the soft earth. Then I took the empty purse to the school office.

"Where did you find this?" The secretary lady peered down at me from the counter.

"On the playground," I said.

"And did it have anything in it?" She opened the little mouth of the purse.

I shook my head.

"Well," she said, "I'm sure the little girl who lost this will be very happy it was found." Her tanned face smiled, but under her chin the skin shone white. "Would you like me to tell her your name?"

I shook my head again and drifted silently from the office, sliding along the hall to my classroom. I kept mum all afternoon, my eyes cast down until the bell. Then I dug up the coins and walked to the variety store. Head down I passed the clerk, passed the fish tank, hobby beads, plastic soldiers, to my new prize—the small red plastic wild Indian and his plastic pony, complete with bow and arrows, shield, and lance. It smelled new, like sage after a rain I thought.

The clerk took my money, blew sawdust from the coins with her pursed lips, and gave me seven pennies in change.

I went straight home, but not to the garage. Schooled by failure, a little sad in my triumph, I thrust the Indian and horse and plastic weapons under the battered cedar hedge between our yard and the lawn of the Mexican kids next door, where I could find it later. Then I fidgeted about. My brother came, and we dug in the cave for a while. When we had exposed a new section of hardpan, I put the shovel down and drifted toward the hedge.

"Hey Bret," I said, "look." I pulled my Indian from the shade. "Those kids must have left this out, but we can play with it for a while, can't we? Do you think it's okay?"

"I guess," he said. "Let's see. Until tomorrow, you mean?"

"Yeah, tomorrow, maybe. We can keep it in our cave so it won't get lost." I could feel him looking at me as I looked at my Indian. "Let's take it to the cave right now," I said.

"Okay, if you promise," he said. I led the way, and he followed.

In the yard, my loot became my favorite toy—I was the Indian boy, horse and rider lawless in the dirt. My boy doll rambled the dust of the earth, lived well, raised his bow and shot arrows into the dry California grass. I could hold up my head with my parents, and in the cave avoid my brother's looks when I picked up my Indian. And on the morning we moved away to Oregon, before the sun rose or the family wakened, I went alone to the cave, fetched all the pieces in a double handful, and circled around the hedge to leave my worn prize on the doorstep of the neighbor boys I had never met.

I felt like an angel then, leaving a magic gift for the children—I who knew how sweet such pleasures tasted in the whole body. I turned on the sidewalk and skipped away. Giving had almost the thrill of taking. Now I was going away, and I practiced the kind of small miracle at dawn that Jesus practiced in my New Testament.

When I look back on my three crimes from a distance of forty years, I see a paradox. When you want more than you can have, you proceed in the right direction in the wrong way. A book of old poetry (the Good Book), the gloves of honorable work, and the talisman of the Indian's bow and arrows—these lie at the heart of my father's most central practices that I obeyed. Each time, I got half the lesson right: lyric words, honest work, the wild. Inventing my own way, I was punished, but somehow confirmed. The cost would be greater for my brother, who never stole a dime.

Once in midlife at a garage sale, I was riveted by a fifty-cent book, *Childhood: The Challenge* by Rudolph Dreikurs. As I read the examples of good and bad parenting that filled the book, I had an uneasy feeling. "Don't Feel Sorry," the book said; "Sidestep the Struggle for Power . . . Action! Not Words . . . Stimulate Independence . . . Take It Easy":

> Our worry about possible disaster in no way prevents it. We can
> only deal with trouble after it happens. Our best refuge is to have
> confidence in our children and to take it easy until such time as our
> talents for coping with disaster are really called upon. . . . Striving to
> make life perfect is futile. We won't succeed.

Why did these lines sound so familiar? It turns out an earlier version of this book, *The Challenge of Parenthood,* had been my parents' bible as they tried to civilize their little tribe of four. But what may have been lost on my parents was that Dreikurs was trying to civilize the parents, turn them into pacifists, teaching them nonviolent means to shape the unruly powers of their children.

I see my father, trying to be stern, looking for an address he could not read as we drove through San Jose. Today I can open my little New Testament to the place I marked then with a Band-Aid for a bookmark:

> To another the working of miracles; to another prophecy; to another discerning of spirits; to another diverse kinds of tongues; to another the interpretation of tongues. But all these worketh that one and the selfsame Spirit, dividing to every man severally as he will. For as the body is one and hath many members, and all the members of that one body, being many, are one body. . . .
>
> —1 COR. 12:10–12

Sometime after San Jose, on one of our long nighttime drives through the Midwest I leaned my little body at the left-hand window of the backseat—my station all through childhood—while my father drove. Everyone slept but my father and me. The straight road had hypnotized the car, and my father's big hands were steady on the wheel. I forget what we had been whispering about, but there was an easy silence between us. The miles rolled softly by. Night was our friend, smooth and endless, holding the secret of morning. And into that silence came the feeling I could tell him anything. I remembered the horse and the Indian, the little bow and arrows. I could tell him now, and it would be all right. I leaned forward, my lips against his hair, just there by his ear.

"Daddy," I whispered.

"Yes, my friend."

"You . . . you're such a good driver," I said.

The miles went on and on, and we talked of other things. Finally, I settled back onto the seat and slept.

# Bows & Arrows

Wood that can learn is no good for a bow.
— "The Sparkle Depends on Flaws in the Diamond"

L IKE MY FATHER I AM A TEACHER who uses writing to assist the painful and exhilarating quest of the willing student. Sometimes in a workshop I invite a circle of writers to describe their job as a child—that task in the maintenance of family balance that fell to them alone. For many, the answer approaches martyrdom: "My job was to make my father happy so he wouldn't leave." "My job was protecting my baby sister—from everything." "I cut up my mother's credit cards—no, really, with scissors when I was ten years old." I have yet to get a simple list of chores.

What was mine? I did wash the dishes, burn the trash, and help my brother mow the yard. But behind the maintenance, I believe my job was to be tame at the right time, then wild; obedient, then surprising; congenial with others, but also happy in my own way. Behind my prevalent equanimity, my real job as a child was to be the family's Indian. That's what I said I wanted to be when I grew up, and I wasn't waiting. Maybe I learned this from my father, for his wild spirit was always somewhere near the edge of any domestic scene. Maybe the doom of every child is to intuit, and then aspire to the suppressed longing of the parent.

My father had his own secluded corner of the yard—behind the bushy hemlock tree he had planted, the fence he had built to hide the place. He would sit easily on a round of unsplit stove-wood and shave lace-like ribbons from a hickory bow-stave with a knuckle of broken glass. He shattered a Coke bottle and took up a thick shard that fit the clenched fingers and thumb of his left hand. Sun dappled the leaves of the silver poplar over him, his felt hat shaded his eyes. There was a kind of hum to the light there, a musical tone of well-being. Our father had come home from his college work to the life of wood. If you stood at his knee or sat close, the fragrance of hickory gave a Midwest tang that flavored a story he might be telling from his childhood.

"Down along Cow Creek one evening, I went with my father to set the trotline. . . ." I sat cross-legged on the ground, my elbows on my knees, my chin on twin fists. I listened, watching his hands stroke and stroke the wood away.

I was eight. From family pictures, I was a pudgy kid, curly hair, often a wry smile on my face. While my brother's face was often pure and distant, mine was caught by the turmoil of the moment. Now I can weasel my way back to that time through episodic moments of pungent memory, and through reference to my father's jotted accounts. From that summer, I find odd things in his daily writing. Reformed from my crimes the previous year, I had become an active little saint that summer:

> BRET: "Mother, I hope you and Daddy don't get a divorce."
>
> I: "Why's that, Bret?
>
> BRET: "Because I wouldn't know which one to go with.
>
> KIM: "I'd go with the one nobody else wanted."
>
> —1 APRIL 1958

> We talked about "the water of life," and each person in the family said he'd like to have some, and then Kim added: "If there was any left."
>
> —26 JUNE

> At Lost Lake, when Kim was charming the baby, saving a baby bird, catching and releasing frogs, helping around camp: "If other people in the world were the way Kim is, God would live here."
>
> —20 JULY

Maybe that was backdrop to my truth: when the bow was done, I went alone to the school yard beside our house, aimed an arrow at the sky, pulled to the limit, and let it go. A fleeing dot, the arrow disappeared. I looked around. Calm everywhere, weekend workers on their lawns and porches. Then Bobby Elliott's father, bent over in his garden, jumped aside. The arrow was buried in the earth beside him. Oh yes, God would have to live here.

As with many things, it wasn't until after my father's death I learned the background of his obsession with a handmade bow and a fist of arrows. Visiting in Hutchinson, Kansas, I talked with an old-timer who had heard a story about the young Billy Stafford from an older-timer of the previous generation. Back in the early 1920s, the story goes, Billy showed up at a service station at the edge of Hutchinson, near where Cow Creek wandered beyond the grid of flatland streets into the loops and eddies of its mystery. That day Billy was carrying a bow he had whittled from a hoe handle, strung taut with a stout shoelace, and in a quiver he had a sheaf of arrows. He had stopped for a drink of water.

"Well, Billy," said the attendant, handing him a paper cup, "that's quite a bow you have there. What are you after today?"

"I'm going to get a rabbit."

"Fine, Billy. Once you get that rabbit, be sure to stop by and show it to me."

About a half hour later, according to my informant, Billy appeared, carrying a big rabbit by the ears. Then came the line the older man passed to the old man who told me: "That young Billy was kind of an Indian."

Kind of an Indian? Not by blood, but by conversion, the intense persuasion of the prairie on his impressionable soul. The persuasion of Cow Creek, his forays as a young camper, his vigil in the breaks above the Cimarron. All his life, he spoke of Wovoka, Crazy Horse, the "people of the south wind." All his life he made vague references to his connection with the "Crowfoot" tribe. After his death, I learned from a cousin this was a joke from my father's childhood. If there was a Blackfoot tribe, he reasoned with his siblings, and a Crow tribe, why not a Crowfoot tribe? They invented the tribe and adopted themselves into it.

Then there was the book my grandmother gave me, *Ishi: In Two Worlds,* the account by Theodora Kroeber of the "last wild Indian" who appeared from the backcountry of northern California in 1911 and lived at the museum in Berkeley until his death in 1916, two years after my father was born. Ishi made bows and arrows, helped his friends the anthropologists understand the primitive, and said enigmatic things that thrilled me as a boy: "You stay, I go." Ishi's physician and friend, Saxton Pope, had written a book specifically about learning archery from Ishi, and this book was my father's preferred reference. Then there were the books of Ernest Thompson Seton—*Two Little Savages, Rolf in the Woods,* and others. I remember being lost in those books, hypnotized in particular by the way Rolf, a white boy, is educated in woodlore by Quanab, the last of his tribe. By the wordless understandings of childhood, when I watched my father hidden in the leafy corner of the yard making a bow, he became the Indian of my life. It was easy to see him that way, more in keeping with his character in many ways than any recognition he might have in the public world.

My father told me once about his favorite teacher, an economics professor at the University of Kansas. According to my father's description, this professor expressed helpless fascination with the subject of economics, but no concern at all about what students learned. My father found that admirable—the purity of the man's love of his subject—even though my father's own teaching style was much more tuned to his students. But I find a parallel in my father's private writings about his obsession with archery. "Some parents," he wrote, "take a benevolent interest in the hobbies of their children. I would build a bow, and shoot the best flight in the world" (Daily Writing, 22 June 1960). He was not making toys for his children. In his hidden corner of the yard he was surrendering to his own obsession. The lesson to us was not about archery, but about loyalty to the self.

Once after returning from a series of poetry readings in the Dakotas, my father said many in the audience had been Lakota people. They had heard he would be reading poems about Crazy Horse. There was a feeling on the Pine Ridge reservation then that Crazy Horse might return. I wonder what they took my father for as he read his ghostly poems:

> All the Sioux were defeated. Our clan
> got poor, but a few got richer.
> They fought two wars. I did not
> take part. No one remembers your vision
> of even your real name.
> —*from* "REPORT TO CRAZY HORSE"

At home, he would sit on a sun-dappled stump working down a hickory stave stroke by stroke, pausing now and again to test the flex of the wood over his knee. He used a rat-tail file to nock the ends for the bowstring and added a lap of leather where his hand would hold the bow. Finally the arrows—birch dowel, vulture quill, a brass bullet casing for a blunt point, and yellow pigment—and a quiver made from a mailing tube with army-green canvas painted onto it.

Then we were somewhere near a bank of dirt. Our father set out a cardboard box at twenty yards. "Let's say that's a rabbit"—he looked at us—"and we're starving. Kim, see what you can do." And I would aim the hickory bow he had made, or the one of lemonwood, or one of several bows of yew, draw the arrow, let it go. No matter our success, he was excited.

"Attaboy! Bret? Kit? Barbara! Take a try. . . ." And last, he would draw his own—the great bow he had wrestled from a stave of the quirky Kansas Osage orange tree, with a backing of rawhide—and I would see his face clench in concentration. Utter attention. It was the kind of look that came to his face in the desert when we sought flakes of obsidian the first people had scattered wherever they worked. He would say on those expeditions, "If I were an arrowhead, where would I be?" We would look around—at the big open of Glass Buttes, or Fort Rock, or the Steens country. His sudden glance knew the world. That was his look when he let fly his arrow, and the world received the exact, slender blur of his purpose.

He didn't always bull's-eye. But his love of the whole adventure was infectious. Our way was private, even furtive. Outside at evening, in the quiet, we hunted a creature older than sport or prey. The target was interior and before.

Once in Kansas, on a visit to the relatives, I climbed to the barn loft and found by pure chance a bow my father had made and mailed home as a gift for the cousins—a short bow of yew, a beauty. I remember my father's big hands, taking the bow from me, then handing it back; they seemed like hands from that other time when everything you needed to survive you made.

We would watch his long preparation—shaping a bow, arrows, a perfect linen string—for the sudden release of the arrow. The jolt of a poem appearing out of a long life went like that.

> The bow bent remembers home long,
> the years of its tree, the whine
> of wind all night conditioning
> it, and its answer—Twang!

To the people here who would fret me down
their way and make me bend:
*By remembering hard I could startle for home*
*and be myself again.*

— "RECOIL"

During a reading of one of his quick, deft poems, someone in the audience once interrupted his reading and asked him aloud, "How long did it take you to write that?"

"All my life," he said.

His bow of Osage orange still hangs on the wall in my mother's garage. And somewhere in a hidden corner of the yard, down in the dirt like an artifact, there may yet lie a knuckle of broken glass.

# *Honorable Work*

I HAVE A MANIA FOR TOOLS that fit the hand, for an ashwood handle that carries a polish only human leather can give. Rummaging in my tool chest, my hand closes on the pruning knife with the rosewood handle, and I go hurtling back—back by way of my father's account to the 1930s when my great-uncle John Stamm, the orchardist in Kansas, gave that knife to my father as a bribe to recruit him as a working man. My father might have joined the farm and worked the orchard at Yaggy. Compared to prospects for an unemployed pacifist poet in the post-war years, the offer must have been a temptation with pull. When my father turned toward the writer's way, the teacher's calling, he left a precious life behind.

"Maybe I should have made shoes," he once lamented, "like Tolstoy. With shoes, you know when your work is done. With teaching, you never know."

"How about with writing a poem?" I said.

"Oh, I know when I'm done writing a poem," he said. "I put the poem aside when the process of revision stops feeling like the wild adventure of the first writing—creation. When it's not creation anymore, I don't do it."

But with tools, with a shovel or a hammer or a drill, his ways were definite. Throughout his life, he maintained a biographical resume for even the most formal use that began with a litany of honorable labors: "At intervals during his schooling, William Stafford worked as a laborer in sugar beet fields, on construction jobs, and in an oil refinery." Then he would list his publications and other bookish things.

Sometimes he would recall with quiet pride the time in his family's economy when his father was out of work and the only income was Billy's paper route.

"Why list the sugar beet fields?" I asked him once.

"It was the hardest work I ever did—you lean over all day with a short-handled hoe. Five dollars an acre—the money was good for those days, but the work would kill you, eventually."

His stories about manual labor were honest about the grueling difficulty, but always tinged with a kind of bedrock dignity he found rare in institutional life. He recognized dignity in individuals, yes. But in a university as a whole, or the government? As he said in his poem "The Sparkle Depends on Flaws in the Diamond,"

> You can lie at a banquet, but you have to
> be honest in the kitchen.

He worked at the oil refinery in El Dorado, Kansas, during the Depression. Again, he felt lucky to have a job that could easily kill him, for he worked all day in an atmosphere so saturated with fumes that any spark, as he would say, could blow you to kingdom come. If a wrench slipped from your hand and struck a spark off the cheater bar, that could be it. Or another time, when his job was holding the star drill while a burly fellow swung the sledge to strike it, he heard the following story from the grunting voice above him, punctuated by blows of the hammer on the slender steel shaft in my father's hands:

> Almost killed a guy one time—uh!—when he held the drill like
> you—uh!—I don't miss often—uh!—but I did that day—uh!—
> sledge to the head, you think—uh!—that's it, he's dead—uh!—got
> him in the car—uh!—on the way to the hospital—uh!—he sits up
> in back—uh!—always a little strange—uh!—after that—uh!

My father told that story with relish, making the motion for turning the drill in his hands before each stroke, giving the staccato grunt with style, and looking up toward the burly giant looming in his mind.

In the war, although the conscientious objectors were promised their alternative service would include "work of national importance," their conscription labor was often of the lowest kind. With shovel and axe they fanned out along a ditch in Arkansas to repair the effects of soil erosion. With shovel and mattock they dug California fire-lines down to mineral soil and fought the blaze. With shovel and bucket in the mountains they planted pines for the long haul, or built roads, or chopped chaparral, or even set out cork-oak saplings because there was a feeling the war might never end. "Our children will need wine," the foreman said. "Plant many, for many will die."

Those years made my father masterful with certain tools. He never traveled without a shovel in the back of the car, and any excuse brought his working hands to the hickory handle. Whether flicking the blade in gravel or earth, his movements were deft with the knowledge of how to do a job with the rhythm of all day.

> Even now in my hands the feel of the shovel comes back,
> the shock of gravel or sand.
>
> — *from* "Life Work"

In his papers I find glimpses into that time he was a working man with a redneck tenderness all his own:

> On vehement-green Southern sod,
> In vital blue dress a girl walks, and tries
> Ten religious men, with a distant nod.
> (Tongues move, heads rise, hoes hesitate.)
> Ten dangerous men fail, pasture their eyes,
> Turn dirt for the glory of God,
> and wait.
>
> Magnolia, Arkansas,
> April, 1942

My father's father was not an educated man, but he was a feverish reader. (He had Poe's "Annabelle Lee" in his pocket the day he died.) My father's mother was distant from sophistication in many ways, but she would go to the library in every new town, check out the same book she always did to start—*A Lantern in Her Hand* by Bess Streeter Aldrich—and go home to read it through in bed before beginning the work of relocation. Exiled from that bookish home by the war, my father was a working man who identified not with literature alone, but with the roots of literature and the other arts in the lives of people—honorable work as cradle to aspiration.

From Arkansas again, I find an unpublished account of the day the boss, one of the "government men," came with his dog Jabo to check up

on a crew of COs at rest beside a ditch they had dug. The ditch was done—
perfectly—but for a pipe they had carefully dug around and left. Caked
with mud, it looked like a root to the boss, and he ordered one of the men
to chop it out.

> Jim leaned deliberately over the side and looked where the boss was
> pointing. Then Jim looked slowly around the group of men, all of
> whom, including Jabo, stood immovable regarding Jim, the axe,
> the boss, and the "root." Jim was a dignified fellow, not used to
> crew work, and he did not relish the way he was ordered around.
> Receiving no look of veto from the group, he jumped into the
> ditch, squared away, planted his feet firmly on the soil of Arkansas,
> and raised the axe in a portentous arc.
>
> Everyone stood motionless, except for Jabo, whose tail waved
> once. The boss, boots apart, hands hooked in belt, stood over Jim
> and willed the blow.
>
> It just had to happen. The axe flashed and freedom smote the
> air with a tremendous whanging sound. There was an instant of
> immobility and silence as Jim stood, the ruined axe in hand and
> looked without expression at the dented pipe and then up at the
> boss. The boss turned, calling out over his shoulder to his only
> slave, "Come along, Jabo."

For my father, physical work offered a context where intention and comple-
tion could be clearly delineated. In other realms, the sense of right living
might be harder to identify. He told of the long Depression summer when
he harnessed up and physically pulled a plow to help a partner plant a gar-
den for wages that ultimately amounted to zero. In several written accounts,
he calls this episode "My Life as a Mule" or "When I Was a Mule." But the
real mystery is the unpublished parallel account he also titles "When I Was a
Mule," from the era when my brother was three and I was two:

> It's strange to me to find myself helping run a whole family—a
> houseful of people—being the grownup responsible one, the father.
> I can't get used to it. The other day when I was hanging up my coat
> after coming home from work, I stopped in the bedroom and lis-
> tened to Dorothy and the kids out in the front room and thought,

"There! It's a family; we're living away off here in Iowa; it's a place I didn't ever expect to be. . . ." And I hung up my coat and went out to be a part of all that. But it seemed strange, and I tried to hear and see things the way it used to be.

The "way it used to be" was partly his freedom as a child, a wanderer, even an exile in America. But "the way it used to be" was also the good work of the physical life, a kind of nostalgia that was transmuted by having a family to a future aspiration: "the Stafford Ranch." This phrase, like a raspberry seed caught in the teeth, slowly released a tantalizing flavor all through my childhood. In the early 1950s, my father wrote home to Kansas, "I am sending out more stories to magazines. If I sell them, I'll buy the ranch and we'll all move on the place—with vine-covered houses for all." (He had written in his daily writing for 2 October 1955, "Any farm on a hill is a rebuke to me, to my way of life.") My mother's father had briefly been a homesteader in Wyoming (he went bust in one season), and her grandfather had been a farmer in Nebraska. Country life was in our family blood on both sides, and so my parents owned the back-to-the-land bible of their generation, *Five Acres and Independence,* with chapters on all kinds of focused husbandry that might enable a better life of work and freedom in the country. Their joke, however, was that instead of five acres and independence they had no acres and dependents.

Somehow I was the child who picked up our father's fondness for the relative ease of hard labor. I was shy, socially inept, and I found small talk harder than hard work. A party? I would rather be whittling a bowl out of oak, or shaping a club from locust wood, or building a fort in the woods. In his daily writing for September 1957, my father records his expedition to the woods near our house, where he found the children divided in their labors:

In the woods at the stockade I visited the kids.

LELA TURNER [a neighbor girl]: "This is a science club now— I'm studying arachnids."

BRET: "And I'm studying the world."

I: "And where's Kim?"

BRET: "Oh, he's down cutting ferns for the roof."

Against this backdrop of long-standing family culture my parents decided shortly after I left for college to buy land east of the Cascade Mountains in Oregon, and build a getaway in the country as a place to roost when they retired. My father talked vaguely of keeping chickens, while my mother favored feeders for the wild birds and the idea of a retreat for sociability with friends. In 1970 they moved to Washington, D.C., for a year, while my father served as Consultant in Poetry at the Library of Congress (a post now called the Poet Laureate). Their move resulted in my elevation to foreman for house construction on the land.

I was relatively skilled with hammer and saw, had puttered seriously with my father and brother throwing together decks and other projects at home, and I loved tools. Undeterred by my profound ignorance—a deck constructed of select cedar is not a house—I established a budget with the folks by mail, hired an architect, borrowed a tiny house trailer, moved onto the building site with my wife, and recruited two workmen at random. What followed was slow disaster, an expensive education in the gritty details of honorable work.

The architect, I found out later, had never designed a house. One representative result of this fact was his habit of specifying boards ten feet two inches long. (Boards come in even-numbered lengths, so we bought hundreds of twelve-foot boards, and sawed off hundreds of twenty-two-inch blocks as waste.) He also specified a foundation system of eighteen concrete columns topped with fastening hardware I had to commission from a crusty blacksmith named Joe Egg. I loved visiting Joe's shop—all that fire and grit and the savvy of old work—but when his bill came we were almost out of business. And then there were the workmen: Lockett the quintessential optimist ("We'll have this baby done by lunch"), and Andy the pessimist ("My father died at 29, and I'll be lucky to make it that far—and as for this foundation corner, it's going to take four days"). Andy was always right, and Lockett was outrageously entertaining—until he lined me up with a friend from Chiloquin for our lumber order, and the whole load turned out to be culls. A six-by-six-inch post broke in half when we lifted it off the stack he had dropped at the building site, and we realized our good old boy, the gyppo millwright, had sourced his timber from what others left to rot in the clear-cut slash pile.

My father and I drove the long road to the dealer's yard near Chiloquin, in southern Oregon, and met with the man. When he took off his tin hat I saw a deep dent in his forehead. He didn't have a lot to say, just offered "anything you find that's better" with a wave of his hand. My father and I stood on a hill to survey acres of rotting boards, some in stacks and some haphazard on the ground.

"Well," my father said, "it was a nice drive." He seemed to shrug off our loss right there. "It's only money," he said, repeating a phrase that echoed through my childhood. There never was much, and so money didn't matter, even when, in time, there was more. My father's attitude was instructive: money is not worth getting angry about. We headed for home—two hundred miles without another word about the loss. Instead, my father spoke with gusto about new projects.

After learning we couldn't get our money back without legal action, we laid off our crew of two and started from scratch with our own revisions of the architect's drawings. This began one of the sweetest times in our overlapping lives: the building of what the family still calls "The Little House."

It was winter and the trailer was gone. We set up the family tent under a pine and stared out at our cemetery in the snow: eighteen concrete piers in good order, each topped with a fourteen-inch spire of hand-forged iron rod. By reading how-to books from the library and guessing and tinkering, we were going to build a shelter for ourselves atop the six piers at the south end, and then stop and take stock of where to go from there. The gas crisis was on, so it took me a long wait each week to get a tank of fuel, but when my graduate classes ended in Eugene on a Friday, I was gone over the mountains to rendezvous with my father who drove down from Portland.

"Erase that line!" he would shout over the whine of the power-saw as I leaned toward a board resting on the most elaborate sawhorses ever built. "Atta boy!" he would urge as I hunched under the floor to sweat-solder a copper water pipe. "Got it?" I would shout as we teetered on nightmarish scaffolding to hoist a post or heft a beam. For we had the scraps of our fiasco still—those selected timbers from the gyppo that were solid wood. One of them furnished what must be the world's largest shim, a six-by-fourteen-inch timber twenty feet long that came in handy when we sawed off a set of posts too short for the west wall. We wrestled the beam to the tops of three piers, bolted the too-short posts on top of it, and were back in business.

I remember vividly the joy we felt when the work went well. I remember gratitude for not killing ourselves with tools and techniques we could barely manage. But best of all I remember the talk between us. Work by hand enabled a mystic freedom of mind like nothing else. In graduate school, I had some brilliant teachers. I was studying medieval literature, and those old stories had me mesmerized. But even the best moments in literature couldn't hold a candle to a resin-scented, snow-sifted evening with my father, who would pause while the soldering flame burned blue to ask a question or make a strange connection that required the co-authorship of the tool in hand, the task before us, and the easy kinship we felt in the work.

I wish I could report them now, those words, those golden threads, confessions, and generous speculations that shaped my being. Childhood had been a foundation. Soon I would go forward into my own vocation. We would not long have times like these. Our work was meditative, grateful, sometimes filled with resonant silences. If I hadn't lived through the whole of the twentieth century myself, I lived closely with a father who brought those years to me. A swinging hammer in my father's hand was a time machine.

Once I almost snipped through a live 220-volt cable, late in the day when I was punchy, even more stupid than usual. I remember the thumb pounded blue, and the loosened threads on the knee of my pants where the spinning blade of the power-saw just grazed the fabric. I remember falling backward when the pulley failed and a giant beam thudded to earth where we had stood. Why weren't we killed?

After some years of intermittent work at Sisters, we had a cozy room, running water, a loft with a bed, and a woodstove roaring with pine knots. We felt no timetable, only pleasure. My mother watched us, helpless in the face of our leisure, as we boarded over a window on the south wall, deciding we liked it snug inside; then changed our minds and installed the window again for solar gain; then boarded it up and built the wall solid so the stovepipe could stand there.

Eventually she hired a real architect, and soon a professional crew had built the north end of the project, "The Big House." She was right to do so; the cemetery of foundation piers had begun to wear on the neighbors, and she deserved her say. When I visit now, I go into the little house we made, my father and I, and admire our museum of tasteful details and nightmarish plumbing. In the loft, I nudge open a wooden latch, swing aside a quarter-sheet of plywood on its piano hinge, and stand up into the sky.

In that snug cabin, one night by the light of kerosene, my father and I played a game like cards, each with a hand of poems we laid down one by one to weave together our book: *Braided Apart.*

# *Vocation*

WHEN I WAS IN MY EARLY THIRTIES and the century in its mid-seventies, I was cruising west through the Cascade Mountains of Oregon in The Duchess, my '64 Chevy wagon, fresh from a weekend at the half-built Little House. My brother had given me The Duchess when he moved to Vancouver Island, figuring he could do without a car on an island. His was the economy of a saint! I was between jobs, having begun my Ph.D. in medieval literature, then a stint as oral historian in a local museum. I did a little teaching, writing, worked as a printer, photographer, and wondered what might happen next. I was puzzled about it all and strangely happy.

In this happy trance, my glance caught a police car in the rearview mirror, lights flashing. I pulled over, rubbed my scruffy chin, adjusted the collar of my coveralls, rolled down the window, and waited. The officer, a little older than me, asked to see my license, informed me the tag on my Oregon plate was a month overdue, and wrote me out a warning. Then he asked a question not customarily in the script.

"What do you do, Mr. Stafford?" He turned his head like a curious dog. It was a friendly question. Without thinking, I replied.

"I'm a writer."

"That's good," he said. "We need writers. Have a good day." He returned to his car, turned off the flashing lights, and drove away. I stared at my hands on the wheel. Was it that easy to claim your calling, an announcement to an official at random? I drove on with a gathering sense of certainty. I would follow the path of the writer! But how?

In the winter of 1979, I was living in the little eastern Oregon town of North Powder, still between jobs. While driving west through the Blue Mountains in his Cougar, my friend Jim Heynen interviewed and hired me on a whim. We had both finished jobs as "artists in the schools"—visitors writing with young children for a week at a time in the backcountry towns of Oregon and Idaho—and had converged to drive back to Portland. Jim was then in the position of choosing a photography instructor for a two-week stint at Lewis & Clark College, and he chose me. Although I had been familiar with the Lewis & Clark campus since childhood, and considered many on the faculty my adoptive aunts and uncles, I came in through the back door. By summer, I was part of an instructional team at the college for the Foxfire Workshop.

I was in charge of the darkroom. When the instructor for the writing portion of the class told everyone to read *The Elements of Style* and then spent the balance of the workshop drinking coffee and reading the newspaper, I could see there was room for my role to grow. Within a few years, by saying yes to every invitation, I became an indispensable itinerant at the college—teaching anything, anytime, to anyone. I taught folklore, Northwest literature, linguistics, journalism, prose writing, the Oregon Writing Project, an invention called Writer to Writer, and a freshman course called Basic Inquiry. I taught nights, weekends, summers. I taught high-school students, undergraduates, teachers, writers from the community both young and old. I had no office, but carried a wooden box with all I needed on a strap over my shoulder, a box my friends called my "shoeshine kit." This continued for seven years.

By 1986, an enterprising administrator decided the cluster of courses I had developed should be named. A month after founding the Northwest Writing Institute, that administrator was terminated in a cost-saving move, but I survived. I have now been on an annual contract for twenty years and hold what I call "self-conferred tenure," which consists of my refusal to leave. There has been a Stafford teaching at Lewis & Clark for fifty-four years. I am a writer, and I teach at the college, often part-time, and still I seek the larger sense of vocation I observed in my father's life.

After my father died, a friend asked me, "Do you know what your father's motto was?" I did not. "Do it now; do it all." But then I remembered another motto of his: "Do the hard part first." And another: "Never touch a piece of paper more than once." He would rip through the mail in one rush, answering everything, the hardest tasks first. No sorting, no delaying, no dithering.

He was a teacher, but he practiced that job within a larger calling: the Writer. But I would say even Writer was part of a larger calling he named the Seeker. Once he came home from a journey and reported an encounter with a Hari Krishna in the Chicago airport. When the young man tried to get him to buy a copy of the *Upanishads,* my father took him on: was this the best translation? How could one know this? What was lost from the original? What was the heart of the text for the disciple—in particular? Was selling the *Upanishads* the best way to live in accord with the teachings of the book? And what ethical perspectives had even the *Upanishads* neglected that by talking recklessly we might learn right now?

"I told him," my father said, "I was a Seeker. I really wanted to know about the best translation. It was so important, I had to be sure I was getting the true thing."

My father didn't meet people, he interviewed them. He didn't teach classes, he activated them. A favorite story was the time he had to leave a class in Cincinnati, but the students were so engaged by the questions he had put to them they went on without him. By later report, the class was still going two hours after he slipped away to fly home.

My father was Matthew Arnold's ideal, the "scholar gypsy." His connection to the college was devoted, but oblique. For one eight-year stretch, he taught a class at the coast one night a week. He told me this journey outward, in the dark, toward working people who wanted to learn about literature and writing, kept him from ever being an insider at Lewis & Clark. His traveling through the dark alone, in service to learners in far places, made him different. His daily writing gave him a rich and continuous inner life; his pacifism gave him a constant alternative viewpoint; his journeys and his reading gave him a broad and unpredictable perspective he focused in lively ways whenever questions of ethics or aesthetics came up. My cousin Ned said of my father's visits to Kansas: "the few times Bill stopped through Kansas, he was obviously different from other Kansans. But, at the same time, he fit right in."

In one sense, my father's greatest services to the college were his regular departures—to Iowa in the 1950s to get a Ph.D. in the Creative Writing Program; to a host of colleges in the 1960s following his National Book Award; to Washington, D.C. in 1970 as Consultant in Poetry at the Library of Congress. He exercised this last sojourner's duty much as he taught, by responding generously to requests for help. One memorable story involved his meeting with Robert Frost's actual "hired man." Contrary to Frost's poem "The Death of the Hired Man," this gentleman had not died, and he showed up at the Library to bend my father's ear about a literary magazine he had launched in Florida.

Beginning in the 1960s, my father went forth as a literary ambassador to all who asked. He rarely turned down any invitation. But it wasn't only his geographical departures that marked his vocation outside the college; it was his conception of himself as both a writer and a seeker, a friend to people of all kinds, and a performer of unusual cultural responsibilities.

In 1975, Oregon's Governor Tom McCall drafted my father to be the state's Poet Laureate, with the understanding the position consisted of "no pay, no duties." It was an honorary slot, with the one expectation that my father read a poem each year to open the legislative session at the capitol. My father began one session this way:

### *Oregon House Session, 13 April 1987*

This hall recalls that one where warriors watched
a sparrow fly from darkness, traverse their banquet
table, and disappear into the night:
that flight symbolized a life, and the warriors
heard, in Anselm's story, how every person appears
from the unknown, enjoys light, and goes alone
away from this world into the dark.

I'm sure the legislators that day took off their glasses and gave him curious heed.

. . . . . . . . . . . . . . . . . . . . . . . . . . .

Only the people voted, but the animals too are there,
and the salmon testing silt in their home rivers.
Even the trees deserve a place, and the hills
maintaining their part, while the rocks are quietly
mentioning integrity.

Once, when he was traveling, he dispatched me to the capitol in his place. As I looked down from the rostrum, in that beat of silence before I began, I felt the power of my father's calling: replacing a religious blessing with poetry. For my own contribution, I chose to read from the words of an Oregon old-timer:

> I used to hunt bear—killed my share. But once—you know
> how old loggers left stumps fifteen, twenty feet high . . . ?

I was learning from my father how to be playful and serious at the same time by smuggling literature and local voice into the formalities of society.

Another time my father had me represent him at the city council meeting in Portland, where Mayor Bud Clark had commissioned a poem about the great blue heron, recently adopted as the city's official bird. While we were traveling together, I watched my father write the poem as he lay on his motel bed in Washington, D.C. He took a tablet, leaned back, gazed far away, and jotted. A month later, I delivered the poem to a puzzled row of overworked public servants in an upstairs room in Portland's City Hall. The council had just finished hearing a complaint about a police error— battering down the wrong door in a raid—then they looked down at their agendas as the clerk called my father's name. I introduced myself, apologized for his absence, and began:

### Spirit of Place: Great Blue Heron

> Out of their loneliness for each other
> two reeds, or maybe two shadows, lurch
> forward and become suddenly a life
> lifted from dawn or the rain. . . .

I glanced up from the page to see a spectrum of responses—from the beaming face of Bud to active exasperation from the clerk and several council members. This was a long way from graduate school, I thought, where poetry was a matter of books, classes, and libraries cloistered from the world.

When I did my taxes the following year, I counted thirty-eight employers. Like my father, I had become a kind of private voice for public purpose, in my myriad appearances and minor tasks—composing, editing, performing, convening, advising. Since then, my work has broadened. Can I write words to carve in stone at the transit mall? Can I write a song for saving a river? Can I write a blessing for an art school? Can I write a play to honor the life of a particular child? Can I write a poem for the wall of the pediatric intensive care waiting room? Yes, always yes.

One thing I learned by watching my father was his readiness to send his writing forth in all directions with the fluid motion of water leaving a hilltop. Publication for him was no anxious drama of submission and rejection. He simply sent batches of poems out constantly, with a verve more in keeping with shoveling gold than tweezering diamonds. He told me at one point he generally had fifty to a hundred poems "in circulation" at all times. Even his most successful poems (eventually recognized, honored, widely anthologized) began as worn sheets of paper often submitted again and again. The title poem to his National Book Award winner, for example, "Traveling through the Dark," he submitted to a succession of almost twenty magazines before it was accepted.

Once after teaching a writing workshop together and hearing my father explain his fluid approach to submitting work for publication, I remember saying to him, "Daddy, we don't really know how it is for other people. We assume a piece of writing we care about will get published—eventually. We have dumb persistence. But for others, it may seem harder. They may not have the creator's arrogance required to keep plugging away until some editor gets it."

"Maybe you're right," he said with a shrug. "The process goes like perpetual motion."

Schooled by my father's example, and by my own inability to find a "real" job full-time, I kept inventing ways to get by. I was low-end half-time at the college, and for years I couldn't see beyond a month ahead how I was going to pay the rent. The constant was writing. This approach begins in one lesson from my father: write inevitable things out of your self. I have learned to obey any request, but with an independent spirit. As my father once wrote, in a fragment that later became an essay:

> If you begin to believe what others say about you, you become like
> a compass that listens to the hunches of the pilot. You may be good
> company, but you are useless as a compass—I mean a poet.

In contrast to the compass too easily persuaded is my father's direct way— the writer of "inevitable" poems, the ones most congruent with the self. He wrote in his daily writing, "We are surrounded by brilliant people who don't do much." I find this strangely consoling: I do not need to be brilliant by anyone's standard, but I do need to be fiercely alert to my own contribution. (A voice in a dream explained this to me: "When others don't understand you, you must be clear with yourself about your own purpose.") About this clarity, my father wrote, "The last star will not know how small it is" (Daily Writing, 21 December 1968). The authentic act of writing is more about clarity than magnitude. This kind of writing I call being "scribe to the prophet." The prophet may be any quiet voice near me—a child, a cloud, a river, an idea in the air. I write it down.

My father ends his poem "Vocation" with his own father telling him, "Your job is to find what the world is trying to be." To do so requires the long view, intuition, listening, patience with your own ways.

When my father wrote in his will, "My literary executor will be my son Kim," he was giving me another compact, cryptic invitation. Within my own ever-broadening vocation, how does this role of "executor" fit? How can I follow this mysterious calling well? After my father died, I confided to a friend I felt alone with the burden of the work. "Why be alone?" she said. "Your family has no shortage of talent—your mother, Kit, Barbara. Let them take on all they want." But I keep it to myself. I can't tell whether it is a virtue or a flaw in my character that urges me to keep this role, abiding by the letter of my father's directive. I don't know whether his selection of me as literary executor was an act of confidence in my ability, or his way of protecting others from the work.

Despite a congenial nature, my father kept his own council in the practice of his craft. "Someone asked me," he said after a journey to the East Coast, "who was on my committee for my writing. I didn't know what they were talking about, but it seems a habit of certain flourishing writers is to have a group of powerful friends act as editors for their work. The writer doesn't put a book of poems together; the committee does. And then the committee swings into action to lean on their friends to get the book published, and even write reviews of this great book they have made, and generally talk it up."

My father said he couldn't understand why anyone who could relish the freedom available to a writer would then abdicate that freedom for mere success. In his world, an artist inhabited an unusual realm of great solitude and rare liberty. Maybe I have seized this independence as literary executor. I want to be the one to decide.

I attend to my father's poems, unpublished writings, voice on tape, video, and sometimes also the hunger of his readers. One letter states: "Your father had a poem about a time in the evening, how everything was all right. I heard him read it once. I would love to have a copy." I try to comply, though such a description might fit several dozen poems. But beyond the words on paper, I now read my father's directive in the will as a welcome life sentence of another kind. This is linked to many other directives that turn up in the archive. For my father, the job of the writer had no confinable magnitude. From his daily writing in the 1950s:

> About poets: Most people don't realize the stupendous attempts we think we are making—to overwhelm by *rightness,* to do something peculiarly difficult to such a perfect pitch that we catch the universe, understand it, *ride* it, and live. Think of the discrepancy, now, between this overweening impulse and the role given in society to poets. No wonder they sometimes act humble, like verse-makers, and sometimes act godlike, like criminals.

I love talk like that—helplessly gripped by the native optimism of the creator, the seeker. My father quietly pursued the utter re-creation of the world.

> I understand that the wrong sound weakens
> what no sound could ever save, and I am the one
> to live by the hum that shivers till the world can sing:—
> May my voice hover and wait for fate,
>     when the right note shakes everything.
>
> —*from* "BELIEVER"

My father saw his calling as both local and vast. My generation wanted to stop the particular war in Vietnam, while my father wanted to soften the hearts of the whole human village. To block a single war—especially by aggressive means—was too limited and misguided a goal. By writing, teaching, and acts of witness, we needed to stop the silencing of souls everywhere. Maybe this could come about through the most tender of our treasures: honest breath filling a right word. For in the words of the child-rearing book my parents used, children (and perhaps nations) "frequently hear more in our tone of voice than in the words we use."

I have a recurring dream that I am about to go on a long drive with my father, and I will be able to ask him everything. "Tell me all about Kansas again . . . spill the family secrets . . . your longings never before revealed. . . ." When I wake, I remember that drive will never be. But after many wakings to a world without his direct presence, I have come to believe this life *is* that long drive. And so I ask my life what I would know from him: What is my particular calling among the quiet voices of the world?

My parents were in the habit of inviting over the group they called "the old gang"—three faculty members and their spouses—for dinner at our house. We kids were consigned to our rooms where we huddled over homework or books while hearing the hilarity of the party down the hall.

At one such gathering my father was questioned about his travels. When he began his usual long list of coming engagements, someone challenged him.

"Bill, why do you travel so much?"

"It's my work," my father said. And that was all.

He called himself "a wanderer among the appearances of things" (Daily Writing, 18 February 1952). And later, "I must help anyone not plan a war" (Daily Writing, 22 November 1967). If he was needed, could he ever say no? I remember in college receiving his two-page, single-spaced record of coming engagements—date, host, duties, city by city, month by month— just to keep me "alerted," as he said, about his doings. The intensity was extreme. It seemed a kind of binge behavior. He would relish open stretches on the calendar when he could be at home, but paradoxically he did not discourage his friendly agents far and wide from putting together circuits that lasted for weeks at a time. At his desk after his death I found a list of sixteen impending engagements—readings, workshops, conferences. Beside this master list, I found his humble set of essentials for the road:

### For a trip

| | |
|---|---|
| ticket | razor |
| watch | change of clothes |
| lecture & reading material | toothbrush—towel |
| pen & notebook | vitamins etc. |
| billfold (with money) | coat—hat |

The great traveler had to remember to put money in his billfold, but did not need more than a single change of clothes, no matter how long the trip. He traveled light, and even at the end he was planning to be a busy man. He had typed the following to use as needed:

### Coming from Elsewhere to Speak:

Often I've heard a visitor speak from authority, from his distance; usually I've been impressed. When called a long way myself, I pause: what could I bring, what values could I carry?—so far am I from having any authority at home. But maybe by care in our common subject I can brush those few little corners which happen to appear....

He brought his poems, his "few little corners"—thousands of times.

One ambitious journey will serve to give the flavor of his work in far places. In 1972 he agreed to travel on behalf of the U.S. Information Agency to present programs on American literature abroad. The itinerary was grueling. He told me the two previous emissaries had become ill on the road. He intended to survive: Pakistan, India, Bangladesh, Nepal, Egypt, Iran. On his first evening in Pakistan, sixty poets gathered to read a poem apiece in his honor. After the first had completed a long, exuberant poem that seemed to go forever, everyone shouted, "Wah, Wah!" When my father asked the writer next to him what that meant, the answer came: "Read it again!" It was a long night.

He went with local hosts to visit the bandits at Khyber Pass. "Is it dangerous?" he asked. "Oh no, they take very good care of their visitors." The party shopped the bazaar of stolen goods in the mountains. In Calcutta, his taxi struck down a beggar—the driver afraid, refusing to stop: "We would be killed." In Nepal my father contacted my best friend from high school, then in the Peace Corps, and they agreed to meet for lunch in Kathmandu. Pointing to my father at a corner table, the waiter said to my friend, "You are here to meet that Japanese man?" My father's oriental mien.

By some fluke, the official report of my father's visit to Iran—then under the autocratic rule of the Shah—showed up among my father's papers. According to the report, my father gave six lectures, three readings, and several "small, private functions" that provided "the mission with a unique opportunity to strengthen our relations with the country's poets— a difficult and critical target group. Iranian poets, perhaps the most vocal element of the left, are often critical of the U.S., its culture and its policies. Poets in Iran take on special importance because poetry is an integral part of Iranian society and one of the few effective mediums of social comment. . . ."

The fact that we have a copy of this document may mean the official report was a different, hidden one. But one part of the report rings true:

> Despite being at the end of a long tour and anxious to be home
> Stafford was cooperative and easy to work with. He was flexible in
> his scheduling, was willing to tailor his presentations to post needs,
> and took suggestions well. He related well to his audiences especially during question and answer periods and was even better in
> small informal groups. He was, of course, best when reading his
> own poetry.

The Iran engagement was ambitious. Two dozen William Stafford poems had been translated into Persian by local poets, and at the reading in Tehran the Persian translations were projected on the wall above my father's head as he read his poems in English.

My father's own account includes one incident not in the official report. When he read his poem "The Animal That Drank Up Sound"—a long parable about a mysterious animal that swallows all voices, silences the world, and then slowly starves to death—students in the audience expressed amazement that a poet in America could get away with a poem so transparently critical of state censorship. When my father reported to them his innocence of this element in his poem, the students were even more amazed.

Early in his career, my father was in the habit of recording on the back of his "documentary copy" of a poem a list of places where he had read it. Presumably this was to avoid boring an audience in a place by reading the same poem again, even if his next visit occurred years after the first, and the audience was new. He read certain poems at colleges, high schools, libraries, churches, conferences, and in the homes of writers when they gathered and invited him. For example, he records a total of thirty-two readings over a five-year period of his poem, "A Dedication," which ends:

> At that corner in a flash of lightning we two stood;
> that glimpse we had will stare through the dark forever:
> on the poorest roads we would be walkers and beggars,
> toward some deathless meeting involving a crust of bread.

I imagine now the listeners to that poem at College of the Holy Names, San Francisco Art Museum, American Friends Service Committee, Reno, Mount Angel, Chattanooga, Simon Fraser University, Missoula, Congregational Church, Guggenheim, Gray's Harbor, Mrs. Stan's ladies in Eastmorland. . . .

My father told me there are three stages in one's career. In the first stage, no one asks you to do anything. In the second stage, more and more people ask, and you have to say yes—for if you don't, they might not ask again. In the third stage, he said, people ask you to do things, and you get to decide if you want to do them or not. He claimed he had never arrived at the third stage.

He came back with many stories from the road, little things he learned from chance encounters. For a child, hearing these stories was like reading a book with characters and lessons you would never forget, even when the book's title was eclipsed from memory.

One time his hosts had a daughter, thirty years old, who had never had a date. One morning, the mother took my father aside and asked him for advice.

"I don't know why she never seems to interest any of the young men," said the mother.

"I know why," my father said.

"You do?"

"When you say something to her," he said, "she leans back. If she would lean forward, people would think she had taken an interest in them, and they would take an interest in her."

A year later, the mother wrote him: the daughter was married and expecting a child.

Another time my father reported after a trip to Alaska that he had learned from a Native man the way hunters in the old days could cover a great distance without ever stopping to rest. They would walk at high speed, and every third step would be a running step, alternating left and right. I remember my father taking me out to the street to give me a demonstration. He had been practicing ever since.

A favorite ruse of my father's was to arrive early, but not make contact with the host until the last minute. He relished the chance to sidle into town, check into a motel, and coast through a lavish day of reading, writing, and exploring on the sly before the work started. On several occasions, he flew to a city, found a motel, explored in secret, and then returned to the airport the next day to meet his host as if he had just arrived.

This is one of the ways he survived, physically, a grueling itinerary. I remember one trip that included readings and workshops in twenty-seven towns over thirty days, all in one circuit around Ohio. He had to preserve what he called his "bounce," his good humor and resilience for the lively give and take of meetings with teachers and writers.

What was he pursuing in the long journey of his work? I don't have answers, but I do have clues. As my own career began to blossom—or should I say, my own career entered stage two: frenetic—one day my father told me about a passage from Maxim Gorky's autobiography. It was a time in Gorky's life when he had no real home, and it was a time in Russia's history when many people were out wandering the roads, searching for freedom, a new place, a revolution the size of one life. Young Gorky was striding along a road thick with wanderers when a great storm came up, and everyone took refuge in a barn. The storm raged outside, and darkness came, but Gorky could not sleep. He became aware that a wanderer near him in the straw was also awake, and so he asked her, "Why do you travel?"

She recounted her vision: "Oh, sir, I am looking for a hill on the steppe, and when I find it there will be a man. We will marry, plant our orchard, and build our house. When everything blossoms, others will see how we have made the earth beautiful, and they will build near us, plant their own gardens, and soon there will be a village there. Our neighbors will look to us for advice; they will name their children after us. . . . That is why I travel. But you who ask me, I ask you in return: why do you travel?"

"I travel," Gorky said, "to see how people live."

To see how people live. Is that my father's story? Is it mine? Impressed by Gorky's story, my father wrote:

*A Vita*

Maxim Gorky:

Dishwasher
Errand Boy
Draftsman
Icon Painter
Rag and Bone Man
Baker's Helper
Writer

1868–1936

In an undated letter from somewhere on the road, perhaps in the early 1940s, my father's father Earl is spending a Sunday in a hotel lobby, just watching the world go by. There is a tone of deep fatigue in the letter, yet a ready interest in what the lonely traveler sees. "Pop" reports to the family back home he has found a comfortable chair near the radio, where he can observe the hustle of other travelers streaming before him, and he has a good view of the mural on the lobby wall, a chronological panorama of "Transportation thru the ages. Elephants, Camels, Rickshaws, Prairie Schooners, horses, trains, autos, airplanes etc." He reports this "is the first day I haven't felt like I had to be in a hurry and on a nervous strain looking for something to happen, first day I have taken time to notice things."

That wanderer, my father's father, died on the road. He died so mysteriously even my father never got the story clear. I sense the way my own father's wandering began had a great effect on his calling, and on his writing.

In his last year at the University of Kansas before war swept him away, my father published a poem in the *Daily Kansan,* called "Communication from a Wanderer," which begins:

### *1. Report of Kansas in Winter*

(To everyone passed in the crowd whose eyes said hello:
    yes, he saw you.
To those hurt by the deeds and the talk every day
    it hurt him too.

To all who hinted what pride or convention or fear wouldn't
    let them say:
        he heard you; he was there with you.
To whoever are wondering if he gets their hopes, fears,
    insinuations:
        he does.
He does from being winter-homeless in Kansas.)

It was May 1941. My father was twenty-seven years old. In his attention to
people threatened and oppressed, he wasn't alone. World War I was still
fresh in the minds of his teachers, and on the minds of some fellow stu-
dents. In one editorial in the University of Kansas *Jayhawker* from June
1941, the anonymous writer describes the predicament my father must
have felt:

> Perhaps the bell will toll for us. You, all of us, are part of a genera-
> tion which in our own persecution complex we have termed "the
> plagued generation." Most of us had lived too little to enjoy the
> 1921–29 prosperity that our elders still talk about. We had existed
> just long enough to feel the "depression." And the draft bill seems
> to be so fate-fashioned as to inclose unanimously our little group.
>
> We were instructed in the folly of '14. We were told that wars
> never succeeded in establishing their ends. We saw the "war to end
> wars" sprinkle fertilizer for an abundant harvest of bigger and bet-
> ter wars. And now we are being led into mortal conflict by these
> same teachers. . . .

I hear good teachers behind this voice—an educated ability to ask tough
questions. As I read the anonymous voice of this student writer, together
with my father's writings from the time, I feel I am witnessing the source,
the headwaters of my father's vocation as writer and pacifist and seeker. It
was a time when certain perspectives were becoming visible in a way the
approaching war would obliterate for all but a few. War, like a bold adven-
ture story, would simplify the nuances of human interaction to a drama of
good and evil, Allies and Axis, winners and losers. Only a few might retain
the deeper questions. The writer in the *Jayhawker* goes on to prophesy:

We demand assurance, that in the event of fighting and dying and winning, we can return to our home and find a nation internally peaceful. We are urged to fight this war to prevent the spread of a foreign evil. Can we be assured that the evils which exist within our own borders will be rationally solved? Or will we return war-weary to find the specter which we had fought to destroy haunting our own hearths?

In this world tumbling toward war, my father's "Communication from a Wanderer" looks beyond the war to a life spent searching for meaning:

This is where the lonesomeness of the world shoulders in and stands.
This is to walk on a frozen dead street in a strange town,
     and there in the graveyard night by the railroad yards,
     and the cold steel wind, and the pitted cement of that doorway
     to lay a life down.
And they robbed him there in the secret ways, the bandits,
     the ones with the final grasp on exhibit A, the swag.
They held him up with their cruel weird pistols—
     the camouflaged ways of forcing the victim down.

He ends his prophecy by imagining, geographically, exactly what his fate would bring: both the poem and the whims of war took my father west, across the desert, to the coast. The poem ends there, with the speaker broken:

. . . . . . . . . . . . . . . . . . . . . . . . . . .
No longer stern, the laughter loose in his head,
     the warm rain falling on his back, he turned,
     the whole world softly turning, visions dead,
     and nothing left but this that he had learned:
Pilgrims turn back from what they can't quite see
     and seek in caves the blind for company.

My father did not seek the soft company of denial. He was a wanderer all his life precisely because he could not strike a bargain with himself to be blind, to settle for things as they were. In another poem, published in the *Jayhawker,* in October 1942 (perhaps a poem he submitted from camp), I hear my father preparing to carry his local allegiances through dark times:

> Tomorrow is darkness and a bomb ticking.
> But peace and yesterday are a still pool.
> Peace and yesterday are a shadow quiet on the wall.
>
> And from the sound of peace I heard a voice,
> A man who raised before the wind of steel
> A wispy tapestry of wondering:
>
> "Why follow half-way saviors, men who kill
> Or lie or compromise for distant ends?
> Marauders come; but no man dares cry 'Wolf!'
> The wolves look too much like our guardians."
> . . . . . . . . . . . . . . . . . . . . . . . . . . . .
> My place is only a little place, lost behind fronds,
> Hidden in the wolf reaches of the terrible earth.
> —*from* "FROM THE SOUND OF PEACE"

Our soldiers look like their soldiers. War is the enemy, not any man.

My father may have written this poem when he was home from camp for his father's funeral. The "man who raised before the wind of steel / A wispy tapestry of wondering . . ." Is that my father? His father? I suspect when my father left home again in the fall of 1942 to return to camp, he carried in his body the voice, the devotions, the responsibilities, and the silences of his father—and spoke from that place.

In these early poems the tone is sometimes overly grand, the language can be clumsy, and the author's views often relegated to third-person. But the ethical imperatives my father would carry all his life are clear.

When I ponder my father's vocation and try to braid these clues together, I think of him following the ways of his father, traveling to notice things, to see how people live. He once wrote, "Let me be a plain, unmarked envelope passing through the world." He would be the one picking up stories in one place, carrying them to share in another, and then "hobbling along" out of sight. In his poem "Retirement Speech," there is an indication of how one knows when to depart: "In courtesy at the end of a visit / one of the older Eskimos hints / time to part: 'I feel rich enough.'"

When my father's National Book Award first took him away from us, far and often, we would drive him to the old airport in Portland and walk him to the plane. There he would stand, his surplus World War II haversack slung over his shoulder with camera and tablet, and a little bag in one hand with his one change of clothes. The good-bye was brief—"We'll get all caught up when I get back." We knew he wouldn't call. Once he turned and walked down the tunnel to his plane, he was simply gone.

We would go up to the observation deck, stand at the aluminum railing, pick out his plane swinging slowly toward the runway. I remember the wind, and often the rain. He was everything to us and growing smaller—climbing, then disappearing into the clouds.

❧

# Strips of the Actual

WHEN I WAS OLD ENOUGH TO DRIVE, it was sometimes my privilege to disappear with my father and learn his distances. I got inside his silence and found a place at the busy table of his private life. When I heard about his need to get to Arcata for a reading or workshop, or to San Francisco, to Chico, Seattle, Bellingham, or Boise, if I could I would announce, "I'll be your chauffeur." And he would reply, "Great! We'll share the swag."

This series of journeys together was an important chapter in my education. I was his driver, and he my teacher, my companion, my listener. Our days on the wanderer's road could be sacramental. At the end of a hot afternoon in Berkeley, when his workshop was over, the reading behind us, the last meetings with students and writers done, we circled back to where we had left the car—planning ahead by parking where afternoon shade would swing east to cover it. The sun was so hot you had to watch the pavement where you stepped, or be mired in molten tar. I was moved to suggest an ancient ritual: I pried a hubcap off the wheel, filled it with water, and knelt on the grass to wash my father's feet. I had never studied his toes before. Ticklish, they wiggled. It was a moment both biblical and domestic. Then we traded places, and he washed my feet. The water was cool, the effect of his hands' touch delicious.

I remember a car screeching to a stop. The driver's electric window glided down. "Man, what are you doing?"

"We're getting ready for the long drive home."

Often our travels took us into complex territory. During one visit to a conservative college where we were invited to perform together, we were to speak to classes, have lunch with selected faculty members, and then give an evening reading. Our ideas converged when we were with the students, witnessing about the life of writing; but when we sat down with the college president and a group of distinguished faculty, I noticed my father camouflaging himself in language congenial to our hosts. The lunch was going along in an easy way when I heard my father say, "I believe an artist should fit in with the people of the time—no special distinctions."

"But you were a pacifist in World War II," I said. "That wasn't exactly fitting in."

"Well . . . yes, that's true." Silence. My father, for once, was stalled. The room waited. The president held his fork in midair.

"Doesn't the artist have to witness with personal truth," I said, "regardless of what other people think?"

"Personal truth. Hmmm." My father let the idea dangle in the air.

"I mean that part of the truth available to the artist," I said, "but for the benefit of others. In the '40s you had to witness for peace, even if you couldn't stop the war." I realized my father and I were having a little symposium, and the others were going to let us go it alone.

That night in our motel, after the poetry reading, I said to my father, "I hear there's a tavern on the edge of town—the place where the sinners go. Do you want to walk out there and get the feel?" My father declined, so I took the long ramble alone, sat in the blue smoke of the bar, drank my beer, and pondered. It came to me slowly there: in our symposium my father had treated me as he treated his students, saying something incomplete and then letting me explore the implications. But this approach wasn't calculated on his part. It was how he thought—taking an idea, a conversation, a class, a child—or a poem—to the brink of difficult truth. I had fallen into his welcoming trap.

We traveled, we tried things out, we traded ideas. Our journeys formed a long tutorial for me, and perhaps for him. Our common vocation gave us a privacy from the world in which to explore the unpredictable:

> If you don't know the kind of person I am
> and I don't know the kind of person you are
> a pattern that others made may prevail in the world
> and following the wrong god home we may miss our star.
> —WILLIAM STAFFORD, *from* "A RITUAL TO READ TO EACH OTHER"

> You took me to the mountains
> where we stood among the corn.
> You covered my mouth and spoke:

*little straight tree, beautiful and happy,*
*not yet turned aside to wisdom.*
    —KIM STAFFORD, *from* "FLOWER DRAWN FROM THORN"

I remember a journey through the dry, open land of eastern Oregon when my father answered my life questions with talk about poetry. (If I had asked about poetry, he might have turned to a subject equally oblique— like gardening.) We were headed for Idaho where he would be part of a televised program about poetry, and I was the driver. Somewhere east of Bend, Oregon, I began to ask for his advice about my working life. I had many part-time jobs, but seemed to be getting nowhere. I wanted to publish my poetry, but was discouraged. Characteristically, he listened, asked questions, but didn't advise. We drove for a time in silence. Then, east of Burns, he began to talk. Perhaps he was answering my questions in his own way. Or perhaps he was practicing for his talk in Boise by talking to me. It was hard to tell.

"When I write a poem," he said, his hand shading his eyes, "it's like I glimpse something far off—just a strip of the actual." He paused. In the distance, I saw the palisades of a basalt cliff, the stone columns where the lava had cooled.

"It's like seeing a strip of the universe," he said, "between the slats of a picket fence. You are passing, and between the pickets you glimpse a little of what's beyond." We were closer to the cliff then, and I could see the dust of lichen on its surface, the dull yellow smudge where a skin of life held on.

"And then I write another poem," he said, "and I get another glimpse, another strip of light through the fence. And then another. Another. But I never know if the successive glimpses are connected. Behind the fence, I never know if all those strips of the universe have continuity, one substance."

"They're connected," I said. "The strips behind the fence are connected."

"There's no way to tell," he said.

For some reason this made me so afraid I turned cold. If my father didn't know how things fit, then maybe they didn't. If he could not achieve this principle of coherence, how could I? Maybe my life would always be a fragmented mosaic, a puzzle, pain.

Since that conversation, I have thought often about that picket fence.

In his world we are alone, we are divided, we die, and we share this predicament as honestly as we can. The blank behind each picket makes the strips of illumination precious. Glimpsing that light, the writer gives us little talismans in a long episodic mystery. In my father's poems, you observe small things in open country. You are safe in that outside place, though you will suffer, be lost, feel the cold, and die. Still you are safe because that's where you should be.

He loved me, so he advised me with such parables: you belong in the world, and you are alone. Each glimpse is true, and successively they shift us in and out of safety. He was offering me observation, warning, consolation, ultimatum.

While listening to his reading in Boise, at the end of that journey, it came to me that my father's poems do not come to rest in assurance, nor in some final departure from assurance. Instead, they take us back and forth. Dawn, storm, sun, dusk, starlight, cold: every sensation is true. You are safe because you have been educated by the world's variety. Yet you know you are not safe, because you recognize the world's terrible variations. Yet you are safe, because you belong in the variable world, though it buffets you. The trail of your life "is one person wide."

That was one journey.

Later, my own life got too busy to travel with him often, and he kept saying he was going to retire. But in June 1993, his friend Robert Bly invited him to take part at the Conference on the Great Mother and the New Father, to be held at a place called Camp Miminagish, east from Bozeman, Montana, and my father decided to make the trip. I was swamped and declined the chance to go along. He would drive it alone, he said. I knew he would relish that—no schedule if he left early, and all that open country to explore. But a few days before he was due to go, I was standing by the window in my house looking out at the new leaves just coming onto the old birch tree, and the obvious struck: I had to go. I was divorced. My brother had died. The family was going its various ways. And my father was seventy-nine.

We left at midday, and the old routine took hold before we were out of Portland: we talked recklessly about everything, with a sense of leisure that only such a drive could give. The hum of the car, the scene unrolling—river, cliffs, forest, then the upland open country that slowly unpacked the mind.

In the car I could feel his years of traveling alone. His best-known poem, "Traveling through the Dark," describes an experience he had while driving home late through the Oregon Coast Range, after teaching an extension class at Tillamook: "Traveling through the dark I found a deer / dead on the edge of the Wilson River road. . . ." The poem tells one night's drama on that road, but behind the poem, and behind much of his life as a writer and teacher, I believe, were those eight years in the 1950s and '60s when he drove to the coast alone every week to teach that class. Once or twice he took the family along. I remember rain, a narrow forest road, and the open trunk of a fisherman's car where a giant steelhead lay on a bed of ferns, a thread of blood trailing from the gills.

My father was always traveling through the dark alone. Maybe those journeys gave him a foothold outside the family. He was objector, writer, wanderer—a three-way isolation by choice. If he led the life of a mule sometimes, working at a college and supporting a family, he was also hawk, ghost from an old tribe, a leaf blown willingly down the road.

We keep finding strange things in the archive, and one that pertains here he wrote in September 1982, apparently while on the road:

### A Report to My Mother

*"Billy, what happened to you today?"*

In the alley by the Royal Motel at dawn
a piece of cardboard lifts, end
over end. Mother, the life of your son
came to this, a wanderer in the wind.

Solitary watcher, unmoving, no sound—
let the blind light come: what passes is only
the edge of time groping along
where you happen to play the lonely one.

I bring this fragment a morning found,
that followed a stubborn child wherever
the world allowed: the cardboard wavers
toward what light there is, and slowly lies down.

He remembered his father's wide loops for the oil company through western Kansas, in the 1920s and '30s. To companion my father on any long journey was to inhabit a space he carried, a space where his father, his mother, his brother and sister, and all of that Kansas homeland—all gone from him by the time we were grown—had once reigned richly in his life.

On our journey to Montana I was hurting. I had been divorced for five years, and my life was in turmoil. I couldn't seem to stay with a woman longer than a year, and feared I contained a corrosive element—an intensity that kindled my writing but burned my companion. My father would listen, there would be a long silence, I would watch the undulating lines of barbwire fences streaming along, and then he might make an oblique, but strangely inevitable remark.

Somewhere east from Pendleton, in the big open hills toward Idaho, my father talked about an idea from Nietzsche, and I asked him to write it down in my pocket notebook. In his characteristic dense scrawl, he wrote, "Nietzsche: In our time of doubt about all 'certainties,' sustained intellectual discourse is hypocrisy." When I look at that notebook now, I see the next entry records my own inner turmoil: "I don't know where I am going. It's a good thing I have many years of practice with this feeling." We arrived the next evening for the Conference on the Great Mother and the New Father, far up a shadowed canyon in Montana.

The conference was most congenial to my father's curiosity. He kept assiduous notes for the full week, peppered with quotations from various speakers, and moments of drama, insight, purpose and reversal:

> Camus says that we can rediscover through art and ritual one or two images in the presence of which a person most lives . . . a "recovering Catholic" . . . Here, you need a shadow . . . You can hurt each other, but only for the other's good . . . Water has disciplined itself to walk upon the land . . . Human beings are no longer at home in the world . . . How can you know something . . . the Grayhairs: "We handle darkness. Complain to us." . . . people blindfolded, make clay objects, pass them along, destroy them without ever seeing. . . .

Some afternoons my father led a writing workshop; he dressed up as Lucifer for a skit; he dissolved an impasse in the debate by quoting from one of his own poems: "Some haystacks don't even have a needle." Robert Bly has since quoted what my father said at one point—what the river says when it meets a rock: "I'll just go around, and think about it later."

Despite my interest in this gathering, my own anguish took me away. I had suffered through the romantic highs and lows of a series of relationships and was in the midst of a clearly doomed but strangely paralyzing passage with a woman I could not understand. Since the topic of the conference had much to say on the blindness of men to the suppressed powers of women, I took notes on discussions of romantic love that my father—by the evidence of his own jottings—let pass without record. When I read through my notebook now, it bristles:

> What the goddess might look like to the small eyes of the ego . . .
> rational ego is president of our interior being—could be a tyrant . . .
> everything you can't control is the goddess . . . male ego splits the
> goddess into the beautiful and the dark one . . . rational ego
> oversees attempt to live an ordered life—eventually becomes a
> puritan. . . .

Was my woman friend the goddess, and I the puritan? I spent days high on a ridge, and later carried my tent and sleeping bag into the forest at night in order to wake alone among the trees. In the messy story of my life I felt the confusion that the writer Elizabeth Woody describes: "Trying to understand the pattern from the perspective of a bead." The wilderness fit each stone, tree, and river into place. Perched on a boulder far up a talus slope, I scribbled questions into my little notebook, then lost my favorite fountain pen scrambling over the rocks. I felt like a fool to be mooning alone over my romance, while wisdom and theater were shared at the camp below. I hiked the Bridge Lake Trail into the high country, and there I came out into a meadow of flowers and butterflies. I was stricken by the beauty of the world my brother had abandoned through his suicide. As I gazed at the shimmering sunlight of that place, from nowhere a sentence came to me, and I burst into tears: "I am feeding my brother."

Feeding my brother? Leaving my lover? My whole life seemed wrong. Higher, almost to the snow, I came into another meadow where an elk was feeding. So as not to frighten her, I lay down to sleep where she could see me. When I woke she was gone.

Down in camp, my father was on his own journey. As he joined with the others, talk swirling around him, he wrote two poems that reveal his grief and his joy in the story he was living. One is for my brother:

> This is for you, Bret, I think; this
> is the way an old man walks who still
> stays vigorous and strong, firm, alert,
> holding on through the years for you—
>
> The kind of old man you could be,
>     or could have been.
>         —*from* "Crossing Our Campground"

The other poem, "Godiva County, Montana," is an erotic reach toward the landscape, a manifesto for joy:

> She's a big country. Her undulations
> roll and flow in the sun. Those flanks
> quiver when the wind caresses the grass.
> . . . . . . . . . . . . . . . . .
> "Be alive," the land says. "Listen—
> this is your time, your world, your pleasure."

These poems represent the double gift my father gave me: helpless suffering and tenderness toward old mistakes, but also a fresh appetite for life right now. A lost soul at the conference asked his advice about what to do with her life. He told her he had met the camp handyman who had all the tools he could need in his truck and found zest in his work. "But that example was beneath her," my father said. "She wanted a spiritual answer." (Was he telling this story to advise me?)

My father stayed for the whole conference, but I had to get back to Oregon. As he drove me to the Bozeman airport, he asked what I had learned at the gathering, and I read him some of the quotations I had written down. "You heard things I didn't hear," he said.

"Daddy, can I ask you about the whole life?"

"Ask me anything."

"If I'm with the wrong person how will I find the right one? What does it take for a partnership to work?" He cocked his head and raised his eyebrows. It was hot. Through the open window, wind buffeted his hair, silver and black. He talked of life with my mother—steadiness, calm, a search for shared support and independence.

"Dorothy knows I let her win many little domestic victories," he said, "but I keep the big one—my freedom. When we have a hard time, she says, 'Let's agree this won't happen again.' But you can't do that. It's part of life."

"Sometimes," I said, "I feel like there is some kind of acid in my character—what feels like a richness to me, an intensity, my whole creative life—that wears another person down and things stop working."

"Dorothy and I have had a good life," he said. "But sometimes I feel sorry for her. She had the bad luck—just the plain tough luck to marry Crazy Horse. She'll forget for a while, and then something will happen that reminds her with a jolt."

"Who *should* marry Crazy Horse?" I said. He looked over at me with that direct gaze of his.

"Another hawk, I guess."

"What happened to Robert and Carol Bly?"

"Two hawks on one farm."

As we were coming into town, my heart sank, and I fell silent. The life of writing, friendship, good work—these I could do. Partnership eluded me, yet I kept magnetically falling in love. I was clumsy, puzzled, failing, stumbling away.

He stopped the car on a shady street, and turned to face me. For all our deep connection, he kept a certain distance. This was one of the few times in my life he did not. Denying his customary respect for my independence, he reached out to touch my shoulder and spoke directly.

"I just want to say I think a good life is possible—lively companionship, and all. Marriages that begin young, as yours did, often suffer attrition. Two grown people have the best chance when they meet later. It seems to me that could be the best there is. Be of good heart, my friend."

❦

# IV.

## *You Have to Explain*

# Negative Capability

O NE TIME, AS WE PUT our tools away in the evening, my father ran his fingers along a length of cord he was coiling. "This string has all kinds of protuberances I didn't see," he said. "I realize: light hides a lot."

Light hides a lot? My father had a Ph.D., but lived as a champion of intuition, peripheral vision, hunch. If you can see too well, he would say, you will miss the nuances. The eye, he said, "tapered for braille," might see beyond present things.

If light hides the world, darkness reveals it. The title of his most famous book ran like a refrain through our early years, *Traveling through the Dark*. And after his death, Robert Bly edited a selection of my father's poems called *The Darkness Around Us Is Deep*. A poem from late in my father's life begins, "A voice within my shadow wakened me, / a glowing voice: 'I love the dark / too much—I cannot sleep.'" He heard a "glowing" voice—as if invisible things make their own light from within, and we must dim the world to see our true path, to find the thread. For it is there, always: "The thread we follow no one spun" (Daily Writing, 14 June 1969).

One evening in the early 1960s, this world of metaphor about the dark and the light became actual when my father and I found ourselves at an unusual garage sale. On a table in the driveway, treasure: a man retiring from the FBI was selling his darkroom. Dusty on the driveway, an old enlarger leaned on its stand with bellows extended. There were film tanks and reels, clips, trays and tongs, a thermometer, a safelight, and a contact printer—all the black shapes and snaky electric cords for this darkroom magic we knew nothing about. We saw promise we couldn't name, and we carried it all home. Soon the backyard hut that our father had built as our playhouse was stripped of toys and converted into a darkroom. He dug a trench from the house and ran electric cable to the new project. Then he painted the inside walls of knotty pine black (I've learned since that darkrooms should be white inside); roughed in a bench for the enlarger and trays; added a light-lock drawer for photo paper; and hammered a nail on the wall to hold the ruby glow of the safelight. It was slipshod glory then—you taped a sheet of black plastic over the door, and once you locked yourself in, you could have the pure darkness any time you pleased.

That hut was Daddy's Darkroom, his refuge from the everyday, where by rights he could lock darkness in and learn his way back into the world image by image, face by face. And like my father, I chose to surrender there to the plea of light in darkness.

In the kitchen, evenings, my father and I would be at the sink, pouring a clear, strangely slippery solution called Microdol X into the film tank. Inside, film lay coiled, spiraling the reel where we had threaded it in the perfect darkness of the coat closet down the hall. My father would tap the tank on the edge of the counter to free any bubbles within that might mar the image, and I would keep time as he turned and turned the tank to bathe its secrets with fresh chemical—"agitation" was the technical term for this meditative practice.

We took to buying our film in ten-meter rolls and hiding in the closet to snip off a fathom at a time to coil into cassettes. That work in the dark of the closet—camera, scissors, church key to snap off the top of the cassette, and then the glassy length of film sprung free—was a prelude. When you peeled the tape from where the film met the spool, a little flash of green fire sprang forth. Static, the small spirit released.

The words, the concepts intrigued me: aperture, depth-of-field, infinity, light making silver black, reciprocity failure, positive and negative. Photography was a world of metaphor, of dream made real, and the perfect negative was our goal. My father would say, as he poured in and out the succession of change agents in liquid form—developer, water, fixer, water, hypoclear, water, photo-flo—"Maybe this time we'll get the perfect negative."

Of course, there were the prints as well. My father had a preference for catching his writer friends off guard—Gary Snyder asleep at a meeting of the California Arts Council; Carolyn Kizer snipping at W. S. Merwin's tie with her scissor fingers. My father's prints were sometimes marred by dusty negatives—maybe he couldn't see that well. But often they were brilliant. He wrote of his allegiance to the inescapable truth of the print:

> God snaps your picture—don't look away—
> this room right now, your face tilted

exactly as it is before you can think
or control it. Go ahead, let it betray
all the secret emergencies you still hold
that partial disguise you call your character.
. . . . . . . . . . . . . . . . . . . . .
The camera wide open,
stands ready; the exposure is thirty-five years
or so—after that you have become
whatever the veneer is, all the way through.
　　　　　—*from* "AN ARCHIVAL PRINT"

But behind any public sharing of a print, my father had a preference for the negative itself. He would hold a hand lens up to the film still wet, find a tiny face captured in the emulsion, and examine the silver grain that formed the image: "Just right!"

The negative held an idea still seed-small, like the first nibbling syllable of discovery, the tooth marks or spore of an animal we were about to glimpse for the first time. Like his own intuitive beginnings in his daily writing before dawn—his exploratory, salty, reckless seeds of discovery— the *negative* was for my father the source of his greatest pleasure in the whole process.

Years later, I came upon that passage in John Keats's letter to his brother where he describes what he calls "negative capability," the forthright avoidance of prior standard or judgment that allows one to receive and experience varieties of character without striving after fact. Keats said that Shakespeare, in his ability to create characters of all kinds, was preeminent in this ability—or nonability. Keats called it "negative" capability because it was the opposite of what one might identify as power or skill. Surrendering to experience beyond oneself might be classified by some as weakness, a lack of consistent character. I find in my father's writing a passage about just this kind of receptivity, dating from the time we began to do photography:

Failures guide. Ignorance is one of our friends. What we can't
see tells us part of what we know. Blunders cry out information.
Prehensile thought survives by welcoming blanks, reversals, falters,
salvation—great stupidities. To disregard what happens, to cringe
at events—including events we did not want to happen—is to
part company with the real world, our guide, our foundation, our

everything. The blur your fallible sight brings is a meaning—the *blurring* means as much as the shape.

—DAILY WRITING, 5 JULY 1959

The readiness of the thin silver emulsion on film or photo paper receives exactly what light stamps. This felt like the pleasure that lay at the root of writing freely, receiving the shock of cold or hunger, living without prejudgment.

For a time in the 1950s, my father joined a group of Oregon photographers who met regularly to talk about their art. He was the only poet in the group, but they all had a language in common. They did not "take pictures," but rather they "made exposures." He did not make poems, he received them, welcomed them, wrote down what came. And by the time we stumbled upon that garage sale, my father was ready to practice his art of poetry with a lens of glass.

The habit of photography, as I practiced it with my father and later alone, was not about ideas, or skill, or equipment. It was light along the railroad tracks at evening, light embracing each wave across a pool, sensuous light. It was dew along a stem of grass, world by world. It was the eyes of the fawn as they dawned slowly onto the paper lit red before me in the darkroom.

As with writing, I seek to understand my father's legacy by examining my own experience. When he taught me photography, I see now, he was teaching me lessons in writing and other forms of being in the world. His way of teaching was to send me forth for a vision, a trial. The secrecy of sensitive film locked safe inside a box of steel spread outward in my life. When my parents gave me a camera of my own, I took a book at random from the family shelf, hollowed its pages with my knife, and secured the camera inside with a machine screw through the spine. (Perhaps my mother will never quite forgive me for the book I chose: James Stephens, *The Crock of Gold,* a favorite.) I saved my scant allowance for a "cable release" so I could trip the shutter without opening the book. Then I smuggled my own FBI secret-agent instrument of adolescent negative capability to school and aimed it as best I could at people I admired.

Increasingly keeping to myself as junior high spit me into high school, I would rove the halls alone, aiming my book with care as Mikey walked by, or Molly, Bob, Anita, Paul, Carolyn. My wrist would swivel the book upright, so the lens piercing the cover was uncovered. I would clear my throat to disguise the sound as the shutter clicked, then swivel the book back down and go my way.

At the sink in the evening, I would hold the film tank, about the size of a heart, I thought, turning it, counting the beat of the seconds until it was safe to open. Then I would strip the film from its reel and hold it stretched from hand to hand against the wan light above the stove. The images were sometimes crooked, blurred, turning away, but in my keeping now. Later, once our whole house had settled into sleep, I would rise and pad my way to the darkroom in the yard, flip on the safelight, and grope for tools to make my prints of people who might, by this alchemy, become friends. Then as the prints washed, the garden hose whispering into a pan in the yard, I might return to the darkroom to practice my clarinet softly. "The Dark Horseman," perhaps, or "Silver Threads among the Gold," and later Mozart. A certain adagio from Mozart, or certain passages in Brahms had for me an elusive silver sound best breathed in the darkroom at night while water pearled across the ghostly faces outside in the yard.

At school I would deliver any remotely flattering print to its rightful owner, getting a laugh if I was lucky, but often a puzzled look. "You what? In a book? Why?" I had no answer.

My father, in his circle of poets, was a famous man by then, and I watched him use the camera to get outside the center, to be a spy among the famous, a mere reporter rather than the prophet his acclaim afforded him. He would come home from every journey with a roll of film or two, and we would talk by the sink as he processed his catch. When he unreeled the negatives I might see Richard Hugo, Linda Pastan, Ann Darr, Henry Taylor, and often young unknowns he bragged of: "a distinctive person I was glad to meet. We sat down and talked about everything! She had this strange idea. . . ." And then my father would unreel a string of insights and questions some new friend had offered to his willing mind.

I was his disciple of light, expressed in darkness. From the work I did with my father at home, I went forth. In college I twisted the intent of an assignment in design class so I could fulfill it by wandering Oregon in my VW bug, driving to the coast to photograph circles on a pond in the dunes, then east to the desert to photograph the weathered growth rings of a pine stump. I talked a gallery into mounting a show of my photographs. Maybe this would be my calling. Maybe I could enter those black-and-white myths to which the library exposed me—where Edward Weston's nudes and Imogen Cunningham's ravishing flowers seemed to be plotting my future.

Years later, I found myself at midnight in a line of travelers disembarking from a Danish ferry on the shore of Sweden. My hair was shaggy, my rucksack torn, and the customs man chose me to shake down completely. I disassembled all I had—my few clothes, my journal, wood recorder, my hitchhiker sign "Dirección Göteborg," my rain cape and hat, my camera, and my sleeping bag. At the center of my tight-rolled sleeping bag was a sealed can of film—a twelve-meter roll of unexposed Ilford FP4—and a dozen film cassettes with the record of my wanderings. This last secret of my whole kit appeared, and I saw the eyes of the customs man widen. Here must be the drugs for sure.

I don't remember our awkward conversation as I pointed to the camera, the lightbulb overhead, the cassettes, the film can in my hand with tape running around its rim. I went through the motions I had so often practiced in the dark with a fathom of film, the scissors, the little flash of fire. The customs man peered closely at me, turned my film can over and over in his hand, shook it, smelled it, looked into my eyes. Since it was midnight, and raining softly outside, the other travelers were in no hurry, and some stood to watch our performance—the threadbare possibility of trust between an official and a vagabond. Finally the man handed my treasure back to me and waved me on.

I slept in a garden that night. The rain had stopped, and it was the only neutral ground in a town of silent houses. Shadowed from any streetlight, I spread my cape and unrolled my sleeping bag on a strip of turf, crawled in, and was gone. Waking sometime before dawn, I saw the stars. A bird I didn't recognize had begun to mutter and then to sing. I remembered when my father got the idea he wanted to photograph the stars with a long exposure. He conducted me out through the dark to ask my advice about setting up his camera under the stars. We stood in a clearing among the pines as he snapped open the tripod by feel, trained the camera upward, got down on his knees to peer through the range finder, opened the shutter wide, and extended the focus to infinity. For some reason, we felt like whispering.

"How long?" he whispered. We both looked up, trying to calculate how much light the stars might offer.

# Smoke's Way

I F YOU WAKE UP BEFORE other people, my father said, you can be free, for a little while. But what about daylight, society, the world of work? How can you maintain your freedom when you are with others? My father's answer: "smoke's way."

> Smoke's way's a good way—find,
> or be rebuffed and gone:
> a day and a day, the whole world home.
>
> Smoke? Into the mountains I guess
> a long time ago. Once here, yes,
> everywhere. Say anything? No.

In a world often directed by required social behaviors, and even by aggression, where people "credit fact, force, battering" (his poem, "Lit Instructor"), my father could be visible, but yielding; present, but elusive:

> I saw Smoke, slow traveler, reluctant
> but sure. Hesitant sometimes, yes,
> because that's the way things are.
>
> Smoke never doubts though:
> some new move will appear.
> Wherever you are, there is another door.
> —"SMOKE"

That other door could be death, I suppose. Or it could be the death of the predictable: a buoyant approach to life by the willing suspension of certainty. My father called a collection of his poems *Smoke's Way* because that phrase identified for him the way of the seeker who must be a fugitive in a forceful world. The poems in this book, significantly, were collected from his small-press publications, not the more prominent books from Harper & Row that had brought him some fame. He favored the small, the hidden, the hard-to-pin-down. For certainty, and its anger, can kill—even a little at a time.

> The reliable animus: it's always alert, the watchdog. Sleeps with a snarl in its throat. I can count on its putting a hidden edge on any reaction to offensive situations. Be sure you are fighting the right enemy.
> —DAILY WRITING, 8 JANUARY 1952

As a pacifist, my father knew more about the power of aggression than any soldier. He had watched its effects all his life, and suffered them—not just during war, but in the daily arrogance of money, manhood, reputation, and journalism slanted by fear:

> I call it cruel and maybe the root of all cruelty
> to know what occurs but not recognize the fact.
> —*from* "A RITUAL TO READ TO EACH OTHER"

He observed the willful denial by his country (and even by many writers) of the destructive impact of aggression for both aggressor and victim, and he felt alone. This isolation, made inevitable by his pacifism, found expression in my father's elusive ways of writing and seeking—ways that were forced on him first by his closest friends following World War II:

> [M]y friends were . . . more antagonistic to my position [as a conscientious objector] than the general populace was. I think it must be some kind of psychological thing. They knew me, and I had done this, and it was kind of an affront. . . . I think that's an endemic part of my life now. How much of the truth is it practicable to allow a person you meet in a hurry? . . . I had always assumed people up and down the street, you know, this is *our* country, this is *our* town. Suddenly, it's *their* country, it's *their* town. And I'm more foreign.
> —AN INTERVIEW WITH WILLIAM STAFFORD, IN
> *We Have Just Begun to Not Fight*

What human allegiance kept my father open, welcoming, and eagerly help-ful toward others in a world darkened against him? What could he do? As with many things, it wasn't until after my father was gone that I began to understand: he could be smoke.

Like my father, I didn't come to understand smoke's way on my own. Others taught me. In November 1998, five years after my father died, my family and others were gathered in the library at Lewis & Clark College to dedicate the William Stafford Room. When several literary pilgrims had appeared on campus years before, asking to see some shrine to their hero, William Stafford, we had to say there wasn't one. I directed them to the bookstore; but alas, the clerk at the register that day had never heard of William Stafford—a famous teacher at the college for thirty years, but now gone. When they reported this to me, I knew we had to act.

With the president's approval and the help of many, we designated a study space in the library as the William Stafford Room, and raised money to appoint it. The room commands a view to the east, and is furnished with a table with a lamp and a set of framed photographs: William Stafford teaching on the lawn in his old felt hat; William Stafford with his bicycle on the campus cobblestone road; and a class in the 1960s, which he printed to help him remember the students' names. There is a copy of his manifesto, "Assumptions about Literature Class," and various poems in multiple versions, from the handwritten start in his daily writing through revision to the published text. Finally, the room's most important feature, a couch where anyone might lie down and write a poem in the spirit of William Stafford. On almost every visit, I have found a student there asleep.

At the dedication, the president of the college welcomed the audience. He reported my father's contributions as a faculty member and a writer, and offered insightful comments on his work, listing his awards, his publi-cations, the profile of his career in that place and beyond. As I listened to the president, I heard a strange reply in my mind: "My Daddy had a lot of yin." Yin? I think that word came to mind because of the way his poetry spoke often of smoke, wind, sky, a river's pliant turning, or the way grass yields in the manner of recurrent images in the *Tao Te Ching*. He was more like the air in a room than the room itself; more fog than stone; more mys-tery than fame. The president's list would have been nothing to my father. Nothing at all. His allegiance went instead to something deeper—the searching, never-completed, immeasurably "rich distress" of becoming a human being.

Robert Bly stepped to the microphone. Tears in his voice, he read a poem and stepped away. Others came to say their own quiet words. At such an occasion, from long habit, I expected to glimpse my father somewhere near the edge of the crowd, slyly taking pictures of us. Later, we might see ourselves as he caught us: "Hold it. Don't move. That's you forever."

As I scanned the room—saw my wife and our small boy, my mother, sisters, our friends gathered to celebrate this mysterious friend—I thought back. I never heard my father brag. I rarely heard him correct another. I don't remember him raising his voice once in all those years. Not once. Instead, he was the receiver of all we did, who we were. But yes, he could be fiercely clear, too, in his own way. When he did emerge from the quiet to speak directly, what brought him into the open?

Years ago on a panel, one luminary held forth at length that it was impossible to really teach writing, since talent was native. My father responded that it would seem wrong in that case to accept a salary as a writing teacher. The point was lost on no one. My father had publicly accused a famous man of stealing from the young. That, to my ear, was a rare aggressive correction—perhaps common for many in his position, but very unusual for my father.

Many of my father's poems are about women, but most of the books on his office shelf are by men—certainly the philosophers, his core collection: Nietzsche, Kierkegaard, Pascal, Wittgenstein. He read those men who, like himself, knew smoke's way, who had a receptive way of being a man. Both in their restless, searching ways of practicing philosophy and in their style of writing, these seekers did not create monuments to truth but rather invitations to mystery. Their quests, like my father's, were based in suffering and its resulting uncertainty, and they sought provisional, dynamic, ever-unfolding remedies that did not retreat into static pronouncements. One of the sheets of paper he kept above his desk was a passage he had typed from a translator's introduction to Kierkegaard's *Philosophical Fragments*:

> [T]hese writings illuminate and bring to a high degree of conscious
> clarity the subjective life of the human spirit, the life of passion,
> emotion, aspiration, evaluation, hope, despair, anxiety, dread, confidence, trust, doubt, faith. This is the problem for thought gener-

ally neglected by philosophers. . .[but] Kierkegaard's writings form
an outstanding exception to this rule; in his case the entire energy
of a great genius of reflection was expended upon the clarification
of the realm of the subjective, which is the realm of the spirit.

My father favored men of pliant mind because he needed their company.
He wrote about women because, as a pacifist, an outsider, a poet of con-
science, a disciple of the inner life, he felt affinity with their way of being.
He wrote a note to himself, for example, that "D. H. Lawrence . . . is quite
ambivalent in his perceptions: I know he preaches masculinity, but he is in
many ways feminine."

Smoke's way, the feminine, pacifism—how did these strands join in my
father's character? Just as pacifism shaped his politics, and intuition his
writing, so his pliant approach to life, which he called "smoke's way,"
shaped his teaching and his parenting. His devotions were to victory
through surrender, eloquence through listening, and becoming a man
through understanding the ways of women. In one poem he reports the
discovery of a new metal—"Christianite"—that bends but does not break
when subjected to intense pressure. Strength through pliability is the para-
doxical source of his character. I follow this flexibility in his life as I search
through a set of clues he left me.

Interviewers would ask him what writer had most influenced him. His
reply without fail: "My mother." Having said this often, in the last year of
his life he was still puzzling over it, noting in his daily writing: "Of all the
people I know my mother was the only one who always realized in entire
consistency something that underlies my own essence: life is inexplicable,
and those masterful people who base their lives on confidence and explana-
tion deserve our sympathy."

Someone once asked him who was the best twentieth-century poet.
His reply: "Emily Dickinson had more to offer than anyone of the current
century."

He recognized his future wife as "the one" on that fateful day in 1943,
partly because she knew the work of Willa Cather.

I sense my sisters each had a spirited closeness with our father quite dis-
tinct from mine. His best-known poem about a child is about a daughter—
"With Kit, Age 7, at the Beach." When Barbara asked if he would write
a poem, in turn, for her, he produced one that began, "In prison, they

would give you the best cell. . . ." He was fond, but unpredictable. Smoke's way.

Aside from his own writing, the only piece of literature in his daily writing box at his death was a quotation recorded by Mother Agnes from Saint Teresa:

> Allowing her to see my fears, I asked her what sort of death I would die. She answered with a very tender smile: "God will sip you up like a little drop of dew."

When he was asked to choose one young poet as his accompanying reader for a major event at the Library of Congress, he chose Naomi Shihab Nye. I find it significant he chose as his favorite a Palestinian American woman forthright in her devotion to conciliation.

If my father had a pliant habit of mind, how did his ways come to me? How does a seeker practice parenting? He and my mother named me "Kim" after the title of the Rudyard Kipling novel she took to the hospital to read when I was born. (Kipling was a favorite of my father's father.) I rarely met anyone who had read *Kim*. The title character is a listener, an observer, a scamp. He is known in the markets of Lahore as "Little Friend of All the World." I learned all this in my thirties when I finally read the book. Until then, I only knew I had a woman's name.

By a strange reversal I learned feminine sensibilities from my father, and something more assertively masculine from my mother. They seem to have struck a bargain by which she would lay down the law at home, while he would contribute prevailing if often elusive ideas of what was right. I once wrote my parents from college I wanted to cut class for a week and drive to San Francisco. Before the trip I got a short letter from my mother telling me not to go. After the trip I got a long letter from my father, a philosophical meditation on the difficulty of making wise decisions.

I know in many families the parents divide their child-raising responsibilities, one parent providing clarity and the other mystery. My parents both recognized the least effective way to be a parent was to get into a power struggle, a confrontation with their children. My father's retirement from all such confrontation, however, left my mother feeling she had to be the one to speak up. In advance of my trip, her position was clear:

Dear Son Kim Most Honored—

1) Do I think it wise to make a tremendous trip to S.F. this week?
   No.
2) Do I think your job is to attend classes & do your best? Yes.
3) Does Daddy agree? Yes, although he wouldn't say it boldly like
   this.
4) Do we love you? Yes!

I went anyway—but not only to San Francisco. Once on the road I decided
to take in L.A., too. The trip was a long lunge and a blast. Falling asleep at
the wheel on the road home, I could have died. My VW bug sailed through
roadside bushes in a green blur before miraculously bouncing back onto
the road. Somehow this didn't faze me.

In due time, my father's letter came—typical in its clarity about the lit-
tle things and its mystery about the big ones. First he sternly instructed me
to return money I had borrowed from a family friend while in California.
He enclosed a stamped envelope addressed to them: "The way to deserve
such good friends is to act worthily." As for the rest—deciding how to live a
life—my father shared his musing at length. He had been to a conference of
English teachers, he said, and during one session he got to thinking about
my journey:

> Robt. Hogan in his speech in the morning identified several kinds
> of "belief" a person should learn, and I now realize that your trip
> to California was good for several things, some related to Hogan's
> points. He said that besides learning belief about the ordinary
> things, that is about the ordinary way we identify belief, one should
> go on: 1) Things are . . . (the ordinary kind of belief in the way
> things are etc.). 2) I can . . . (the realization that one is able to do,
> try, live with, certain things, a growing number of things). 3) People
> can help when . . . (the awareness that many occasions or situa-
> tions are the kind in which one can ask help of others and get it).
> 4) These are fun . . . (the encountering of new experiences that it
> is fun to get involved in). Well, when I got to thinking of Hogan's
> speech and your trip, I saw. . . .

He ends his letter to me with an ellipsis—four dots. He saw . . . what? His advice was . . . what, exactly? Perhaps he saw I was learning, and his advice was to go on learning, thinking, wandering: smoke's way.

My father's poems, like his letters to me, often speak as a witness to power rather than in the language of the one with power. The world-citizens who inhabit his poems are often women, a series of hurt people who would not be known but for the poem's notice: Althea, Berky, Bess, Selina, Lorene, Ruby, and on through the pantheon. His poems *refer* to men, of course—Dag Hammarskjöld, Thomas Jefferson, Hitler, Jesus—but the subject or activating muse of many poems is a woman. The poet is the listener who watches hard things, has limited power, but knows a better way. His poems offer homage to women who have not been seen by the world, until the poet sees:

> we found each other alive,
> by our glances never to accept our town's
> ways, torture for advancement,
> nor ever again be prisoners by choice.
> —*from* "MONUMENTS FOR A FRIENDLY GIRL
> AT A TENTH GRADE PARTY"

> But Lorene—it was a stranger maybe, and he
> said, "Your life, I need it." And nobody else did.
> —*from* "SAINT MATTHEW AND ALL"

An early poem ("At Liberty School," 1953) begins, "Girl in the front row who had no mother . . . the taxes of Rome were at your feet." My father's regard for the girl—injured at the margin of life, but cherished by the quiet observer—led him in 1968 to track down Catherine, the woman who had been the actual "girl in the front row." He sent her a letter gushing with homesickness for Kansas, and expressing hope his family could someday visit hers. After a sketch of his life since Kansas, he yields to a loving evocation of home:

> I turn to a long-anticipated attempt to reach out a memory toward
> you:—remember Liberty School! . . . Hutchinson. The Arkansas
> River. Cow Creek. Farmington. The sandhills. Several times we

"No one told us where to put the signs."
(Stafford at a peace rally in the 1960s)

"This is the hand I dipped in the Missouri . . ." (photo by Jerry Johnson)

"The bitter habit of the forlorn cause is my addiction." (faculty colleagues at Lewis & Clark College, c. 1965: [l-r] Steve Knox, Leon Pike, William Stafford, Ted Braun, Jack Hart)

"Priest of the imagination" (Stafford teaching at Centrum in Port Townsend; photo by Don Hunter)

"Mine was a Midwest home . . ."
(Stafford, top, with his sister
Peg, brother Bob)

"That Billy was
kind of an Indian."

"Within the citadel of myself . . ." (Stafford in his childhood fort in Kansas)

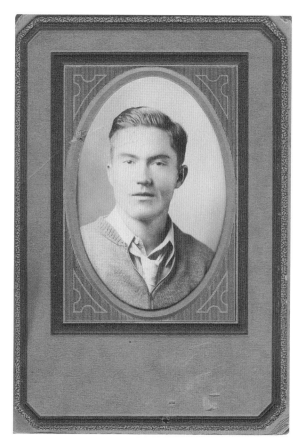

"Hold it. Don't move. That's you forever." (Stafford as a student in the 1930s)

"My father could hear a little animal step . . ." (Earl Stafford)

"My mother, who opened my eyes . . ." (Ruby Stafford)

"When are men dangerous?" (photo by Stafford of two fellow pacifists before the mob arrived, McNeil, Arkansas, 1942)

"I couldn't stop the war."
(at camp for conscientious
objectors during World War II)

"In camps like that, if I should go again, I'd still study the gospel and play the accordion."

"My wife, a vivid girl from the mountains . . ." (Stafford with his wife Dorothy on their honeymoon)

"We were living in Iowa then, in the Quonset hut of tin." (William and Dorothy, with their children Kim and Bret)

"I don't remember questioning why we moved every year until I was eight."
(Kim left, Bret right)

"The target was
interior and before."
(Kim and Bret)

"A Saint from the Kingdom" (Stafford
family, with friend Betty Hosking, visiting
pacifist Glenn Coffield at his handmade
house on Mount Hood, 1950s)

"Our Ways Those Days" (left to right: Kim, Bret, Kit Stafford)

"My father had a preference for catching his writer friends off guard."
(Stafford photo of Stanley Kunitz, with Barbara and Dorothy Stafford)

"Our work was meditative" (Kim and Bill working on the house at Sisters)

"What great rope current braided us apart?" (Bill and Kim at Sisters)

"When I ponder my father's vocation . . ."
(Bill and Kim at the Fishtrap Writers Gathering in Oregon)

"My brother Bret was otherwise . . ."

"We call him Guthrie, and we play him Woody Guthrie tunes to start him right."

"I don't need to hold on to Bill . . ." (Kim with his daughter Rosemary)

"In 1993 the festival was dedicated to my father."
(Stafford with festival poster; photo by Mike Markee)

"I went alone to my father's study to sit in his swivel chair, turn slowly and feel —
his absence, or his presence?" (Stafford's typewriter at his study in Lake Oswego;
photo by Mike Markee)

". . . the quiet, poised, welcoming, hawkish, friendly-but-not-tame czar of my childhood." (Stafford's self-portrait on the back of *Stories That Could Be True*)

"The Bond" (Bill and Dorothy)

*and all my love* (Stafford in the last month of his life; photo by Mike Markee)

have swerved back through that area. I vibrate. Some of those vibrations have become writings, and I might enclose two or three examples that link to Hutchinson. . . .

The place makes him "vibrate," and I remember a line from the *Tao Te Ching* (76): "Whoever is soft and yielding / is a disciple of life." Brittle strength breaks, but the yielding, the pliant can heal itself. My father was such a pliant disciple. To Catherine, he reports his own odyssey away from Kansas by way of war, marriage, career, and says, "I don't know why I spell out all this to you, though. It's a long way off; it has been a long way to go."

Did she ever write back? I don't know. But I do know this: in Kansas, by sheer chance I met Catherine's grandson. We spoke of this poem and my father's letter.

"Did your grandmother remember my father from school?" I asked him.

"Oh, no," he said. "She didn't remember him at all." I felt the pain of that truth, my father's habit of speaking to a silence.

My mother told me once, "Bill's acne in high school was so bad he felt isolated in some ways. Some good friends—but alone." I find this confirmed in a line from the first draft of "At Liberty School," a line lost from the final version: "There were runners and fighters, phalanx of review. . . ." His way was not through such achievement, but was instead more marginal. He was a wanderer in the loud combat of the world. In his poem "Vocation," my father's father shows a "groove in the grass" of the prairie that had been the Oregon Trail. He tells of the young man who "dreamed the trace to the mountains, over the hills, / and there a girl who belonged wherever she was." The link between my father's personal aspiration to find the girl who belongs wherever she is and his life in art is signaled in his consistent allegiance to the ways of smoke, intuition, the lost girl in a busy world.

He said at one point, "I don't want to write *good* poems. I want to write *inevitable* poems—to write the things I will write, given who I am." Again, I am reminded of the *Tao Te Ching* (52): "Seeing into darkness is clarity. / Knowing how to yield is strength. / Use your own light / and return to the source of light. / This is called practicing eternity." Even the actions in my father's poems are most often the acts of welcome, opening, acceptance: "I listened and put my hand / out in the sun again." The rituals described in his poems, the "little ways that encourage good fortune," are customs of attention, devotion, or simple witness against hard stories he can't change. He says again and again to a quiet feminine character that he sees her, remembers her, honors the fragile treasure she offers to the world.

This way of acknowledging the quiet voice is in keeping with his practice as a writer—accepting the beginning line, the glimmer of an idea, the clumsy opening as a way of honoring "what the world is trying to be." Someone asked him once what his favorite poem was, out of all he had written. "I love all my children," he said, "but I would trade everything I have ever written for the *next* thing."

As a writer, he was a mother to beginnings. The "next thing" may be a kind of latent epiphany ready to be born. A friend told me my father's "imagination was tuned to the moment when epiphanies were just about to come into being." At such a moment, ambition could be fatal to what we seek. Take a deep breath and wait. What seeks you may then appear.

In my life as a writer, I see the effect of my father's approach in my own blunders and allegiances. Shortly after the publication of the book my father and I made together, *Braided Apart,* I felt the need to find a completely different voice in my poetry. Richard Hugo's introduction to that book had made direct comparisons I believe he meant as compliments, but they troubled me:

> Kim has good instincts for a young poet. He lays down forceful
> rhythms and he keeps moving. He will not risk being boring or flat,
> or even pale, as Bill often will. Kim flashes well on the surface. He
> risks the whole poem coming to nothing but the memory of energy.
> That's a way of saying both are good poets—both are taking risks. . . .

Did I want to be forceful, to flash well on the surface, to be a memory of energy? The comments themselves did not bother me so much as the experience of being compared. My father championed my work as its own. He was more likely to note our differences.

Against this backdrop, I had one recurrent and unsettling experience: sometimes I heard my father's voice in my mind when a poem I was writing began to gather momentum. At first I found such an echo assuring. But if my voice rested on my father's voice, why write? He could do it better.

When I turned from poetry to essays, my father's ghost-voice in my writing disappeared, and I was able to find my own.

The same year as *Braided Apart,* I published a book with Copper Canyon Press called *A Gypsy's History of the World,* and as we were designing the title page, I asked Tree Swenson at the press if we could omit my name throughout the book. (William Stafford: "Read my lips, forget my name.") I wanted the book to simply be "a gypsy's history." She laughed and said no. So the book came out with my name, and several reviewers talked about the feminine experiences "Ms. Stafford" had captured.

Even when I have diverged from my father's voice—by writing essays and stories—I seem to adopt his ways of seeing the world. Recently one of my students asked me a brazen question: "Do you ever think you could be a better writer than your father?" My response to this question was instructive to me, for it felt in keeping with what I learned from my father about the essential life of art. It seemed to me the real question is this: "Is my way of writing closer to my essential character, and more successful in expressing what is in me to say—than William Stafford's (or any writer I might admire)?" That is, compare the approach to creation, not the product of creation. This way of seeing is useful to me because I am driven to compare what I have written only with what I would like to write, and this leads me forward directly into my own work.

It is reported I told my father when I was a child, "You rubbed my head when I was little and now I think like you think." Perhaps this is a form of filial piety—or what Lao Tzu called "practicing eternity."

So my father offered me an intuitive model of writing, and then intuition led me forth to find my own way. Another thing he offered as a parent was his concept of "happy problems." I remember standing at the open sliding door to his study when I was young. He had made his writing place in the garage—a long plywood table under the window facing south, functional bookshelves above the window and along the north wall, and a woodstove on the brick hearth he and mother had built. His fingers would be flying on his monster Remington manual typewriter. A hefty stack of incoming mail sat to his left, the outgoing mail on a shelf above, and the wastebasket to his right. He was always a working blur, but would swivel his chair invitingly when one of us kids appeared at the door—though his hands didn't stop typing at high speed. The door was always open, and we knew what would happen if we asked for advice. Most difficulties in writing or in life, according to our father, were "happy problems."

When we would come to him in anguish, lamenting some difficult decision that loomed before us, he would respond, "Poor kid—you've got happy problems." This meant all our choices were good ones, and our anguish lay in our inability to see this. An early version of this conversation (when I was ten) might go like this:

"Daddy, I really want to just go down in the woods and make a fort, but Pat says his dad wants to take us swimming, and we don't get to go very often."

"My friend," he would say, "you have happy problems. Don't worry, you'll figure it out."

A later version—when I was thirty-nine, and passing through my divorce—went like this:

"Kim! Bring me all up-to-date."

"Well, it's like this: I meet a woman. It's not right. She gets hurt. I get hurt. We part. I keep searching."

"It sounds great," he said.

And it was, and it wasn't. Happy problems.

And what about those moments in my life of his utter silence? Sometimes my father's reticence was so intense it felt coercive. He used this silence sparingly, but its effects were memorable. You had to figure out what he thought, wanted, resisted, and then you acted in keeping with your hunch. This was reflected in a book on horse-training he loved, *Think Harmony with Horses,* where the author described how to get the horse to want to do what you want. You learned to understand what my father believed was right, and then, by acting on that, you felt free. Was this manipulative? It didn't feel so. At his best, he created a zone of fearlessness, teaching us to listen for our own inclination, which would be the world's hidden intention as this was available to us.

Even at this distance, I can feel my own gyroscopic guide, little-affected by the opinions of others. I can imagine this book affecting readers both inside and outside the family, where they may say, "That's not the William Stafford I knew." And I can hear my father saying in reply, "Good! I hope you will write your own ideas, and then we'll have a lot to consider."

He only rarely told us out loud what to do. Paying a debt, always. And little things. You would know of his irritation, for example, if you failed to clean the lint from the dryer vent. For some reason that was a big thing. Or if you failed in a promise to someone outside the family, you would hear about that. But within the family he stepped back, made very few direct suggestions. I would hear a voice inside my mind—part his and part my own. He relied on our own observations to instruct us, which could result in slow learning for the young. Sometimes he could drive us wild by refusing to venture an opinion. On a family journey we might travel for miles in some arbitrary direction, trying to get him to tell us where he wanted to go.

"I'm just the driver," he would say. "You all decide." A long silence would follow, and he would drive on and on. But in our more common showdowns at home, he could be aloof but watching. Or he might venture a few words only. When I "pretended" to burn my sister Kit at the stake— tying her willingly to the tetherball pole in my friend Van's backyard, but then producing a real lit match and holding it to her shoe—my father's response was brief but clear. When Kit told, and my father confronted me, he said simply, "Maybe you aren't old enough to carry matches." I threw my matchbook into the fireplace and stalked away. No more was said. It never happened again.

The power of "maybe" was our corrective from him. Silences spoke in sufficient detail to guide us. A direct look, like a wolf's, kept us on the path. "Maybe" meant "yes" or "no." We knew the difference.

If he was sometimes hidden, silent, or even harsh with others, in his private writing my father could be particularly tough on himself. He constantly accused himself, challenged himself to be more honest. Toward the end of his life, while far from home, he wrote up a manifesto about what real equality means, and later typed it up and gave me a copy. As often, he glimpses something in the world that begins as a brooding, interior assessment:

4 May 1993, at Columbus, Ohio

Seeing four people together this morning, one of them slightly confused, "inferior," disregarded, I felt a thunderclap realization: injustices recognized by those around me are grossly misguided, inadequate, invalid. Not possessions, not race, or gender, or rank, not any general classification identifies one's place on the scale of justice. Absolutely surpassing such trivial considerations are intelligence, physique, internal drive, other personal qualities. . . .

The power of the conventionally lucky will have sway in the world, he seems to be saying, but this only clarifies the plight of the weaker citizens among us:

> Why toy with . . . conventional discriminations? The nature of
> being has fastened our essences on us, and other groupings and pro-
> grams and animosities are diversions from what each of us has to
> face.
>     Within the citadel of myself I will maintain vigilant court: my
> kind, all people, all beings; no more blundering classification. Each
> of you, you equal beings, will be judged in this bright light that
> perceives either total equality of headlong, unpitying, individual
> assessment. . . .

Against such judgments, characteristically, my father returns to yet another variation of smoke's way—the "side wind."

> Certain people feel the gentle touch of a side wind in their lives.
> Through what seems a miraculous good fortune, leading by way of
> a myth to a truth, certain people attain to the stance in life that
> validly recognizes equality of other lives, their legitimate place in
> regard to each other. These certain people—Pascal, Kierkegaard,
> purity-of-heart people—find through their faith an attitude con-
> gruent with both rationality and religion.

Superior to the rational, the "gentle touch of a side wind" identifies where my father's experience lay, whether in his own welcoming practice as a writer, his gentle engagement with students' inner lives in his teaching, his pacifism directed at "the unknown good in our enemies," his sensitivity to the natural world, or other realms of responsive experience. Even his long devotion to photography finds root here, I believe, in the way a camera receives the bite of light from outside itself and retains exactly what the world has offered.

One of his last acts as a writer was his review of Carolyn Forché's

*Against Forgetting: Twentieth-Century Poetry of Witness.* Reading his notes that led up to the published review, I see him wrestling with the difficulty of challenging the work of another. But finally he does this, questioning not only Forché's book but a culture that blames, generalizes, and responds to cruelty with anger, rather than a search for conciliation. He writes:

> I feel a bump when the explanatory text says, "The Germans de-
> cided." All Germans? And similarly when Carolyn Forché says,
> "My new work seemed controversial to my American contempo-
> raries?" (Who, me?) The labels in the book, the assumptions, and
> the speed of assessment almost inevitable for a book with a thesis
> like this one, put a torque on me, snagged my attention, kept me
> wary of living on the emotional high of atrocity hunger.

I hear in these lines the responsive soul of my father, "bumped . . . torqued . . . snagged . . . wary" in the grip of reading about the "poetry of witness." He was in a strange predicament. His was a life of witness; his writing was a sustained campaign against forgetting about essential human connections, no matter the confrontational situations the world may offer. Yet his approach to conciliation is utterly different from Forché's thesis. He concludes by offering his alternative view:

> Nietzsche speaks of "the use and abuse of history." How heavily
> should we load up with the past? For how long? In what size doses?
> On whose terms? . . . A poet, a person, a fallible human being, has
> to step carefully through a puzzling world. We have to remember
> our own surges of anger, how we sometimes choose a country or a
> people and load our hatred on them, how we go to war—and then
> how later we come to our senses and perceive that ills are not to be
> so simply projected on an alien group.
>     Remember?
>     That is what I don't want to forget.

By seeing and honoring what others don't quite see, my father invited into our world a kind of truce. In the clarity available to the seeker, he remained ready for conciliation to the end.

Both sides of my father's nature came together in his tenacity to "follow the thread" of intuitive writing, philosophical inquiry, and pacifist conciliation. The intuitive feminine and the forceful masculine become one when you have to be tough to stay loyal to the tender. His late poem beginning "There's a thread you follow" echoes a dozen earlier poems that identify the fragile but essential line, the trace of something almost known. In Kansas, his father fixed the phone lines that kept distant people connected; my father never forgot. "A telephone line goes cold;" he wrote, in a poem about the death of his parents; "birds tread it wherever it goes" ("The Farm on the Great Plains"). "I follow a trail so old," he wrote in his daily writing, "the hounds lost it years ago." And "Writers work . . . from the end of a golden thread: they find progress longitudinally in thought" (undated note for class). The "golden thread" is from Blake's *Jerusalem,* which my father quoted often in class and in his book *Writing the Australian Crawl:*

> I give you the end of a golden string,
> > Only wind it into a ball,
> It will lead you in at Heaven's gate
> > Built in Jerusalem's wall.

The artist—like the world-citizen—was for my father a person who knew how to trust something initially fragile, but more true than steel for the ultimate connection it promises. "If you pull that string too hard," he would say, "if you try to direct it, if you ask it to do too much, at first, it will break." Being responsive to a quiet signal might be his first step in the direction of right action, but daily writing and perennial conversation with others will be required, because we will always need the next quiet signal.

My father's idea about following such a thread is thus inconsistent with any kind of permanent authority, including his own. His poem that begins "There's a thread you follow . . . ," for all its apparent certainty, follows in his daily writing a dream of great confusion. And a year earlier, he had begun a poem "One of the threads led the wrong way / in the labyrinth, toward the false light. . ." (Daily Writing, 4 November 1992). You take up the thread trusting, but not knowing, where it may lead. The habit of the seeker is never to rest.

One scene fascinates me in the Haydn Reiss film, *Robert Bly and William Stafford: A Literary Friendship.* Robert and my father are locked in conversation as they start down a precipitous set of stairs above fast water—

a cliff over the Sandy River. Robert doesn't notice my father is on the out-side of the stairway with no handrail, and he is unsteady, he's getting old. They go down the stairs, Robert holding the rail on his side as he talks, and my father listening, stepping, teetering.

After my father died, I spoke with the cameraman for that project. "Your father said the strangest thing," he said, "as he started down those stairs: 'Whatever happens,' he said, 'keep that camera going.'" My father was ready to embrace exactly what happened, and asked for no one to swerve aside when the time came.

The way of the warrior.

Once my father and I converged in Vienna, following his literary jour-ney through Denmark, Germany, and Poland with my mother, giving read-ings and workshops in half a dozen places. My father confided in me what he had witnessed in Berlin.

"Just outside the hotel," he said, "on the street two men were fighting. I looked around to see if anyone was going to do something. It amazed me—no one. That's what a city can be like."

After he died, I asked my mother about this incident.

"Did he tell you what he did?" she said.

"No."

"He made them stop."

"How?"

"He went between them. If they had had guns, they would have killed him."

My father confided in me late in his life that he took an active interest in Tai Chi. He had ordered an instructional video by mail and would practice before the TV screen when he was alone. One time on the road he joined a group of practitioners in Union Square outside his San Francisco hotel. And his interest in this tradition appears in the opening lines of his poem, "Annals of *Tai Chi*: 'Push Hands.'"

> In this long routine "Push Hands,"
> one recognizes force and yields, then
> slides, again, again, endlessly like water,
> what goes away, what follows, aggressive
> courtesy till force must always lose,
> lost in the seethe and retreat of ocean.

The earliest tributaries to my father's allegiance to smoke's way? Perhaps the reclusive habit of his mother was an influence, as well as the plain ways of the prairie he haunted as a boy. But his brother, the bomber pilot, absorbed those same beginnings without exhibiting my father's overt pacifism. His family had great variety, peopled by characters of all kinds. The archive contains the text for a speech by my father's grandmother, for example, which she delivered to the City Federation of Clubs in 1905—a speech on "Woman in Modern History," a stirring suffragist talk. Fervent, yes, but that talk is a standard profile of Elizabeth Palmer Peabody, Mary Lyon, Fannie Crosby, Clara Barton, and others. It tells of the stars among women, the famous, the powerful voices. By contrast, my father's poems speak for unknown women without voice who need a listener to help say what silence means:

### When I Met My Muse

I glanced at her and took my glasses
off—they were still singing. They buzzed
like a locust on the coffee table and then
ceased. Her voice belled forth, and the
sunlight bent. I felt the ceiling arch, and
knew that nails up there took a new grip
on whatever they touched. "I am your own
way of looking at things," she said. "When
you allow me to live with you, every
glance at the world around you will be
a sort of salvation." And I took her hand.

"I am your own way of looking at things." To my eye, that line is the psychic marriage of smoke's responsive way and the prophet's assertive way—to be forthright in honoring and telling what one receives and must say. In this, I find what my father called "smoke's way" was actually neither feminine nor masculine. It was what might be called the inevitable self. The muse for my father was first an affectionate loyalty to one's own way of seeing, a native genius sensitive to the quiet of the land, to a resonance best heard in the silence of a hurt person.

Early in his writing career, my father's daily writing includes frequent jotted ideas for fiction. He produced several dozen short stories, mostly unpublished, and I remember him reporting to me he may have alienated a number of writers in his newly adopted state of Oregon when in one year he won both the short story and the poetry contests sponsored by the *Northwest Review*. In his winning story, "The Osage Orange Tree," my father tells the predicament of a prairie girl living at home on a farm, where poverty and harsh parentage imprison her young soul, a soul the story's narrator is unable to save, or finally even to know. At the end of the story, having failed to connect to the girl, the narrator stands alone on the prairie: "Near me stood our ragged little tree—an Osage orange tree it was. It was feebly coming into leaf, green all over the branches, among the sharp thorns. I hadn't wondered before how it grew there, all alone, in the plains country, neglected."

My father carried a double knowledge that grew heavier as he grew older: you can't save the lives and spirits caught in the machine of our time; but you will regret what you can't save, all the same. His poems sometimes offer the simple pain of that fact. (From his daily writing: "What you like will suffer.") I remember Robert Bly once telling me that in my own writing I have more authority when I talk about my failures than my successes. Was he telling me a truth about myself, or about himself—or about all art, in his view?

This predicament is typified in an exercise my father shared in several writing workshops, with instructions: "The Project—Think of something you did and then write not what you did but what you wish you had done. Or, think of something you said, but write not what you said but what you wish you had said." His own workshop example follows, first what he said to protect everyone, and second what he should have said to tell his own way of seeing things:

Two Letters from College

Dear Home,

We study by the lamp you sent, and Mrs. Wilson sends cookies upstairs sometimes. Norman and my other roommate Frank are good company, and our bull sessions—as the guys here call them— are fun.

I made a B in the last psychology test. Did you ever hear of Freud and Jung? They know what we are really like, I guess. I'll try to learn and explain when we meet at Christmas.

Thanks for your letters.

—Bill

Dear Home,

I hate it. Every night in the stale-cabbage smell upstairs we gather to make fun of Charley. He is so pale and dumb—he believes anything. Frank the medic has him terrified of diseases; Norman delights in telling him shocking stories about scoutmasters and ministers, the heroes Charley used to have. These years will mark Charley for life.

It's so cold in our room that the inkwell froze. Noise from the frat house goes on all night. The psychology teacher snickers about people like you, and I sit there holding my smile still so he won't know I'm hurt.

I want to quit and be yours again.

—Bill

My father's "own way of looking at things" included attention to the assaulted spiritual life of ordinary people. Charley, the girl in "The Osage Orange Tree," or the scattered congregation of troubled lives in other poems ("Priests and sisters of hundreds of unsaid creeds") were the voiceless authorities that caught my father's attention early and in sustained ways. They caught his attention not because he could save them or make them worthy, but because their predicament was his own. The just ways of the world seemed invisible to many around him. His pacifism could not stop war. The world honored loud, forceful ways foreign not only to his custom, but more importantly, foreign to his sense of "what the world is trying to be." And so:

Smoke's way's a good way—find,
or be rebuffed and gone:
a day and a day, the whole world home.

# *Early Morning*

W HEN MY FATHER DIED, I thought my relationship with him had ended. Then the dreams began, and memories of him from my childhood forward began appearing out of nowhere, as if summoned to fill his absence. As I took over the management of his literary estate and delved into his private writings, he addressed me directly from the page:

> Wisdom is having things right in your life
> and knowing why.
> If you do not have things right in your life
> you will be overwhelmed:
> you may be heroic, but you will not be wise.
> — *from* "THE LITTLE WAYS THAT ENCOURAGE GOOD FORTUNE"

When my father was alive, that was a poem. When he died it became part of a conversation that would go on and on. Our relationship would continue, and I felt the beginning of a second life.

Within a few months I met the woman who would become my wife. As Perrin and I began our life together, I settled into a new and productive routine in my own writing—poems, essays, stories. Perrin helped me record a CD of my songs. I helped her complete her dissertation. Our child was born in the midst of it all: the good, difficult life together. Part of our steadiness was my access to the unpredictable, for I had returned to my father's habit I had adopted in college of rising early to write. This practice, which he pursued without fail, has been intermittent for me. My father's example was there all through childhood, but largely invisible. We knew he rose early, and we knew the poems kept appearing in magazines, and every year or two he would hand us each a copy of his newest book, but the relation between the invisible practice and the visible performance was a mystery.

You have a family you love. You have a job you do and some days love, if you are lucky. But you also have an inner life, a quiet voice, a realm of intuition and expression that may be largely dormant through your busy days. In my father's practice, this inner life happened first. As he once wrote, "To get up in the cold, then make a warm place, have paper, pen, books to hand, look out at gleaming rain, shadows, the streetlight steadfast. You could stay awake all night, not give away these hours" (Daily Writing, 9 January 1968). When you read my father's poems, you are with him there, in the early morning. Others are sleeping, but you are with him to discover something independent of frenzy, word by word before dawn. You can have a piece of that anytime you open one of his books.

He has begun to live with me in recollection and dreams, and more and more in the new projects that I and a small band of helpers draw forth from the archive. When we began to work our way into my father's papers, we had specific tasks we wanted to complete. By 1998, we had published five books by William Stafford: *Even in Quiet Places,* and *Crossing Unmarked Snow: Further Views on the Writer's Vocation,* and *The Way It Is: New & Selected Poems,* and the two reprint editions, *Down in My Heart: Peace Witness in War Time,* and *Traveling through the Dark.* The shaping of *The Way It Is,* in particular, benefited from the generous help of many writers and friends. In addition, we helped others to produce films, audiotapes, and a host of unpublished or reprinted poems and articles by my father.

All this work, however—this mosaic-like fitting for publication of texts my father had finished—was different from our encounters with the holograph pages of his forty years of daily writing in the early morning.

His handwriting, with the favored ease and fluidity of a fountain pen, was a dense difficulty. His lowercase "e" tends to be as tall at an "l," and sometimes a sequence of letters seems undecipherable at first. But every stroke has purpose, every intent is recorded—every letter, comma, dot. It's all there, if we stare long enough. People have accused my handwriting of looking like my father's; I accuse his of looking like his own father's. Inheritance can be heartless.

His daily practice produced about a handwritten ream a year. The yearly ream went into a box, was sequenced with other such reams into a bigger box, and eventually placed in the attic at home. A decade of my father's mornings fills one archival carton you can carry in your arms.

A page of my father's daily writing often included brief news from the day before, often a dream, observations on the life of the family, odd quotations from the children, infrequent ideas for fictional stories, single lines of trenchant observation (we call them "aphorisms"), examinations of his place in the family, society, and the world—and a poem or two. The poems are densely written, with indents rather than an open line to signal a new stanza, titles scribbled beside them, and if judged worthy, labeled "copied." Any poem so labeled will turn up in typescript elsewhere in the archive.

Taken as a whole, the daily writing constitutes a symposium with the self, where questions of ethics, aesthetics, education, aggression, and creation are posed, debated, and then practiced in poetic form by one intelligence—my father's academy of one. This writing practice reveals the critical and intuitive faculties of a fertile mind in conversation with itself almost every single day for over forty years. Out of this meditative practice, what he called his "compost pile," his poems appeared at a rate of about one a day.

It's curious to me what my father did *not* record in his daily writing. For example, the day we moved into the house in Lake Oswego, in July of 1957, would seem worth consideration in his record. As far as I can tell, this is the first house my family or my father's family—our long heritage of modest means—had ever owned. Yet this milestone gets brief mention only: "first morning in the new house," with no elaboration. The daily writing was not a diary; what might be considered important events by others were nothing to him. Rather, the daily writing is a realm for the timeless. Ownership of a house might be a landmark for some, but before dawn my father had more important quarry.

Sifting through the daily writing I came upon the day of my earlier wedding, at age twenty. Did my father notice? Well, yes—but just.

29 August 1970

Today at 10:30 a.m. at the Episcopal Church in Carmel Kim & Beverly were married.

    "God, He"
He reached into the world.
He ranked mountains that froze the sky. . . .

And he is off into a poem of cosmic speculation. In contrast to a mere wedding, a real event—a story, in his eyes—might get his attention, as with this sobering glimpse of me when I was not yet three:

> Kim heaped coals of fire on our heads. Because he wouldn't drink
> his milk promptly, before getting something solid to eat, we made
> him get down from his high-chair. He whimpered, and I seriously
> told him we were trying to teach him not to be that way, because
> people didn't like that kind of little boys. "Oh, I see," he said. He
> played so nobly all alone while we three ate, that Bret finally said,
> "Why don't we give Kimney that old piece of cheese?" Kim stopped
> playing and looked at us. I went on eating my berries and ice cream,
> and deliberately looked into Kim's eyes, then said "All right." He
> clambered excitedly up his chair. I put the little old dried piece of
> cheese in front of him; he picked it up eagerly, and then looked
> around happily, clasped his hands and said, "We 'got [forgot] to say
> a-men!" He bowed over the piece of cheese, and we all joined him
> in a long *a-men*.
>                                          —DAILY WRITING, 30 MARCH 1952

We have had a delicious time with the isolated aphorisms—lines that stand alone on his writing pages and never became part of poems or prose texts. We tease them out from those dense pages, and ponder what life experience may have led him to bury such jagged diamonds:

> Off a high place, it is courtesy to let others go first.
>
> It is legitimate to crawl, after the wings are broken.
>
> Actors, their relief. I have to be myself with no vacation.
>
> Successful people are in a rut.
>
> Aggressive people do not appeal to me; I yield them scorched earth.

At what high place did he stand? What broke his wings? What was the faint path he followed? Who were those successful people? In what ways did he yield scorched earth to the loud and forceful? The only answer I can give is that these aphorisms exemplify at a maximum voltage what he had told me about poetry being made of contexts, not words. And I would reply to those who found my father too prolific with a glance at the aphorisms; he simply had more gold than he could use, even by writing every day.

His ponderings about his place in the world ranged from self-accusation to speculative witness about his beliefs. Sometimes these speculations were expressed in prose, and sometimes in unpublished poems:

> A divide comes in a life. At first you
> don't know, and then looking back you see
> before and after. That's what they mean
> when they say you can't go back home:
> it's the same, but half-closed eyes have opened.
>                   — Daily Writing, 3 August 1993

One morning he wrote, "Every day something keeps me from the main business of my soul." His remedy was to give attention early to that soul — by writing — and let the day unfold from there. My father reported on his early-morning habit often, for example in his poem "How These Words Happened":

> In winter, in the dark hours, when others
> were asleep, I found these words and put them
> together by their appetites and respect for
> each other. In stillness, they jostled. They traded
> meanings while pretending to have only one.
>
> Monstrous alliances never dreamed of before
> began. Sometimes they last. Never again
> do they separate in this world. They die
> together. They have a fidelity that no
> purpose or pretense can ever break.
>
> And all of this happens like magic to the words
> in those dark hours when others sleep.

Originally published in *Passwords*, my father's last book with Harper-Collins in 1991, this poem was the one we selected to reprint at the close of

*Crossing Unmarked Snow,* the collection we edited of his writing about writing. The poem acts innocent, saying this is how words happen. But I find the explanation increasingly mystifying, as the control of what has happened shifts from writer to words to alliances, and finally to a kind of destiny. The language is of hunger, marriage, international treaty, legend. That early-morning practice, like the cloistered devotions of a monk or nun, seems quiet on the surface, but invites extreme possibilities, adventures, and wrenching discoveries. Memory is not always benign. As a friend says of my father's practice, "Memory—at 4 A.M., what else is there?"

> In those reaches of the night when your thoughts
> burrow in, or at some stabbed interval
> pinned by a recollection in daylight,
> a better self begs its hands out to you.
>                   —*from* "MEIN KAMPF"

My father's total welcome of struggle in the early morning was the source of his artesian productions. It's true some critics blamed him for being prolific. That may be like blaming another for taking too many breaths or having too many dreams or having too many friends or living too long. Being too happy. Mozart's too many notes. The writer of my father's obituary in the *New York Times* referred to him as a "noted regionalist," a gentle nature poet. Had that writer read *"Mein Kampf"?* "Thinking for Berky"? "Serving with Gideon"? Had that writer read my father's work at all?

Even on the days when he wrote a painful poem, my father seemed happy when we joined him at breakfast. The accomplishment of saying a harsh thing clearly seemed to allow him resolution and sometimes exhilaration.

In his last years, he told me he was surprised he kept this early-morning habit of writing. In fact, his retirement from teaching had enabled him to rise even earlier—he no longer needed to save energy for work on campus. He could squander everything before light and take a nap later in the day. So he would rise at 3 A.M., instead of 4, go for a run, and then write until daylight. As he got older, he took longer to complete the running distance he had set for himself—several miles. I urged him to set a standard running time—thirty minutes, or sixty—and accept the distance he covered in that time, whatever it might be. But he said no, he had to complete the distance he had established years before. You could call this stubborn. I prefer to see this in light of his writing: consistent practice as mother to the unpredictable. He just had to get up earlier to do it now, do it all.

For my father, the partnership between rising early to run and write and then devoting time to an afternoon nap worked well. The earlier he rose, the more possible the work, and the more delicious the nap. Why did he write lying down, on the couch? When you get up early, he would say, you have the whole world to yourself, and you get to do it exactly as you please. He once said many of his poems were happy because he was so comfortable as he wrote. But were they?

> First, this face—history did it,
> winters, two world wars, long
> days bent in the fields in the sun,
> a few blows, fear, sorrow.
> —*from* "EVIDENCE"

Two world wars provided harsh schooling for one life. But even when he was being hard on himself, or others, my father's impulse was to go for the richest things by being open to everything. I remember waking to watch him through half-shut eyes when we shared a room on the road. He would settle at ease, take a sheet of paper from his daily writing box, write the date and sometimes the place where he was writing at the top, stare off to the side, hold the pen ready, and then begin. When you look at the daily writing sheets, you see him begin with a note about what happened the day before, or a dream, or a single observation that never became a poem. (For example, "I blame others for acts and impulses much more forgivable than my own," or "When a whale gets away, you're willing to range far to find it.") But then, after brief preliminaries, his writing takes the shape of a poem.

One secret of his practice can be related to the idea of a "latent image" in photography. When you trip the camera shutter, the exact light that is a scene outside the lens rushes in and makes an invisible change in the silver of the film's emulsion. If the lens is the spirit of William Stafford and the invisible change is event-become-memory, that latent image remains poised for development as long as the spirit of the writer lives. So in my father's last days, he wrote of some of his earliest recollections:

An instant sprang at me, a winter instant,
a thin gray panel of evening. . . .
   —*from* "AT FOURTH AND MAIN IN LIBERAL, KANSAS, 1932"
      (WRITTEN 27 AUGUST 1993)

Pondering this effect, once when he was on the road, he wrote:

Last night, sleeping on the floor of the Episcopal Church at Valdez
[Alaska], I dreamed that some old, exposed roll of film had turned
up. I held it, ready to develop it, and thought of the scenes, the
people, ready there to be mine again, from that vivid, precious past.
Without knowing just what they would be I yet hungered for them
all.

   Writing is like that, I realize: to hold the pen and wait, then
start, is like holding that roll of film. Something will come; it will
bring from the past. I wait deliciously. And the thing that occurs
depends partly on how much I hunger!
                                    —DAILY WRITING, 28 JULY 1968

Those lost things "ready there to be mine again" reveal an affectionate, om-
nivorous writer. He once wrote on the eve of the rebellious years of the
1960s that he saw himself as a Greek chorus of our culture, there to remind
others of the central things of life that stupefied citizens all around him
seemed bent to destroy:

Yesterday in a discussion . . . students asked whether an artist had
to be a rebel. My impulse was to say that it is the society which the
artist feels to be rebelling. I feel that I am like a Greek chorus—
speaking deliberately and measuredly the central truth of things,
while all around me people—bankers, generals, kings, my children,
everyone—all speak the wildest kind of impulsive, mistaken things.
                                —DAILY WRITING, 12 FEBRUARY 1959

Shortly before my father died, I had a dream of my own that touches on a
particular quality in his daily writing. In the dream I am at my father's
childhood house in Kansas, a rustic cabin—oilcloth on the table, the worn
floor swept spotless. Others are at work, but my father sits with me to con-

fide: "I've made them mad again because I'm not staying longer." Then he turns to me. "When you marry . . . ," he says. I lean toward him, but that's all I get. The dream ends with a sense that I am going away and won't see him again.

Waking, I realized that my father's writing practice in the early morning, every day, year after year through a long life was a return, again and again, to something like that old house, a place of elemental things, sparely kept. I had a glimpse in my dream, and this quality is everywhere in his poems. In that native place, if he didn't stay long he went often.

I have written important parts of this book in that quiet time before first light, and I know from this practice that one of the secrets of writing, as my father taught me by example, is the welcome—the hunger—for just the words that come. Perhaps the most telling aspect of my father's daily writing is the faithfully written *weak* lines of his beginnings, which enabled the subsequent revised lines of great power. For example, the lines that eventually led him to one tight, exacting poem began as soft, vague, searching:

> Children of whisper grown, the war cry,
> we can't say truth, because the saying
> changes it. One time we met and the truth
> was there, Ever since, the truth has flooded
> the town. . . .
> —DAILY WRITING, 15 DECEMBER 1960

And in revision:

> The Apache word for love twists
>    then numbs the tongue:
> Uttered once clear, said—
>    never that word again.
> —*from* "IN THE NIGHT DESERT"

Some readers have assumed my father did not revise—fiercely revise— because of his stated attitude of acceptance in first writing. But his welcome that first brought the poem onto the page was his abiding friendship with his craft. My father did embrace major revision when necessary—as in the poem above—when revision led to further creative discovery. He said once, "If you don't welcome all your ideas when they first appear, pretty soon even your bad ideas won't come to you. They will learn to stay away."

While on the road in 1966, he wrote "The Importance of the Trivial":

[T]he beginning impulses too are often so colorless, so apparently random, so *homeless* and unaccountable, that most people would neglect them: they don't seem to amount to much. It is by lending faith and attention to these waifs of thought that we allow their meanings to develop, sometimes. And their mutual reinforcement is the composition of the poem, or the realization of any creative endeavor.

He was alert for extremely intimate beginnings:

As a writer do you find interest in words? In *syllables*.
— DAILY WRITING, 8 JULY 1957

How can we help each other toward that condition that enables the sustained zest and readiness to fall with endless dives and disportings, and flops and recoveries, the way an otter plays and invents on the bank of a stream?
— CRAFT LECTURE, 1990

Seeing the art students picking up their boards, I felt the push on the left shoulder down—the signal of need to write something about them. It was separate from *knowing* what to write: it was the sign that something was there.
— DAILY WRITING, 4 MAY 1957

One of my father's most quoted ideas in teaching is his invitation, "If you are writing and you get stuck, lower your standards and keep going. And my standards," he would add, "can get really low." Some teachers and writers champion this advice; others think it is the worst advice one could give. (Perhaps they don't know his own corollary: "When you are writing and it gets hard, don't stop. It's hard because you are doing something original.") The principle of "lowering your standards" sounds "wishy-washy," as my father himself would say. Is it? After his death a friend pointed out to me a deeper dimension to this attitude. She had looked up the meaning of the phrase "lower your standard" and found it had been a technical term in medieval warfare. To lower one's standard (i.e., flag) was a signal for a truce; to raise one's standard was a signal for attack without quarter. My father would have been delighted by this. To declare a truce as a writer is to be utterly ready for what comes. To raise one's standard in order to force a poem into being was not his way. This integrated attitude toward creation, teaching, and the life of witness appears often in his writing, as in his poem "Report to Crazy Horse":

> Crazy Horse, it is not fair
> to hide a new vision from you.
> In our schools we are learning
> to take aim when we talk, and we have
> found out our enemies. They shift when
> words do; they even change and hide
> in every person. A teacher here says
> hurt or scorned people are places
> where real enemies hide. . . .
> . . . . . . . . . . . . . . .
> when I salute
> I hold my hand alertly on the heartbeat
> and remember all of us and how we depend
> on a steady pulse together. . . .

As a friend said to me, William Stafford had learned by writing and living not to demand answers or utterances before trusting the language to lead him. "Understanding too soon is overrated."

In his thousands of early mornings, my father was the pacifist with a lowered flag, the receiver in a quiet field, alert witness to the whispered word.

❧

# Priest of the Imagination

IN THE EVENINGS NOW, when it's dark and time for a story, I some-
times sit down with our son to pore over his *Encyclopedia of the Animal
Kingdom*. He favors the pages with sharks, monkeys, and snakes. At five, he
lingers over the pictures, and I over the words. For the authors of this book
emphasize what they don't know. The great white shark disappears into the
deep to breed, they say, and we don't know if its young are born live or
in eggs. We don't know why the hammerhead shark has its eyes positioned
wide—does that structure of the head provide lift in swimming?

I paid college tuition for twelve years and often received the opposite
approach: erudition. At first I felt I was really getting my money's worth.
My professors' brilliance cast my own ignorance in bold contrast. I couldn't
take notes fast enough. Then one day, visiting home, I watched my father
"interview" his class. He was puzzled. The students helped him. But then
he pushed the questions deeper. Alive to their power, the students fol-
lowed, then led my father further on. Suddenly the conversation turned in
a surprising direction. Who had turned it? I couldn't tell.

I remember in particular a student from Iran telling the class about fear,
how in his country the wrong word could make a person disappear. The
wrong poem could kill someone. As I listened to this student and looked
around the classroom, there was definitely a hum in the room, but it was
not coming from a single source.

When I began to teach, I felt tugged in two directions. Should I have
answers for my students like my professors; or should I have questions—
and a hum—like my father? Sometimes in class I would feel drunk with
insight. Sentences spilled forth from my reading, my pondering, my pure
invention. But when I finished we all dwelt in the trance of "so what?" So
what if all these ideas were important to me? What question was bigger
than me? What question would require the students to help me?

But if questions were all I had, was I cheating my students?

I became a student of my father's ways, then an apprentice. As I watched him teach, I witnessed multiple rivers flowing into one. For the place in my father's life where writer and parent converged, where yin and yang came most seamlessly together, was in his teaching. If you are a pacifist and can't stop the wars your country launches, how else would you practice the teaching vocation but in gentle, sustained questioning of what my father called "intellection used as a weapon"? For all his influence as a writer, I suspect my father's more lasting influence may come through his approach to teaching. He observed in a poem in 1968 ("A Test You Do Not Need to Take"), "Every person you meet has a god / and is an animal. Find both." As a teacher, he did.

Robert Dusenbery, a colleague since the 1940s, reported my father's habitual description of classtime: "Well, it's time to go dance the minuet." He worked hard—I remember him heroically responding to mountains of student papers. At the same time he believed true teaching was a different ritual. It was an adroit following of events in class, events that could not be fully predicted in advance, nor described afterward: an improvisational dance.

> My first impulse, when confronted with a student's writing, is to become steadfastly evasive until some signal from the student indicates a direction where the student is ready to go. I want to become the follower in this dance, partly because of some principles about what can be truly helpful in such an interchange, and partly because I have learned that the air between us is full of booby traps: the writer may have many kinds of predispositions, hang-ups, quirks, needs, bonuses. How the student comes toward me across that area is a crucially important beginning for whatever dancing there is going to be.
> The first move is the student's move, not mine. . . .
> — *You Must Revise Your Life*

How do you dance with someone who is "steadfastly evasive"? You have to lead. My father made the students lead, just as he followed the lead of imagination when he wrote. He was loyal to that realm between intuition and accomplishment, between student and teacher, beyond doubt but this side of certainty. The intuitive, searching, ambiguous work of the writer, by his long practice, was my father's best preparation for his ways in class.

He observed that most writing classes—as taught everywhere—were about revision rather than writing. The now-standard practice of teaching by the workshop method, where student writing forms the basis for critique and response, was a departure from his primary interest in writing directly out of your own life. My own motto as a teacher derives from observing his practice: my students are making writing, but I am making writers. Their work is with pages, words, stories, and poems. Mine is with silences, glimpses, hints, and insights "out of nowhere."

I find this common approach to teaching and writing implicit everywhere in my recollections of my father's teaching, and in the notes he left behind. His classic statement from *Writing the Australian Crawl: Views on the Writer's Vocation* typifies his practice:

> A writer is not so much someone who has something to say as he is someone who has found a process that will bring about new things he would not have thought of if he had not started to say them. That is, he does not draw on a reservoir; instead, he engages in an activity that brings to him a whole succession of unforeseen stories, poems, essays, plays, laws, philosophies, religions, or—but wait!
>
> Back in school, from the first when I began to try to write things, I felt this richness. One thing would lead to another; the world would give and give. Now, after twenty years or so of trying, I live by that certain richness, an idea hard to pin down, difficult to say, and perhaps offensive to some. For there are strange implications to it.
>
> One implication is the importance of just plain receptivity. . . .

A famous teacher called this attitude and this book the most dangerous in America. Or maybe the publication of this book was the worst thing that had happened in American education. I can't remember. The critic was right about one thing—the idea of open receptivity that seems natural to a certain kind of writer and teacher will seem like sacrilege to another. For without preconceived intention, without set standards, without models and the guiding method of an instructor, how is a writer to get oriented? How will a writer know what good writing is?

My father told me, "A student comes to me with a piece of writing, holds it out, says, 'Is this good?' A whole sequence of emergencies goes off in my mind. That's not a question to ask anyone but yourself. Others may be able to accept standards from another. But an artist is a person who *decides*."

Was he witnessing about his teaching, advising me about my own, or giving a rare piece of advice about my writing, and the conduct of my own life? All realms of learning were simultaneous with him.

Simply put, my father advocated freedom, which is harder than it might seem. He told me once, "You can legislate freedom of speech, but you have to learn how to accomplish freedom *in* speech." Yet his approach was often viewed as insubstantial. He wrote in his daily writing (16 June 1968), "This country has not yet been made." He was a patriot of the truly free and socially conscious country he could imagine but did not yet inhabit.

My father, then, was in pursuit of issues deeper than writing as he approached a workshop, and this is evidenced often in the notes he jotted quickly for his own use. In one instance, an undated statement titled "Thoughts on a Workshop," my father articulates his primary interest in what all the participants don't yet know. He will suppress both what he knows, and what they have written—but hope to fix:

> The 'quality' of writing cannot be assessed by an inventory of what is there and what is well managed. What *isn't* there? What achievement here has come from suppressing *another* kind? What ultimately sacramental value is linked to this piece? Is this act of writing *healthful*?—for the writer?—for the reader?—for the universe?

For anyone afraid William Stafford's standards weren't high enough, I find clear evidence here that his actual standards were stellar. He is approaching his task as a Wordsworth, a "priest of the imagination." What other writing teachers ask if the poem under discussion is good for the universe? For my father, this was fundamental.

Another example from the archive demonstrates a more playful, but finally an equally serious approach:

Writing Workshop—1st session

1) Most workshops are *revision* workshops.
2) "You can't make a mistake" in your native language.
3) We do not "correct" a piece of writing; we question a life.
4) We consider what the language says—but also what it *does*.
5) The secret language inside the usual "meanings."
6) Harness all the sled dogs.
7) Uh-uh . . . ;—ok in your life, but in your *writing* you can catch the unintended obstructions to your self.
8) We are all exactly equal (your critics too). In a workshop there are no bad (or good) poems.

I've discussed the first item: my father's allegiance to bold beginnings. The second—"You can't make a mistake" in your native language—comes from a controversial statement put forward by the National Council of Teachers of English, a view to which my father subscribed: native speakers of any language are its arbiters, not the professors. The third ("we question a life") is congruent with my father's book about teaching and writing, its title paraphrasing an idea from Rilke: *You Must Revise Your Life*.

The fourth item—what language says and does—spins off, I believe, from a conversation my father and I had about words. We had been discussing our hunch that little storms are one-syllable words—rain, sleet, snow—but big storms are two- or three-syllable words: blizzard, tornado, hurricane. Words are not names, but events.

"The secret language inside the meanings"—the fifth item—identifies a kind of recurring aria for my father: the river of possible meanings surging along beneath what we can label and claim to understand. The sixth about the sled dogs is one of many graphic ways my father talked about getting a poem going: "the sled-dog pull for a strong opening line". . . "the attention required when you are starting a car on ice" . . . "the writer getting the drop on the reader" . . . "the need for immediate and sustained rewards. . . ." And the seventh item, "Uh-uh," was my father's customary, noncommittal response to hearing a piece of student writing read aloud. Instead of praise or any hint of advice, my father would say "Uh-uh," and then wait for the *writer* to start the conversation. *"Uh-uh"* was an indication the writing had been heard, a way to delay any qualitative response, and sometimes a prelude to a series of open-ended questions if the writer delayed taking charge: "How did this piece start for you . . . ?" and so on.

It may be that the last idea—"there are no bad or good poems"—most grates on teachers who regard their contribution as precisely the ability to sort the good poems from the bad. Don't we all want our students to succeed?

I can hear my father say, "Well, yes. . . . What is success? How do you feel when you have it? Can you be successful without helping others. . . ?" Socrates—and my father—loved to turn the tables on expectation. For my father, true success was each writer's authentic surrender to individual process. Here his practice as a writer paralleled his approach as a parent:

> Your exact errors make a music
> that nobody hears.
> Your straying feet find the great dance,
> walking alone.
> And you live on a world where stumbling
> always leads home.
>
> —*from* "YOU AND ART"

A writer, a child, a human being in touch with most essential ways could not make a mistake, could not "stray." This is, by turns, reassuring and very demanding. The poem, the child, the life goes forth alone.

My father mostly taught literature in his thirty years at Lewis & Clark College. On the first day of class, he would customarily invite students to write him a note about what they hoped to learn—a piece of writing he took very seriously. "In a few words," he told me, "they stand revealed." When he did teach writing, he conducted experiments like his classes "Easy Writer" or "Notes on the Refrigerator Door." The class anthology for "Notes" includes a kind of syllabus-as-poem by my father that makes a claim for the daily experience of language, as opposed to the refinements of literature beyond daily life:

> In any house there should be much reading that
> has never been published, that is in all states—
> notes, a start, a stop, the pieces that got
> said without presuming to be more than they are.

> Most things aren't finished, and most things
> haven't yet found their right beginning. Beyond
> poetry there is a prose of the way things happen.
> —*from* "PARAGRAPHS TO TACK ON THE WALL"

My father's obituary for his friend Richard Hugo honors Hugo's poetry while savoring the home source of Hugo's utterance:

> The heavy, shambling spirit was Hugo, who conducted excited con-
> versations about craft and substance in class—and around the bottle
> on the kitchen table in his old house near the campus, besieged by
> Montana storms, but made cozy by pictures, messages, clippings,
> broadsides, recipes, manuscripts of poems, reminders, and odd in-
> decipherable scraps of paper tacked, nailed, clipped, pasted, wired,
> hooked, and magnetized to cupboards, walls, refrigerator, and
> stove.

My father's ideal environment for learning to write would not be a class-room, he said, but the kind of "poetry reading room" he suggested we create at a college or in a town, where everyone would bring writing of diverse kinds for mutual benefit. He would often bring a box of the literary journals that flooded his life to a workshop, and invite everyone to take copies that interested them, scattering them about the room like seeds.

"Mutual benefit" comes closer to what he sought in class than "instruction." A quirky mimeograph he distributed to students in the 1950s reveals the early version of this attitude, his "Assumptions About Literature Classes." He sought freedom for the private writer, but with benefit of company:

> *Writing:* Any person in the class has a claim to participate in the fre-
> quent occasions for writing in class. No one will be forced to write.
> And no one will be "corrected," though as in talking any request for
> particular reactions will be honored.
>
> *Ratings, rankings, grades, records, etc.:* The course is designated as
> "credit, no record"; any person wanting a grade can follow proce-
> dure set by the Registrar's office. . . . The instructor will go into a

trance at the end of the course and provide a mark, if requested to
do so.

*"Difficulty" etc.:* The course is easy, no hazards. Minimum involve-
ment can be very light. At an extreme of involvement, the course
could become a career.

The last point is the core of my father's teaching: start the utterly authentic
life right now. We are not practicing to be writers; we are entering into the
*practice* of the writer, revising our very lives, yielding in each moment to
the vocation that demands our deepest allegiance.

A student would stop my father on a campus sidewalk and say, "Can I
come talk to you about my writing sometime?" "How about right now?"
my father would say. And he would begin his questions to get at the heart,
the origin, the authentic source of the student's life in writing. Sometimes
they would stand there for a good long time, delving deep. It wasn't about
texts for improvement, but about the pure beginning. His approach to the
ethical life ("When all you are trying to do is the right thing, it isn't hard to
act. . . .") would apply equally well to his approach to writing. Once you
decide to write in your own voice, for your own purposes, in your own
way—then the act of writing is your teacher. Other writers, perhaps some
in the role of "teacher," become companions in our common search for un-
common things.

In responding to student writing, my father did not correct or make
suggestions about the writing. Instead, he posed questions. He offered
strangely pertinent information in keeping with the student's own direc-
tion. He might quote Pascal, or Nietzsche. He might suggest a student read
a particular paper by another student. He might remind the writer of an
idea that had come up in class. The class was a village honoring each stu-
dent's native discoveries, and learning occurred as a process of mutual
discovery in which the teacher's principal concern was to avoid the occupa-
tional hazard of hoarding authority.

Was he teaching philosophy? Was he teaching writing? I believe he
most wanted to teach the power of beginnings—where the perennial acts
of writing and philosophy reside, along with ethics, empathy, and joy. Was
he teaching literature? Yes—his many favorites from the past and present,
and also the not-yet-written literature of the students' own lives in direct

companionship with their friends Montaigne, Keats, Dickinson, Saint Augustine. . . . But behind all this, he taught what he called "the little ways that encourage good fortune." He was teaching justice: the gift of each seeker in a quest for mutual allegiance among people.

In an essay he published in 1946 in *Compass,* a pacifist magazine, my father showed how fully formed was his approach as a teacher from the start, and how his teaching grew in the cradle of his pacifism:

> If the ABC's are not to become symbols for Atom Bomb
> Construction, if the typical instructional situation is not to become
> a soldier on one end of a rifle and his pupil on the other, it is gener-
> ally presumed that the world is going to have to wise up pretty fast.

In a series of ideas he had developed in conversation with fellow pacifist Glenn Coffield, he goes on to outline "education designed to disregard or transcend national boundaries," based on a search for "creative citizenship" from the youngest student forward, avoiding "any situation where orders come down from above." He recognized, in 1946, that this educational agenda "is not done, will never be fully done, and will remain as a project calling for the best efforts of those . . . wanting the long, good life for every-one, and will sacrifice to achieve it." In another early essay published in the *California Journal of Secondary Education* in 1947, my father told of a con-versation with a fellow high-school teacher, a former Marine. They both realized the conditions in an American high school were in many ways con-trary to ideal for student learning—and teacher survival:

> From sheer lack of time, your own relations with students will be
> more de-personalized than you would like them to be. You will be
> telling other human beings what to do all day. Even though you
> may have ideas of maintaining a human and neighborly relation-
> ship with your students, you will have them for only one hour a
> day; and during the other hours, they, in all likelihood, are sub-
> jected to the authoritarian regimen crowded conditions make likely.
> If you let up for one hour a day, you may fall heir to the pent-up
> frustrations and tensions built during the other hours.

To my ear, this could be a teacher's lament today. My father's solution was to establish conditions of true inquiry with his students, conditions of respect, deliberate process, and open dialogue that matched his approach as a writer. This approach was radical in postwar America, and despite the loud proclamations of freedom in the 1960s remained radical until my father's death. All his life, he was a witness for the restraint of those forms of instruction he found foreign to learning.

There is one core claim for the conscientious objector, a piece of language I heard from my father as a child, and ultimately typed into my own application for conscientious-objector status during the war in Vietnam: "I will not engage in war in any form."

In military terms, this means one will not bear arms, nor even serve as a medic attached to a military unit, where the purpose is to aid the war effort, however indirectly. But in a life of writing and teaching, this claim takes on a deeper and more mysterious intention. When I watched my father teach, I was watching the educational equivalent of the pacifist's creed. There is a sentence I don't believe my father ever wrote down, nor do I remember hearing him say it, but I sense it everywhere behind his practice as a teacher. This sentence would join the standard vow of the pacifist to the aspiration of the responsive teacher:

I will not engage in war in any form *upon my students—using an approach to learning that does not match my own experience as an artist.*

In 1991 an article about my father in *Poets & Writers Magazine* outlining his approach of welcome to student writers was energetically contested by Stephen Minot, who viewed free inquiry by writers in a class today as passé. Stafford's approach might have been appropriate following World War II and the Korean War, Minot said, when veterans filled classrooms with their mature life experience. According to Minot, now students are less experienced and need more guidance. My father's response:

A Guide for Modern Teachers of Creative Writing

Students are beginners or advanced. Beginners haven't learned the skills and views that creative writing class offers. . . . With a few timely words a good teacher can make sure that students receive in class the clear perceptions of the teacher. . . . The teacher can assess, and once a student learns that bad grades will tag bad writing, the writing will get better. As a mentor, the teacher will induce a kind of writing that succeeds. But even in these classes many students will of course not succeed. Their use of language will result in failure, despite the superior teaching that flourishes in good, up-to-date writing programs. It is a good thing to give these inept writers a clear signal so that they know they can't make it. Thus they can get out of the way and try something else. . . .

I find that rather wicked. Through contrast, my father charts his own approach, knowing many will not agree.

After my father died, I got a glimpse of his world when a spectrum of writers far away and unknown to me began writing letters as if to an old friend, sending me their poems, reporting their literary activities. Several writers reported their long-standing correspondence with my father. This was an exchange, they said, that I would be welcome to continue. I had to decline, but I was touched by their invitations. The letters were so trusting, so generous with the riches of the inner life, and full of faith in the act of writing. One writer told me that for years he had been sending his poems to my father, and getting letters in response about gardening:

> I kept asking for advice about my poetry, but his letters in reply
> were always about these two kiwis he had in his yard, how he hoped
> they would flourish. I would send him more poems, and he would
> write back about the kiwis. I didn't realize until after he died that he
> was talking about poetry the whole time—how things grow.

Toward the end of his career as a college teacher, my father began experimenting ever more freely in his quest for the best kind of writing class. He cultivated his sense from Nietzsche that the teacher requires "a certain courtesy of heart." In my father's words: "There is a touch of cruelty in teaching—and in forcing ourselves to learn, to know. Writing, the process of it, turns away from that cruelty."

Central to his late classes was "The Box"—a simple cardboard box on reserve in the library, an empty box to which students would turn in papers early in the week, and then a filled box students would check out late in the week in order to read everything it held. The Box, filled with student essays respectfully marked by all, would then come to class, students would nominate texts to discuss, and the nominator would lead the discussion. By all reports I had from his students, the discussions were lively, attention to the work in progress was detailed, and everyone was fully engaged.

Was this a workshop about revision? Yes. But it revised primarily the students' sense of shared responsibilities, rather than revising the writing per se.

In his last semester at the college, in 1978, my father decided at the end of his first class session that he had talked too much. He announced that for the next class he would not say a word. He got a volunteer to agree to start the next class session, and made sure everyone was clear about the reading. When the next class came, the volunteer was overprepared, my father said nothing, and the hour consisted of every student trying to keep up with the volunteer leader by pitching in ideas of their own. My father reported it was one of the best class sessions he had experienced, and for the balance of the term, every Wednesday was scheduled as the instructor's "Dumb Day." He listened to learning happen.

His bushy eyebrows, of course, his wise gaze, and what he called his "rubber face"—contorting wildly in response to student opinions, denoting wonder, scowl, rueful puzzlement, wild enthusiasm—all helped. But the classes represented ever-radical notions of freedom in expression and democratic participation, and the possibility of experiencing, through literature, the opening vista of the creative imagination. In my father's words:

> Is it my first endeavor to teach others toward an objective I have for
> them, or should I make the primary effort be to get right myself? If
> the latter, how much disguise of this second effort is justifiable in a
> life given over, vocationally, to the first? This concern is peculiarly
> strong in our time, when increased consciousness of social techniques
> has made us continuously involved in the political and
> rhetorical endeavors rather than the devotional and poetic.
>
> —DAILY WRITING, 7 APRIL 1954

In any of the hundreds—perhaps thousands—of different workshops my father conducted at home and around the world, it was his devotion to the simple, central, delicate, and yet adventurous task of truth that most engaged him. Writing was important, but secondary to how we live, as he articulated in an interview in 1989: "I think you create a good poem by revising your life . . . by living the kind of life that enables good poems to come about." Or, as he told a friend, "That poem is best that is most congruent with who you are." He learned this early, and never forgot. Back home in Kansas, the family glory was the library, and the Staffords felt the world belonged to them through books, no matter how shabby their rented house. My father, from first to last, listened in a quiet place for what each soul might begin to say:

> I would hear that one intended lonely sound,
> the signature of the day, the ratchet of time
> taking me a step toward here, now, and this
> look back through the door that always closes.
> —*from* "A GESTURE TOWARD AN UNFOUND RENAISSANCE"

*V.*

*Tragedies Happen*

# Sleeping on Hillsides

A T AGE FOUR I TOLD MY PARENTS I wanted to sleep with the rab-
bits. We were living in the Oregon house with the picket fence, a
bungalow now gone, replaced by a mansion. Ours then was a humble ref-
uge across the road from the convent, the Sisters of Saint Francis. The sis-
ters held devotion in their cells. I had my own way.

Behind our house, a grand old maple presided over the rabbit hutch.
Was that the house where my father butchered a chicken and prepared a
feast to welcome my mother home from the hospital when one of us was
born? I can't remember. But I said I wanted to sleep with the rabbits, and
my parents said okay. I left the house at dusk, and all was still.

As the sky grew darker, they heard me open the back door and come
inside.

"Did you decide to sleep in your cozy bed?"

"No. I just forgot my pillow." I rubbed my eyes, fetched my pillow.
Outside, in the straw with the rabbits, I slept the night.

My mother has preserved a drawing of mine at age three—a series of
lines and dots that represent, according to my father's annotation, "some-
one walking in the rain . . . stars . . . footprints." My own world apart. Even
when the family camped out, I often took my sleeping bag and tramped at
dusk to some remote promontory to sleep alone. At Cove on the Crooked
River in central Oregon, it was up on the mesa above the canyon. In the
Malheur country farther east, it was above that cliff where we found the
cave. At the Metolius River in Oregon's mountain forests, it was as far up
Green Ridge as I could stumble before full dark to make my nest on the
ground.

I had to get away because when I woke—often in the night, and finally
at dawn—I had to feel the place uninsulated by comfort or company. I had
to lie on the ground and sip the pine scent of morning.

In his book *You Must Revise Your Life,* my father tells about a similar impulse when he was young and living in western Kansas. He reports riding his bike beyond the edge of town, climbing into the breaks above the Cimarron River, and waiting for night:

> On that still, serene day I stayed and watched. How slow and majestic the day was, and the sunset. No person anywhere, nothing, just space, the solid earth, gradually a star, the stars. Quail sounds, a coyote yapping.
>
> In the middle of the night I woke and saw a long, lighted passenger train slowly pulling along across the far horizon. No sound. Steady stars. The morning was dim, sure, an imperceptible brightening of sky with yellow, gray, orange, and then the powerful sun. That encounter with the size and serenity of the earth and its neighbors in the sky has never left me. The earth was my home; I would never feel lost while it held me.

When an interviewer asked my father, "What religious experiences have been most meaningful to you?" he replied:

> Every religious experience I recall that impressed me greatly has been in the presence of influences that combined several senses— no merely verbal experience, in a church, has provided a full religious experience. The most impressive such experience I recall was on the banks of the Cimarron River in western Kansas one mild summer evening . . . the feeling of being sustained, cherished, included. . . .

And in a poem he wrote a year before he died, he seems to attribute both his good luck and his isolation to such an experience on the prairie.

> Why did you come back a dreamer, never to contend
> like the others, always a little strange and alone?
> *It was those afternoons there in the open,*
> *it was the whole world: I was drunk on the world.*
> —*from* "APOLOGIA PRO VITA SUA"

Such a life in the open was mine when my parents entrusted me to the dark. I remember waking in the forest high on a ridge to see the full moon pouring silver over a buck strutting, crazy with rut, through the young pines. After *The Winter's Tale* at the Shakespeare festival in Ashland, I walked along the railroad tracks until I came to a dark pasture and could pass the night in the continuing dream of what I had seen. At the desert place called Sky Ranch, where we stayed with our friends the Ramseys, I had to take my sleeping bag and find a place on the hill alone, free from interruption to the rustling starlight overhead. After that night, our host Jerry Ramsey wrote a poem:

> It is a preference indicative of wit,
> self-reliance, and indifference to the vulgar comforts.
> Cantilevered there in your bag above us on
> this rocky hillside in the dark, you are keeping
> famous company in your chilly solitude—
> . . . . . . . . . . . . . . . . . .
> the generations of Indian children
> who came alone from far off
> perhaps to this very hill in quest of the spirit
> that would tell them who they were
> and give them a power to be—
> shivering, thirsting, famishing all day and night
> so still in the grass that buzzards might land
> at their feet, or Coyote come and breathe in their faces.
> It could happen to you.
>
> —*from* "SLEEPING ON HILLSIDES"

Another time, I remember my vigil under a lone oak on a Kansas hill. It must have been a family visit when I was fifteen or so. I had left the house while the others slept and wandered as high as I could for a look around. After midnight I leaned my back against the oak and watched lightning strike wheat fields to the west. The air was alive with the breath of damp earth and ozone smoke. I felt closer kinship to the oak, the wind, and even the lightning than with any human life. Mesmerized by the storm, I watched until in a close flash of fire I remembered the rule about the highest tree in a thunderstorm—and suddenly there was a ball of fire hanging in the air above me, spitting and swinging slowly back and forth. I ran, another flash, I fell on the pavement, put my whole hand into my mouth for fear, and the rain came gushing down. I was on my hands and knees in the gutter, drenched. Flash. I ran. Regained the yard at Aunt Peg's house, crept into the family car, the backseat, and shivered myself asleep.

In the morning, I went into the house for dry clothes.

"Got wet, did you?" my father said, looking up from his writing. He put his hand on my shoulder.

"Yeah, caught by the storm." I looked down, exhilarated by what I wasn't going to tell.

"Well, better get cleaned up," he said. "The others ought to be waking soon, and you can help with breakfast."

I never told. That seemed the best way to honor the immensity of such a night. It wasn't about words. You can write a letter describing a day of your life, a poem describing a war, a haiku about the moon—the increasingly compact density of the utterance keeps in balance with the growing immensity of the subject. Finally, the story is so huge only a silence will do it justice.

I remember one of the family's cross-country drives, how we stopped at the bank of a river on the prairie that seemed an empty place. My father stood a little apart, looking around. Eventually we all piled into the car, and after a while, he joined us.

"What river was that?" I asked my father from the back seat.

"The Cimarron."

The Cimarron. Now I see: he was there again, on his night of epiphany when he watched the train and felt "the size and serenity of the earth."

In my own search for such encounters, I remember leaving the family where they lay in sleeping bags and slipping away into the dark. We were camped at the Metolius River in Oregon, and I had to find that precious pocket of time before the others woke.

Tall pines against the stars. The sound of the river to my left to navigate my parallel way through the dark. With my stick I felt the ground ahead and held my free hand before my face to fend off low boughs of pine.

An hour later I settled on a ridge above a bend in the river. The time was approaching for that familiar tension between two worlds: I had not seen what awaited me, and others might be rising soon. I needed to get back.

A fawn appeared from somewhere, stepped toward me, stopped and stared. Jumped in place, frisked about, disappeared. Came back, reached a wet nose toward me, jumped, was gone.

By the time I was back in camp, I had managed to clear the grin off my face. I never told. And why am I telling now? Am I telling this story to you, to myself, to my father?

The water tank across from our house was a hundred feet high with a steel ladder that reached nearly to the ground. Nights I learned to shinny up to the lowest rung and pull myself sweating with terror to the top so I could lie under the stars and ponder. Below me spread the town that knew me not. Down there, the house, the family, Oregon. In this place my mind sprang free.

When the family traveled, some nights I would vow: "I will keep walking until I see no human light." From the "Y Motel" on the north edge of Madras, Oregon, sometime in the early 1960s, I slipped out the door and started up the road. Behind me, my father and my sisters were asleep after a day of exploring the desert. Maybe 1 A.M. The world was too good to squander in sleep, the night too velvet and cold, my body too restless. Striding along the centerline of Highway 97 by starlight, I shied off into the sage whenever car lights appeared. Then I stumbled back to the centerline and went on. Finally, maybe five miles out from town, I left the highway, clambered carefully under a barbwire fence, crossed a ridge of sage, and had my wish: only the stars to give me light. I turned around once in place, looked up, photographed the galaxy with my whole being. Then I could return.

There were darker secrets in our family, things some wished had been done, or said—or not done, not said. But for me, the most important secrets were moments of joy so intense they could not be shared

When we crossed the country I rose before the others, eased out the motel door with my shoes in my hand, got laced up and strode away along our road. Later, I'd be picked up by the family car. Can you imagine letting a child do that? Idaho, Wyoming, Nebraska, Iowa. We would do five hundred miles a day, but I did the first two or three each morning alone. On one of those mornings I found an arrowhead of white flint on the road shoulder in Wyoming; in Edinburgh I traded it to an old man for an English penny from the time of George III. Alone in the early mornings, wandering wide in the world, I had my own currency for the economy of this life.

At age three, I announced, "I'm going to go jump in the daylight." And "I'm going out to get the nice feel of the night." "Well," my parents would say, "better take your jacket." The world awaited me outside the circle of family, civilization, and safety.

Sitting in a faculty meeting now, often I remember, imagine, leap. Out of nowhere I am standing on the ridge or kneeling at the stream. In that distant place I find exactly what I need to contribute to the matter at hand. Or sometimes, with family, when everyone else gets up to go, and I am alone for a moment—say I'm waiting to pay the bill, or setting out to get the car—I hear wind in a pine, or glimpse perfect circles of rain in a puddle, or reach out to put my hand on the bark of an old cedar.

In one discussion of his creative process, my father describes his search for the "periphery of justice," just beyond the edge of what he knows or can defend. Even in the collective work of developing justice, sometimes he had to set out alone:

> An intentional person is too effective to be a good guide in the tentative activity of creating. I think it takes a certain kind of irresponsibility . . . I find a paradox in my present role. I'm supposed to be responsible in what I am saying, and of course in a way I am being responsible. But I'm being responsible in a pretty reckless way, because this is an odd activity, creating.

To my chagrin, I can't find the source of that passage. I was reckless when I copied it in the archive, knowing I needed it. But sometimes, that's the idea: you have to get beyond pattern—by intuitive exploration and "being lost willingly"—in order to find the new design.

One thing those nights gave me, with their treasuries of starlight at the pinnacle of independence, was a great puzzlement when my friends spoke of getting "high." I remember a kid bragging to me he had a six-pack of beer buried in his backyard. I imagined him grubbing in the dirt for that pale buzz. I wasn't better than him. I did my share of stupid things. But my childhood gave me unusual resources. Wasn't bold illumination available everywhere? I now see my wanderings were an intuitive parallel to my father's writing practice. Something invisible was always going on at our house. Our father's daily writing wasn't a secret, it was just at the edge of our awareness. His writing struck me more like a life practice than a literary one, and had more to do with independence than with poetry. By the time the rest of us appeared from our rooms at six or so, he would be in a fine mood. He had accomplished the best of what the day might be, but he kept it to himself.

I've told how during World War II, when my father was in the camp for conscientious objectors, the group made a decision to rise early and devote their best collective energy to the life of mind and spirit, instead of squandering all they had on the physical labor their keepers might devise. My father's habits never changed. In Cold War America, his day-work could feel like an illusion. Writing in the dark was real.

When I was sixteen and assistant moderator of the Presbyterian youth group, one evening the assistant pastor closed the doors for our Bible study class, and gave us a top secret lecture on sex and love. "For your first time with another," he said, "you must be alone. You must know you will not be interrupted." The twenty or so young men and women froze in their chairs. "You must have a sense of privacy and calm," he said, "for you are with another person in a way that is very precious, but also fragile. It is not a time to hurry." I was afraid to look at anyone in the room. I felt utterly naïve.

"The first partner you are with," he said, "will hold a special place in your heart forever. She or he may become your partner for life. Or he or she may not. In any case, take care and be tender."

Maybe my love affair with night was a rehearsal for that. I knew nothing of women, had been on one uneventful date to a football game, had never attended a dance, never held hands, never kissed. That beautiful terror lay somewhere in the dim future. What was I to do in the meantime?

In the spring of 1967, I wanted to hear my clarinet in the sanctuary alone. I had to hear my own breath wail past the reed, press warm along the ebony tunnel of the instrument, and fill the room that had contained our silence weekly for years. I wanted to pray this way and love this way. I wanted Mozart to climb through the silence and carry me.

Our church was several miles from home. Sometime after 10 P.M. the house grew still, and I eased out the front door, hiked down the hill where Iron Mountain Boulevard ended in a whiff of swamp, crossed the dark hills of the golf course, and followed the railroad tracks that curved through the dark. By midnight, I had arrived with my clarinet at the southeast corner of the church. I climbed a drainpipe, with help from the wisteria vine, and stood on the flat roof over the fellowship hall. There I tried to pry up the skylight with my Boy Scout knife, certain I could find a way to flip it open, drop to the floor, thread my way to the double doors with their brass-plated handles, and into the sanctuary to play Mozart for God.

Kneeling in roof gravel I tried the screwdriver blade on the rivets through plexiglass, then the can-opener blade against the tin flashing. The skylight was well made, and in the dark I cut my hand on the tin. I wrapped the wound with a scarf, then tried the leather awl here and there, then the whittling blade. Nothing worked. I was stumped and sat back.

After trudging around the roof, trying the windows of the Sunday-School wing, and the padlocked roof-access lid, I saw it was late and clambered down the drainpipe to scurry along my blackberry path toward the tracks. Halfway home, on a long curve I lay down to sleep on the gravel just below the rails, and was startled awake when a freight train thundered past my head. I crept back into the weeds, shivered, waited. When the red light on the caboose dwindled away, I plodded on in the quiet and dragged my way along Sunningdale Road just as first light came up in the east.

At home, there is a way you can turn the front-door knob so it makes no sound. You pull it toward your belly, and lift slightly, and then lean forward. I turned, and lifted, and leaned—and there was my father stretched out on the couch, looking at me over the top of his writing pad.

"Hello," he whispered.

"Hello," I whispered.

No questions, no stories, only his wide gaze, his smile. I turned away and went down the hall toward my room, slept awhile in my clothes, then rose with the household, gathered with the others at the table for breakfast, and drifted in my trance to school. I said nothing. My father said nothing.

I tried the church again and again over the following weeks. It was not an option to play my clarinet during service. As a musician, I struggled. I would make mistakes, clumsy with the high notes sometimes, or that challenging maneuver with the clarinet called "going over the break," where the performer shifts from the lower register to the upper notes. That's where the instrument, in my hands, would squeak in pain. But I knew the place in Mozart where the clarinet's blind voice climbs a ladder, hesitates, and climbs again, and then, high and thin and pure, steps tenderly down. There, exactly there, God would recognize me.

So, at the end of Sunday service, I would climb the stairs to open a window latch and slip away. After midnight I was back, up the drainpipe to the roof, across the roof to that window, confident, ready. But the window was locked. I had to pad my long way home again. The next Sunday, I unlocked the window again, and that night found it locked again. This went on for three weeks, until one Sunday I found a note the janitor had taped to the window, just for me: "Whoever you are—leave this window locked!" I could read his anger by the stroke of his pen. And so that chapter in my religious education came to an end.

I remember a story the novelist Ignazio Silone tells about riding the train at night down through Italy and noticing the woman across the aisle is reading one of his books. Turning as if in sleep, he manages to see which page she is reading, and it makes him cringe. He recalls he didn't get that passage quite right. She closes the book and looks out into the night. He has failed her. Darkness is her only consolation, for his book cannot be her worthy friend. But then she opens the book again and begins to read. Breathlessly, he watches. What is she receiving? Suddenly, he is humbled. *This* is the reader he was writing for. This is the reader he would speak to on the page, the reader by this miracle he might see, but never the reader he might know. The distance across the aisle between them was too great, though his book was close to her heart.

Writer—what a lonely profession. They would never meet. It was his privilege to write for her. The woman on the train, like every traveler through time, needed the simple companionship of a story to put beside her own.

I have read poem after poem of my father's that reaches out for kindred intelligence, an understanding heart. The reach was real for him, but connection elusive. I find a kind of religion in his poems in this yearning imagination: "Forgive me these shadows I cling to, good people" ("Some Shadows"). Poetry was his school to practice the reach, and suffer the defeat of absolute connection he intuited. In his poems and in our conversations I try to understand my father's particular rehearsals for connection. How did he teach me? And what did I learn?

I remember a girl I so admired all through junior high I carved her name into the bark of trees, and gazed in her direction out of the corner of my eye for years. In the preeminent silence of my adolescence that formed the native waters of my writing life, I don't believe we ever spoke. After high school I didn't see her for decades. Then one day, across a crowded

room, following a memorial service for one of my students, I saw a distin-
guished woman approaching me.

"Do you remember me?" she said.

"Help me. . . ."

"I'm Molly," she said, and my heart, from that great distance in time,
faltered. She was dressed simply, but elegantly. Her hair was bravely begin-
ning to gray.

"I have read your book," she said. "I felt it spoke directly to me." We
shook hands, looked into each other's eyes, and she drifted away.

Isn't that the premier dream of childhood, that someone you admire
would understand you—without a word said directly but in the beam of
light that travels outward from the soul? In many of my father's poems
there is a felt connection, a moment of recognition, a departure. "If only
once in all those years," he wrote, addressing his father, "the right goodby
could have been said. . . ." ("Elegy"). For all his friendships and close affini-
ties with family, friends, students, readers, and fellow writers, did my father
achieve the connections in life he so clearly honored in his writing?

> Even on the last morning
> when we all tremble and lose, I will reach
> carefully, eagerly through that rain, at the end—
>
> Toward whatever is there, with this loyal hand.
> —*from* "WITNESS"

In that time of my life when I went wandering nights and mornings, I
didn't need to write things down. Only to get away into the dark and dwell
there. The forest, an open horizon in the desert, or any empty place: the
sound of water, wind in the trees, the glint of stars.

# Braided Apart

A T HOME, EVERYBODY WROTE POEMS. I remember my sister Barbara coming from school with her lyric about the frog. The one puzzling line was the last: "Then the frog would be sublime." Sublime? It turned out Barb's teacher longed for her students to win the poetry contest and sometimes fiddled with their scrawl as she typed things up. I remember my sister Kit's far-reaching lyrics, and my mother still has a poem by brother Bret on the wall of her sewing room. Mother, too, holds a skill with words that she discounts but others recognize. Our creative democracy in the household—poems here and there from everyone right along— was in keeping with my father's refrain when asked about the beginning of his career as a writer: "The question isn't when did I start writing, but when do most people stop—and why?"

We all wrote, but I don't remember talking with my father about my own experiments. Writing happened, here and there, now and then—from the short-lived family newspaper of the 1950s, *The Happy Reporter,* to the note I Scotch-taped to a crystal when I was eight (which my mother saved): "This is a rock that a boy found in 1957."

My own beginnings were unremarkable. "Snort, snort, snort down the snowy road," I chanted at the age of three, and my poet father wrote it down. Though my own paper evidence is slight, I have a host of memories of those preliminary writing fits. Walking down a particular road at dusk just as the first star showed, I began to chant: "My house shall stand where I can get a good view of the night sky. . . ." By chance, the other day I found a typescript of the whole poem, its ending a classic instance of meter running out of gas:

> And when I die at least I'll know, that these great things will
> Still go on, even though, then, I'll be gone.

Miss Scholastica Murty, my high-school English teacher, would be proud of my command of the comma there. But the sentiment may have been expressed elsewhere—for example, by my father:

> I would be everywhere, as I am right now, a thin tone like the wind,
> a sip of blue light—no source, no end, no horizon.
> —*from* "SOMETHING THAT HAPPENS RIGHT NOW"

> You will bring me
> everything when the time comes.
> —*from* "SKY"

> And where I stand, no one.
> —*from* "AT OUR HOUSE"

A concluding farewell is frequent in my father's poems. He started saying good-bye early and kept at it. I think he was surprised in his later years to have lived so long. For he lived long enough in his art to write amazing, lasting things, even though his beginnings, like mine, like the beginnings of most writers, could be feeble. Witness the early William Stafford:

> And I will raise my head and care:
> Oh orphan world, I love you dear.
> —*from* "COOL WORLD," 21 MARCH 1944

He had written stronger poems earlier, in college. But successful writing wasn't as important in those early years as the consistency of his practice, with ever deepening results. The page on which that last couplet resides is an undated document my father sent home, apparently from CO camp, a page that includes a statement of intention to become a poet, a series of poetic fragments, and his own commentary on these attempts. Titled "A Page of Specialized Communication," it reads like a personal declaration of independence from war, from despair, and from what others thought of his writing. Apparently addressed to his soldier brother, it begins:

> There is a large part of my life—poetry—that not many know
> much about, because so much slush is put out about the general

subject. My attempts, however, are meant merely as intense efforts on my part to communicate thoughts or experiences. Some day I'll be a poet, I believe; but even if that time never comes I'll have a few bits to share with those I want to get into touch with.

What follows is not a great poem, but holds in embryo the folded bones that will unfurl in more powerful ways farther on:

*Home*

Our father owned a star.
And by its light
We lived in father's house
And slept at night.

The tragedies of life,
Like death and war,
Were faces looking in
At our front door.

But finally all came in,
From near and far:
We had to sell the lock
To own the star.

This was written 21 June 1944, under the spell of his father's death. He is liberated—or at least insulated—from paralyzing grief by the balance and buoyant invention possible in poetry. Later in life, he would let similar ideas germinate in more skillful ways:

Halfway across a bridge one night
my father's car went blind. He guided
it on by no star but a light he kept in mind.
—*from* "THE SWERVE"

And finally, in another look back to the walls of a house where his father had held the world together, my father follows to the end his "intense efforts . . . to communicate thoughts and experiences":

My father could hear a little animal step,
or a moth in the dark against the screen,
and every far sound called the listening out
into places where the rest of us had never been.
                                    — *from* "LISTENING"

When I read that poem aloud, a strange short circuit occurs, and the words refer to my own father. "*My* father could hear. . . ." I wait for a time when something in the night will touch me from that other place.

In high school, I remember the *feel* of writing. My father used to say when he began a piece of writing, he didn't know what a poem was going to say, but he sometimes knew what it might smell like—juniper, wheat stubble, an old tool handle. And I remember those moments when syllables crowded in my mind, and I took up a pencil to jot. Once on Orcas Island I walked on ahead from our family's camp at Moran, and the wind moaning in the wires beckoned me to chant. Another time seeing convicts on hands and knees beside the freeway planting iris bulbs—their predicament needed me. And once in high school the flavor of a northern California morning came back—maybe from our trip to Mexico in 1964. "Quail call, a soft flute note on the cool morning air." I remember that line, but more than the poem that followed I remember the feeling then: this is how to live twice.

On a page of lecture notes from high-school history class, 1966, my words compress America into shorthand:

> 19th cent.—laissez faire—land grants—tariff inflation, lower the
> tariff—economic oligopoly—La Follette, T. Roosevelt—break up
> big business—use Sherman trust—politician = mouthpiece, not
> talented. . . .

On the other side of the page, a similar shorthand, but my own:

> wild laugh, wild dance, wild cry,
> never stay, never sway, always shake
> always leap—
> back and forth, rise and fall—
> frenzied feet, where to go
> there—there—there. . . .

Aside from the few stray texts that survive, I remember the feelings that preceded writing and the tools that made it happen more than the poems themselves. I remember the late-night stab of anguish, or the morning twinge or whim. I remember the backs of envelopes, whittled pencil stubs, the dawn raids on the recycle bin at the computer center for those dozen blank sheets that a long program spits out at the end, folded in an endless Z. I would tear away the whiffle holes, cut the sheets in half with my pocketknife, and be a poor writer rich in open pages.

If I showed my father the poem about the quail, he probably talked about quail, or California, or mornings, or that trip to Mexico. The poem would be an occasion for a conversation about ideas, or events, or even language—but not poetry, and most emphatically not the poem at hand.

Sometimes in a writing workshop, after a writer in the group had shared a poem, especially what he would call a "distinctive" one, my father would say, "How I envy you. . . ." And then he would list some of the surprises in the poem that caught his eye and ear, some of what the poem had almost said that sparked his curiosity. The poem was distinctive, he would observe, because it broke rules we didn't know we had. With the common language the writer did uncommon things. Then my father would try by question and nudge to invite the writer to be even more surprising, quirky, and unafraid. He would encourage the writer to venture a beginning so strange no one in the room could predict what it should become. Not even the writer. And that is where my father wanted to be when he was writing on his own—and what he wanted, finally, for us.

There came a time in our lives together when a college might invite the two of us to give a workshop or a reading. For the reading, my father and I often traded off at the microphone at an interval of about three poems apiece. Or he would read three poems, and I would sing a song, or read a passage from an essay, or tell a story. His poems were concise, or to use his word, "trenchant"—or they were playful—but always compact. It was as if the hardships of his life had whittled away any fake crust the culture might have allowed to another. My offerings tended to be rambling, exploratory. When he took his turn at the podium, after one of my forays, he would shake his head, and say *to* me but *for* the audience, "Kim, you're really something else."

I take that as his own strange praise—or rather, his act of recognition. He believed as a teacher and as a parent that approval can hurt as much as a put-down. Approval, praise, or any kind of superior conferring of status implied a power structure foreign to his understanding of art and life.

When he shook his head at my writing (or my life), I understood him to be saying: we are working side by side in our different ways. The point was not to be the kind of master who directs the beginner toward successful ends. The point was to be a companion in a world haunted by distracting fame and despair, to be good company instead of a directive force.

When I turned to writing essays, "lyrical prose," I found a writing voice independent of my father. Shortly before he died, we were talking about what we had been reading, and my father shook his head and sighed.

"Baroque prose," he said. "First Annie Dillard did it, and now everyone." (He favored the plain style of Santayana, after all, the directness of Pascal—but also the complex speculations of his beloved Nietzsche, Kierkegaard, Wittgenstein. He was hard to pin down.)

"But Daddy," I said, "baroque prose . . . that's what I do."

He shook his head. "You're one of the worst," he said.

Was this a devastating remark, an insult? Well . . . it wasn't approval—or disapproval, exactly. It was the kind of enigmatic moment with my father to which I had become accustomed, a moment in keeping with the respect he directed toward my independence. At least that's how I took it. No praise, no blame, only notice taken of inescapable character.

After all, my father could be baroque when it suited him, as in a poem he published in the *New Yorker*:

> Awake, like a hippopotamus with eyes bulged
> from the covers, I find Monday, improbable
> as chair legs, camped around me, and God's terrible
> searchlight raking down from His pillbox on Mount Hood,
> while His mystic hammers reach from the alarm clock
> and rain spangles my head.
> . . . . . . . . . . . . . . . . . . . . . . . . .
> I gradually become young, surge from the covers,
> and go to work.
>
> —*from* "MONDAY"

This kind of language was not foreign to his taste. His beloved Nietzsche, for example, could be quite extravagant. And my father had watched my preparation for baroque ways from the start. I find in his writing from the time I was three that I practiced a kind of swagger he enjoyed:

Kim is one of the luckiest people in the world. Not in any one
endowment—his little pig eyes, his pudgy face—but the whole as-
sembly of Kim is irresistible, dauntless, and happy. Going across
the street, even, he sings: "Hippity hop, puddles of rain, walk on
the bricks, hippitity hop. . . ."

—DAILY WRITING, 20 MARCH 1953

I love that: pig eyes, pudgy face. Maybe my father faulted Annie Dillard,
and me, not so much for a fancy prose style as for missing the point of a di-
rected life. Plato banished the poets because they strayed from their exis-
tential calling as philosophers, and were awed by golden language. Though
my father could be playful in his own writing, and though he advocated an
elastic, responsive approach to creation, he also required that writing be de-
voted to a search for truth. This could make him stern. He was calling me
back to work, for he could never quite accept the heroic, the beautiful, or
the elegant if these qualities were separate from the real sources. True grace,
real poetry happened in fearless confrontation with mystery.

In many contexts, my father was the master of understatement, as
when, in what is obviously a love poem, he concludes, "Remember, Tom?
She's that girl we once spoke of." Hardly a passionate declaration (though
the unspoken "love" is rhymed into the reader's mind). In other contexts,
however, my father relished the obliteration of expectations when his own
talk went over the top. "Since we're speaking recklessly" was one of his fa-
vorite invitations to "up the ante" once a discussion really got going. He
couldn't help it. He was a brilliant man, deeply wise, with a keen sense of
humor, and sometimes this gushed forth. After all, though a Midwestern
pacifist, he was Crazy Horse at heart, setting out to save the world. Not a
job for whisperers alone.

So he said, "Baroque prose . . . you're one of the worst!" And I heard the
bold encouragement his own poem proclaims: "I say Crazy Horse was too
cautious!" I heard a corrective: *Friend, writer, son—tell the kind of truth that
is hard to see.* But I also heard: *Kim, don't be timid about who you are.* Maybe
all honest parenting must be contradictory. As I do to my own children,
maybe he was lecturing a wild and cherished part of himself.

What can I do about my extravagant character? Midwest heritage,
Oregon childhood: I am doomed to be who I am. My father must have rec-
ognized this. I, too, was writing in an inevitable way, not a calculated one.

About difference, he would not approve or disapprove. He would observe from early on:

> Kim got to talking among the people waiting in Dorothy's Dr.'s office: "How much does it cost here?" etc. Then he got curious about a door: "Where does it go?" The other people, once he wondered, began to wonder too. Kim ran over & opened the door. It was a closet. "If all the doors were closets," he said, "we'd have to go out the chimney." Typical Kim thinking: fantastic difficulties; optimistic solutions.
>
> —DAILY WRITING, 12 NOVEMBER 1952

I was three years old, and already baroque. My father could joke about this kind of destiny, as he did in these lines from "An Archival Print":

> Now you want to explain. Your mother
> was a certain—how to express it?—*influence.*
> Yes. And your father, whatever he was,
> you couldn't change that. No. And your town
> of course had its limits. Go on, keep talking—
> Hold it. Don't move. That's you forever.

So he wrote his way, I wrote mine—baroque, plain style—and we enjoyed each other.

In 1975 I agreed to meet my father at the Little House near Sisters to sit at a table by the light of kerosene and weave together our common book, *Braided Apart.* There was a new independent outfit in Idaho, calling themselves "Confluence Press" for their location in Lewiston, where the Clearwater River joins the Snake, and our book was to be their first. A man of boundless welcome—Keith Browning, the editor there—had asked us to make him a manuscript of poems joined out of our two lives, and he would bind them into a book. The production eventually included a scattering of black-and-white photographs I had taken over the years: a pool at Wuthering Heights, a fence in the wheat field near Stonehenge, reeds at Orcas Island, fog along the Willamette River. The binding glue has not held up well. My copy is bunched together with a double loop of linen string. To me it is a landmark in time, my father's life converging with mine. That night we sat at a table late, with the stove stoked and crackling with pine.

I remember holding forty or so of my poems typed on half-sheets of paper, while my father sat across from me with a sheaf of his own. We each held our poems fanned like a hand of cards. "You first," he said. "Are you sure?" I said. He nodded. So I put down "The Lock":

> Like two hands related by birth
> let's clench, a pair folded
> around shared scars, palm lines
> singing for breath, love, offspring.

He leaned forward to study what I had, brood about it. "Hmmm." Sometimes a response to student writing, his first comment revealed no judgment, but signaled the writing had been received. Then he pulled "Attenuate" out of his hand and put it down:

> Some time, following out a sound,
> the way to come back will disappear,

Kerosene burned steady. Outside, we could hear the pines passing their comb through the wind. The fire muttered. My father's eyebrows twitched almost imperceptibly, to signal, wolf-like, that he was having a good time. The shadow of his shaggy head was big on the wall behind him. I put down "The Small Hours":

> First we learned to dance, then to fly,
> then to fall and hide in the grass like quail,
> then to creep away low on earth. . . .

Those lines sound like a William Stafford poem to me now, but then the poem felt like neither his nor mine. "The small hours" was an idea that had occurred to one of us in the early morning, and we were braiding it loose from our life to give away. He put down "Shells":

> When they turn the dial to "know"
> there on the beach or the grass
> they speak low. . . .

We had built the house where now we met. We were surrounded by our errors and our small victories: a crooked juniper limb whittled into a drawer-pull, a ladder to the loft secured to the wall with the U-bolt from a car's muffler, the coiled manila rope of the block and tackle arrayed by the stove to dry. That life was a rude contraption, and our own. I put down "At Night near the Coast," with its tavern lore:

> At the bar I watched an old man
> catch a fly by the wings, drown it
> in a capful of beer, lay the tiny
> carcass on his palm and bring it
> back to life with salt. . . .

When I look back on that night, I see it was a quiet farewell. For our connection, kinship, common interests were at the same time a basis for lives independent from each other. That is the troubling paradox of right love, of intimacy practiced at a respectful distance.

As if playing the trump card, my father put down his next poem, "Aquarium at Seaside":

> Groping stars called up from a field,
> in silence curled these languid creatures,
> abrupt as truth's edge, wander their schedule.
> What great rope current braided us apart?
> Into that night we follow those lives,
> lonely like ours. With my tongue
> I touch the glass: millions of years.
> It divides the world.

The fluid, octopus-like syntax of his voice in that poem could not soften the hurt I began to feel—my departure, finally, from home We were linked and divided, braided apart not as a rope unravels, but as two sinews of DNA might part their bond to seek new connections. We finished our task, numbered the pages in a folder, and went to sleep—he on the couch downstairs, and I in the loft above.

That farewell in poetry, the night we set out to braid ourselves apart, preceded my father's death by almost twenty years. But it marked a new chapter. The book we made was quickly out of print. We went our ways. Being of one source, we could travel different roads without ever letting go of the thread.

After my father died, I met Perrin, the woman who would be my second wife. She recalled a night years before when she had been in the audience as my father and I gave a reading together, sometime in the mid-1980s. It was a big event; I couldn't see the audience against the stage lights. As always, my pieces were different than my father's. He read poems; I told stories and then sang an odd song about my daughter. It was a lullaby I had written when she was three years old and I was giving her a bath:

> Oh my, my belly button's in your eye—
> Oh my, what am I gonna do . . . ?

After the performance, backstage, my father turned to me. "I don't think you should sing that song in public ever again," he said. "People will get the wrong idea."

I understood his view, but was caught by surprise. It was the only time in my life he had given me direct advice about my writing.

After he died, I asked Perrin, "Do you remember that song I sang at the Hult Center in Eugene?"

"About the belly button?" Perrin said. "I do. I had a strange sentence go through my mind as you sang that: 'I should marry a man like that.' I wasn't thinking I should marry *you,* of course. You were married then. But I thought I should marry a man who could be that tender and happy about his child. I should marry a father like that."

❧

# The Lost Child

THE BULLET WAS ON ITS WAY. I had pulled the trigger, but my brother, running frantic through the trees below me, had not flinched. A gray wire of speed connected us, a spiral unraveling who I was. I prayed to bring that bullet back. Alder trees blurred in moss, a silence of birds. His head down, open mouth, leaning into his rush. The rifle solid in my hand kicked against my shoulder. His soft animal eyes turned down.

After I won the pellet gun from my father for rising into the top reading group in grade three, my visits to the woods to play "Indian" changed. Targets, then birds became my quarry, and finally on this worst of adolescent days, my brother. In the heat of play that gun carried me into a crescendo of excitement as my tribe chased my brother's tribe—everyone else with sticks for guns or spears, but I "pretending" with my pump-action pellet gun. And in the rush of the moment, I pulled the trigger, and missed, thank God.

Why did I have the gun pumped and loaded, if this was play? What made me aim a loaded gun at my own brother? What made me pull the trigger? What did the other kids do? And why did my brother never tell?

I've bragged I never fought with my brother, and for the most part, this was true. Our father always referred to Bret as "Number One Son," and I could never tell whether this was what our father believed, or what he thought my brother, older but smaller and shyer than me, needed to hear.

Now I look back. My father's daily writing includes an anxious meditation from August 1968. Despite his confidence about many things, he recognized mortality. As he often does, he begins with roving thoughts and then shifts into a poem, in this case a kind of prayer:

Yesterday reviewing plans our children have, suddenly I felt fear, for
them. I was driving, and all was well, but a passenger was with me

194

then—the thought of what could happen any time, just chances. The good things carry possibility of their opposites. I did not dwell on this, but for an interval I saw it more vividly than before.

Let me find all by myself that mold
the forest has for me, that crag.
May all those reaching plans men
set up, miss me. May I find the still
place.
       Let me die at the right time.

My father begins with fear for his children, but arrives at his own. The focus is finally his own journey, something apart from his connection with others. I am reminded of a classic revelation my father once made, a typical demonstration of his independence from the sentimental. Driving south at sixty on Interstate 5 with my mother, he had dozed at the wheel, drifted onto the right shoulder of the road, struck a light-reflector post, then over-corrected as he woke—sending their little Honda skidding sideways at probably fifty miles an hour across three lanes of heavy traffic. Tires squealed, rubber burned, cars swerved, and my father somehow brought the car to a stop on the left shoulder, facing backward. When they told us about their near-death moment later, my mother said, "I was thinking of the children, Bill. Weren't you?"

"Not at all," my father said. "I was thinking, 'What great tires!'"

My brother Bret was otherwise—a sensitive man, but with a crippling habit of self-sacrifice. His sweet liability surfaced early, when in junior high he announced that in lieu of any Christmas presents he would prefer that friends and family donate money to the United Nations. In high school, he served as Special Projects Chair for his class, and arranged a heroic volunteer effort that resulted in the planting of a mile of flowering cherry trees along the road between town and school—trees now tall, about twenty feet apart, with the full blossoming bounty of spring.

Riding along that road as a child in blossom time, my daughter once asked me, "Did the world thank Uncle Bret for all those trees?"

"No, little friend," I said, "I don't believe it did."

Maybe it was hard for my brother the way I shared obsessions more directly with our father—the selfish pleasures of carpentry, photography, writing—while Bret was the boy more studious, thoughtful, serving others. We two drew forth different strands of paternal character.

We went to the University of Oregon together, but after that, though he won his status as a conscientious objector from the Draft Board, the tensions of American life during the Vietnam War drove him to Canada, where he earned landed-emigrant status and taught anthropology in Victoria. Later, he lived in a series of small Oregon towns, where he worked as a land-use planner. He told me once, "I have become 'They'—'*They* won't let you do what you want with your own land.' It's like I'm the enemy of many people I meet. They sit in my office and cry."

By the time I had left my wife in summer 1988, after eighteen years of marriage, Bret and his wife and their two children were headed to Canada again, to a very remote place 600 miles north of the border. Before he left, I asked him why he had to go. To my confusion, he quoted back to me a line from my own book, which I had arrogantly titled *Having Everything Right*: "Part of our love must be to teach each other how to live alone." It was an idea I believed in general, an approach that felt right for others, but not for him.

"No," I said. "You don't have to go that far."

"I do," he said.

And there, in the north woods, far from us, out of work and brooding, he lost his psychic grasp. He stopped sleeping, took antidepressant medication, spiraled out of focus. When he visited me in the fall, he wanted to return to Oregon, and I offered to help him get his resume together and scan the territory for jobs in land-use planning. When we went to my office at the college together, and I showed him my kingdom there, I could tell it was a blow.

"This is my desk," I said, showing him around, "and my secretary sits over there, and my assistant down the hall . . . and here are brochures about our program, and. . . ." I looked at him. He hadn't immediately held out his hand for what I was offering, then he caught himself and took it.

"This is great," he said, his voice a listless monotone. It was as if I had fired another bullet at him as he ran—this time my success, my world, my own Northwest Writing Institute at our father's college. He was unemployed, living far away, and falling apart.

We went to the house where I lived alone. In the night I woke to hear him whimpering, then sobbing. I went to the couch where he lay, held him against my body. He did not respond. He was rigid and thin, cold. I could feel his ribs.

Earlier that year I had sat down with my brother at a place called Boone's Tavern to tell him I was leaving my wife. I needed to live alone, I said, sort things out. Without a word, he reached for his wallet, and pulled out a well-worn slip of paper from a fortune cookie. I held it up in the tavern's dim light: "Learn to cut your expectations in half."

"Don't," I said, handing it back to him. "Don't do that." It scared me.

"I have to," he said. "Some nights at dinner the only sound is the clink of the silverware."

The morning after he woke me with his sobs, we talked and talked, we jogged, we ate, we laughed. Our morning seemed to cheer him up. He would return to Canada, he said. Then when an Oregon job came along, he would come home to apply, and it would be like it used to be.

"I'll go to Canada with you," I said. "We can have a great drive. I'll help you pack your stuff and get back here."

"No," he said, "it's okay. I can do it."

The day after he departed, I looked on a high shelf and found he had left me a birch bark basket, made by the native people of northern B.C. Inside he had drawn a canoe with two paddlers, and a note in his quick scrawl:

Life's an adventure—what's around the next bend? Thanks for the good time.

I was glad for his visit, and yes, despite his pain, it had been a good time. It wasn't until later—after everything changed—that I read the note again and saw the little loop at the end that might have vaulted me to action, had I understood it then:

. . . Thanks for the good times.

He was saying good-bye to his younger brother.

When Bret did come home, I was away—off on a work circuit of Boston, then San Diego. He came to Oregon, had a job interview in the central Oregon town of Redmond with people who liked him but found him so helplessly depressed, almost catatonic in response to their questions, they could not offer him the job.

By then, I was home in Portland, but he was across the mountains, in central Oregon. He went to my sister Kit's house while she was away. He searched the house until he found a pistol belonging to her boyfriend, carried it downstairs, and in that sleepless trance he had been living for months, he took his life. She found him at the door.

I look back now. There was a moment during his last visit, in the night as he sobbed, when I knew I had a choice. I could take over his life, take command of what he must do—I could force him to live with me, or even arrange some kind of hospital stay. Or I could offer all my help, but leave the initiative to him. The second way felt more respectful, but was not wise. I didn't tell the truth—that my efforts to clarify my own life were not superhuman. I did have a girlfriend by then, but did not tell my brother this. It was another of those pointless secrets, a tremendous silence at an intimate time. I had confusions of my own, but also help, and joy—but I didn't tell my brother this as he cried in my arms.

The family went into a spin. My sister Kit, who found him, could not talk about it. Our father was away, flew home, retreated to his study to read Wordsworth, and then could not bring himself to sit with us at the memorial service. He stood in the back of the room while the rest of us rose in turn to speak of Bret. When I turned to look, I saw my father by the exit door pacing alone like an animal. And at the end of the service, when everyone stood up, I looked around the room, over the heads of friends pressing toward us, for my father. He was gone.

Without him, we struggled, could not get back to what we had been as a family. My mother needed my father to grieve with her. My sister Kit needed something neither Barb nor I could provide. Barb struggled, and I felt weak. Everything was different. I looked around to see who could help. Now I was the oldest child. Maybe each of us forged the private bargain I did with myself: we will never know what happened to Bret (was it his antidepressant drugs, together with no sleep, that triggered the end?), but I accept responsibility for my part in our failure. I sat with the family, cried, and then took on the practical things: obituary in the *Oregonian,* contact with friends as the word spread, a memorial fund for a place called Rowena—an ethereal nature preserve my brother had loved.

When friends came to the house to mourn with us, my father was strangely lively. His hospitality was upbeat, his conversation deftly turning away from the death of his child. His account of the event in a letter home to Kansas, to his sister-in-law Margaret, is straightforward, chronological, and then he turns toward life: "I don't want to end talking about this dire event, for we face forward now, still thinking about what if, what if we had done this or that; but we face forward." And then three paragraphs of chatty news.

By his lead, we rarely spoke directly about what had happened. I wonder now at a family that lets this happen: we suffer a tragedy that shows us there is great need for more talk, clarity, and honesty about hard things. Might more talk have saved Bret—even awkward, difficult talk? Even with that question hanging in the air, we maintained a continuing habit of silence, all the same. It felt strange, but I know it is often so with families. And I knew my father.

> how about the boy who always
> granted others their way to live,
> and he gave away his whole life
> till at last nothing was left for him?
> Don't tell that one.
> —*from* "STORY TIME"

I remember a few times when I broke through my own reserve. Several months after my brother's death, I abruptly asked my father, "How come I survived and Bret did not?"

"You're too mean," he said, "and that's good. Bret was a saint. Don't be a saint."

Yes, Bret was a saint. And no, I am not. Clumsy, selfish, I take care of myself at the expense of others, if I can't find any other way. Perhaps in that, I am like our father. But still his suppression of grief was a mystery to me.

Another time my father told a strange story about one of his last meetings with Bret, before the move to Canada. Bret was visiting the home place with his two kids, and they were feeling boisterous after a long drive. When they ran out to the yard, my father asked Bret, "Do you love your kids more when they are being good?"

"No," my brother said, "I love my kids all the time."

At this point in his account my father told me, "A writer would have told the truth."

What can I make of this? That my father judged my brother harshly for not being mean—for not being a writer, his own particular kind of truth-teller? Was my father telling his whole truth? Did my father love his own child less when that child said a saintly thing? Did he resent that my brother *could* love his kids without a moment's faltering? Was my father simply mystified that my brother did not withdraw into himself to recover when things got hard, and so reached a point of psychic exhaustion where he could not go on? My father, the writer, the reader of Wordsworth, the traveler through the dark, had a place to go when the world attacked, as he said to my mother when the hard news came: "Sometimes the world reaches out a paw." He went to his books and his writing. Is writing a retreat from life, then, a place to hide?

Years later, I found out my father could confide in friends far away, even as he was not able to talk with us at home. He could not sit with us at Bret's memorial, could hardly talk with us about Bret's death. Yet on the road, he could level with people, wrestle out his thoughts. He wrote poems about Bret that came back to us over time, indirectly, some not until years after his own death. Here's one he gave to Frank and Peggy Steele at Western Kentucky University:

### A Spring Day at WKU

Somewhere here—doves and cardinals
weaving songs, tall limbs pointing everyway—
we may find a clue we lost:
    we lost one last year.

What worked for others failed; what hid
where lightning lines came down.
Gone before we could reach or even know,
    we lost one.

I stand for hours where sunlight tells me
it forgives. A golden shaft pours down.
The air waits. A cardinal sings and sings.
    I stand for hours.

To my ear, that last line is not just about time, but is saying "I stand for ours"—our boy, the older, puzzled one, brave and lost. My father could write that. Why couldn't he sit down and say that to me, to my sisters, to our mother?

I know now I could ask this in another way: When my father did write poems about Bret, and when we saw them, why didn't we talk with him about them? We had poems like "For a Lost Child," where the father says to his child, "Nowhere now, you call through every storm, / a voice that wanders without a home." We had "Consolations," where my father counsels himself, " 'The broken part heals even stronger than the rest,' they say. . . ." We had "Long Distance," which begins:

> We didn't know at the time. It was
> for us, a telephone call through the world
> and nobody answered.

Nobody answered. Shall I fault him for his silence and forgive myself for mine? My mother has said, "It's a wonder I stayed put." But she did. He did not stand by her, accompanying her grief in overt ways, but she stood by him. I feel his weakness, his retreat from us all, his public paralysis. One kind of courage in him died.

Once in a workshop the writer Teresa Jordan asked us to follow a sequence: "Remember a photograph from the family album . . . adopt the expression of that face with your own . . . find a place in your body where that expression puts pressure . . . have a dialogue with that point of pain or joy. . . ."

I followed the instructions. For me, it was a photograph of my father at CO camp during World War II. His expression held a kind of plucky sorrow, a resignation so deep it contorted his young face to early wisdom. At least that's how I remembered the image. When I asked my heart what this look could mean, in my mind I heard an imagined conversation with him. My father's voice:

"I couldn't stop the war."

"But Daddy, you couldn't expect yourself to stop the war. It was huge."

"I didn't stop it, that's all. That's what you see in my face. That's what I'll carry to the end. Family. Career. Love. And that—that will be there: Hiroshima."

Maybe my brother's death joined that place in my father's life where the deepest failures cling together with a crippling weight. I'm sure Bret's death brought back the death of our father's own brother Bob, who took his own life more slowly with alcohol. Bob's was a loss for which my father may have felt as helpless, as mystified, and in his own mind as directly implicated. For Bob, like Bret, required special care, and we didn't know how.

> Do I remember kindness? Did I
> shield my brother, comfort him?
> Tell me, you years I had for my life.
> . . . . . . . . . . . . . . . . .
> "You said you would be brave," I chided
> him. "I'll not take you again."
> Years, I look at the white across
> this page, and think: I never did.
> —*from* "REMEMBERING BROTHER BOB"

Did I and my brother replay the quiet drama of our father and his own? For Bob, too, had great promise as a child, but in a story my father published when his brother was still alive, there was a sense there, too, of care for a fragile soul. The story uses my father's family's actual names, and seems to describe their early hard times directly at their arrival in a new town:

> Pop had his work. Peg began to acquire a circle of friends in the
> high school. Mom had her house. And I had the high school and
> the books in the library. It wasn't so bad for us. But Bob faced the
> new town the most alone. He was too young and sensitive to force
> his way, and he was too sociable to be satisfied with solitude.

In the end, the mother manages to get Bob into the Boy Scouts, and secretly she goes with the story's narrator, the older brother, the one who had school and books as companions—the young character of my father—down the alley to spy on Bob's performance as bugler in the troop:

> Beyond the town was the plain, bleak and endless. But in front of
> the little shack across the street were the ten or fifteen Boy Scouts,

lined up at attention; and in front of them, straight—proudly, tri-
umphantly straight—was Brother Bob. As we stood there by the
tumble-down barn. . .we listened to the bugle call. Probably, to
others, the call was not well done; but to us it was Bob blowing the
horn in the new town; blowing a ringing brave tone out at the dark
horizon; blowing a sound that echoed and echoed.

In this story, "Answer, Echoes," my father shows me his care for a brother
hauntingly like my own. For my father, his brother Bob is a ringing, brave
tone isolated in a dark world.

In our father's study alone, as the rest of us addressed one another and
faced the world, what was it in Wordsworth my father may have sought, or
found? Why didn't I ask?

> "But they are dead; those two are dead!
>     Their spirits are in heaven!"—
> 'Twas throwing words away; for still
> The little maid would have her will,
> And said, "Nay, we are seven!"
>     —WILLIAM WORDSWORTH, "WE ARE SEVEN"

Or "Lucy": ". . . She lived unknown, and few could know / When Lucy
ceased to be. . . ." Or maybe "Tintern Abbey," with its lines of impending
loss in the face of kinship's glory, the darkening of the world. Within what
he called "the citadel of myself," my father pulled at the skein of his grief,
as in his poem "Young": "The best of my roads went wrong, / no matter
my age, no matter / how long I tried."

We took my brother's ashes to the slopes of Mount Adams and walked a
path to scatter them. I don't remember a word we said as we walked—up
through the forest, to a crag overlooking a deep blue canyon, a still place
where we built a cairn and sifted Bret through our hands into the earth.

My brother left a wife and two young children to struggle in the world
without him. He took the permanent solution to the temporary problem
of depression. I remember one of my students telling me, when we spoke
of my brother's suicide, that "many people commit suicide a little at a
time—by not living fully who they are. They kill the parts the world does
not welcome, and soon they are as good as gone." I felt the truth of that.

My brother took his life, but why did I let him? Was his silence, after all, any worse than mine? And our father—his own feelings must have been overwhelming. Where my brother used a bullet, our father used silence, distance, a spiral inward to brood and to blame himself.

I turn to what my father wrote, in his time before first light, a month and a day past my brother's death. His pain resonates in the words, and yet his writing on the page is steady, pouring out his accusation of himself, his devotion to his child. Here is exactly how it came to him; after the first writing he changed one verb—as if this were the whole story of his learning then—from present tense to past:

### A Memorial: Son Bret

In the way you went you were important.
I do not know what you found.
In the pattern of my life you stand
where you stood always, in the center,
a hero, a puzzle, a man.

What you might have told me
I will never know—the lips went still,
the body cold. I am afraid
in the circling stars, in the dark,
and even at noon in the light.

When I run what am I running from?
You turned once to tell me something,
but then you glimpsed a shadow on my face
and maybe thought, Why tell what hurts?
You carried it, my boy, so brave, so far.

Now we have all the days, and the sun
goes by the same; there is a faint
wandering trail I find sometimes, off
through grass and sage. I stop
and listen: only summer again—remember?—

The bees, the wind.

There would be good times after that. The family would gather, my father would keep writing, there were things to do. But the shadow of my brother's death never quite left our father's face. He carried it to the end. For even his syllables, writing, were haunted by the good.

From our earliest book, *Lost Words,* there was one puzzle we could not solve. When my brother and I were first learning to talk, we would chatter to each other again and again a question no one could understand, and then we would laugh and laugh.

What you call *beese!* What you call *gotchadaweddah?*

Our father simply tried to write it down. All his life, he was listening:

and listen: only summer again—remember?—

The bees, the wind.

# Shadow by the Library

M Y OFFICE AT LEWIS & CLARK COLLEGE, where our father had begun teaching in 1948, the year Bret was born, was moved by 1990 to the cabin called "The Engineer's Hut" on older campus maps. It was a tiny house in a canyon filled with native salal, huckleberry, vine maple, sword fern, and tall second-growth Douglas fir. When the breeze came from the north in early spring, the fragrance of cottonwood was intoxicating. And just outside my window sprang a thicket of wild rose; in spring, our hummingbird might visit, then whiz away. The dark Douglas squirrel barked somewhere, an elusive towhee called low-octave questions, sometimes a winter wren would unfurl an endless song, and on quiet afternoons you could hear the gnawing of carpenter ants in the wall, slowly taking the place apart.

After occupying this humble dwelling for a year or so, I learned it had been my father's office in the early days. But I did not learn this from him, for he was long retired by the early 1990s and rarely came to campus. Sometimes I would find a note on my desk when I returned from a meeting or class. He had come by to see if I was in. The note would imply my absence spoke well for my assiduous attention to college affairs. There was always some little irony.

The office, despite its humble size, was a hive of frenzied work in those days. In addition to the Northwest Writing Institute, we were engaged in our greatest pride and difficulty, the Oregon Folk Arts Program, which had huge aspirations and was a constant struggle. So I did go to many meetings. And my office was filled with folk art—a Hmong story cloth, old iron tools from the heyday of logging—choker bell, kerf-wedge, stove-oil bottle on a hook. There were beaded moccasins, cedar baskets, mysterious tinkerings from the printing trade, the Columbia River's salmon-trolling heritage, and other old ways. I fought the weedy growth of files, boxes of papers, notes, and syllabi. My father caught me once getting ready for class with a stack of a dozen books on my desk ready to carry to my seminar, each with a card or two marking a passage I wanted to weave into my rambling lecture.

My father perched on the chair I offered. I could not get him to settle back for a long visit. He was always full of apologies for interrupting me, even as I urged him to stay and bring me up-to-date.

"It's so rare I ever get to see you these days," I said.

"You're a busy man," he said.

Such a remark from him was always suspect. Once, when I was out of work, he said, "People who have a steady job think they have it solved." Implication: the real mysteries of life don't accompany a job defined by anyone but yourself.

He gestured toward the stack of books. "Do you have enough there? Are you sure you're ready?"

"Well," I said, "these will keep me going for a while, but then I'm going to have them write."

"When I went to class with a big stack of books and papers," he said, "I knew I wasn't ready. When I went with a single question, or one quotation on a card, I knew I was. You have to leave room. . . ."

"And what was on that card?" I said.

"Oh. . . ." He laughed. "You'd be surprised." I wasn't going to get the answer.

"Daddy," I said, "I can't believe I've never asked you this before: Could you cover my class next week? I have to be away."

"Next week?" he said. "So far as I know the calendar's clear. Tell me when, and I'll dance the minuet." We went over the details of time and place, and he scribbled them down. Then I looked at him. He had sagged in the chair. Weakened. I put my hand on his sleeve.

"Are you okay?" I said. He took a long breath, exhaled through tight lips.

"Well," he said, "a strange thing happened. I went to a play the other night—downtown. I can't remember the name of it. There was a character who tape-recorded everything people said, and then manipulated the tape, distorted what people had intended, and played it back in ways that caused all kinds of damage." He took another breath.

"Someone there," he said, "after the play, said, 'Bill, that's what you do in your writing. You use what people say in hurtful ways.'" His eyebrows went up. He seemed amazed he had told me this.

"Daddy," I said, "I don't think that's what you do."

"Maybe it's true," he said. "I don't know." His face was ashen. He looked old. He had never looked old to me. "I went back through some of my writing," he said, "to find out if that was true. . . ." Suddenly, his voice rose in pitch: " . . . and while I was at it, I found some wonderful things I had forgotten about!" His whole body had straightened, alert again, and I interrupted him.

"That's the greatest gift you have given me," I said. "No matter how bad it gets, you're always open to the next thing, ready to see what could happen."

He sank down, and his voice dropped. "Maybe so," he said. We were silent for a time. He looked to the side, put his hands on his knees, about to rise and go. To stop him, I asked the question I'd wanted to ask ever since my brother died, years before.

"How was it for you," I said, "when Bret died?"

"It was the darkest night of my life," he said without hesitation. "I got the call at my motel in Iowa, late. And then all I could do was wait. I couldn't sleep, of course, and I caught the earliest flight—looking down on all that darkness of America. I didn't know how to think or feel. . . ." His voice rose up again, and his body—" . . . and at dawn when we were coming in over Denver, there's this strange buckskin light in the clouds there—I've seen it before. . . ."

"There it is again," I said, "that way you're alert to what the world is doing, even when you are defeated—just to notice, be alive to it."

He slumped down again. "Well. . . ." He bit his lower lip. "I better leave you to your work," he said. And he was gone.

When I returned from my journey and met my evening class, I asked about my father's time with them. They looked at one another.

"He teaches really different from you," said one.

"Yeah, quite a bit of the time, he didn't say anything. We had to do most of the talking."

"And when he got us writing, he let it go on forever. Like, we were done, but he wasn't, so we had to keep going until he was."

"Did he bring any books or anything?" I asked.

"Nothing. He just started asking questions, and then we took over."

"That's because he wasn't getting paid," I said. "He could relax. It was easy."

"I wouldn't exactly say it was easy," said one student. "He heard everything we said—every little thing, and he kept turning it back to us. It's like he couldn't leave out the slightest idea that came up . . . oh, and he wanted us to give you this." She held out a paper. "He wrote it while we were writing." I took the page with his familiar scrawl.

"Thanks," I said.

During class, I tried to be more reticent, my students told me to be myself, and we made good use of our three hours. When I got back to the office, late, I flipped on the light, put his paper on my desk, and worked through it. It was yet another farewell, but this time it seemed not only a farewell to the world and to the college, but to me.

Or did it include me? The voice on the page was free: "no prize, no penalty." Maybe it asserted for both of us a farewell to regret, to haste, to distraction from the pure witness of a soul in residence here: "we turn, easily, . . . and go on." I studied the script again: three stanzas, no title, his customary # mark at the end. I thought how this would be his way, intimate at a certain distance, "in dear detail, by ideal light," to write a message in my class for me to find when he was gone. I looked up at one of his notes I had wedged into the thick display on my wall:

Hello, son Kim.
　　I'm just wandering—off for
　　　　home.

And then back to the sheet before me. He knew how to be very close at a great distance.

From the soft Oregon night a new shadow
converged with our walk near the library.
In dim light the figure moves easily
along, not toward us or away, but living
its own actions, flickering toward a car
nuzzled to the curb. And it's all easy,
no need for meeting or not meeting this
moving, unknown being.

And a voice comes from the shadow,
tentative and mild: "Is it you? Is it the one
who was here in those years when I
lived in this town?" And the figure
turns quietly and faces us, not moving now,
not reaching out or going away, but waiting.

And whoever it is then quietly rocks
back and forth, and we know it's because
those years have gone, and this person
carries them, simply brings them here
and offers them, no prize, no penalty,
just a reminder the night allowed us.
And we turn, easily, no haste, and go on.

# *Garlic*

AMONG THE THOUSANDS OF POEMS my father put forth into the world, there was one kind for which he held a boyish affection. He called them "stunts," and they had a vaudevillian tone—a Buster Keaton kind of a poem, a "Fibber McGee and Molly" gag:

> Maybe someone comes to the door and says
> "Repent," and you say, "Come on in," and it's
> Jesus. . . .
> — *from* "EASTER MORNING"

Unlike his more formal pieces, these showed affection for the everyday and glints of tragic surprise. He told me these "stunts" could be useful if a poetry reading were becoming too serious, too literary. Or you might dish one out to an editor in danger of reverence for a writer's fame, a wild card to break up the mix.

The list poem "Sayings of the Blind" would serve in this light, or these lines from "Purifying the Language of the Tribe":

> "Maybe" means
> "No."
>
> "Yes" means
> "Maybe."
>
> Looking like this at you means
> "You had your chance."

An audience might laugh, and then wonder if the poem was supposed to be funny. Or there might be an awkward stillness, as if they didn't get it. But maybe they did. These poems were odd. Why not read straight, strong poems, of which he had plenty? But the more I look at the stunts, the more I see them do things a "straight" poem could not. His poem "Things I Learned Last Week," for example, with its welcome of the domestic, the ironic, mortal declaration, literary inside joke, and political terror—such a low-key list can offer a wide spectrum to a reader. At the same time, the poem exemplifies an unusual kind of welcome to its materials, in effect presenting in its very structure a demonstration of how to write. If an artist is "someone who knows how to decide," then maybe a listener, too, could be invited to embrace enigma:

> Ants, when they meet each other,
> usually pass on the right.
>
> Sometimes you can open a sticky
> door with your elbow.
>
> A man in Boston has dedicated himself
> to telling about injustice.
> For three thousand dollars he will
> come to your town and tell you about it.
>
> Schopenhauer was a pessimist but
> he played the flute.
>
> Yeats, Pound, and Eliot saw art as
> growing from other art. They studied that.
>
> If I ever die, I'd like it to be
> in the evening. That way, I'll have
> all the dark to go with me, and no one
> will see how I begin to hobble along.
>
> In The Pentagon one person's job is to
> take pins out of towns, hills, and fields,
> and then save the pins for later.

After my father's death, I found the folder with his will and other final things. It was labeled "If we ever die. . . ," a reference from this poem with its strange humor about the inevitable. The appreciation of Schopenhauer; the oblique challenge to Yeats, Pound, and Eliot; the quiet assessment of the Pentagon; and, strangely, Eli Weisel (the Holocaust expert my father was thinking of, as I remember); the camouflaging matters of ants and doors—all these deft references, like a fencer's thrust and parry, can be gathered in a William Stafford "stunt."

One of his personal favorites in this genre was his "Ode to Garlic," which he wrote at the request of a Portland restaurant. The poem was printed on the napkin there for a special dinner to which my parents were invited as guests of honor: eighteen courses, from appetizer to dessert, each based on garlic. At a poetry reading, my father would talk about this dinner, then read the poem, and everyone would smile, even as the deeper substance of his message—like garlic itself—pierced the heart:

> Say you are dining and it happens:
> soaring like an eagle, you are
> pierced by a message from the midst of life:
>
> Memory—what holds the days together—touches
> your tongue. It is from deep in the earth
> and it reaches out kindly, saying, "Hello, Old Friend."
> . . . . . . . . . . . . . . . . . . . . . . . . . . .
> Like a child again, you breathe on the world, and it shines.

Some things, like war or death, or the embrace of personal defeat, required in my father's writing practice this kind of slant, good-humored, but mortal imperative.

Shortly after he had met my class, as summer drew to a close, I was moved to invite my father to my little house for lunch, serve him garlic pasta, and grill him about the family past. I had realized there were simple things I didn't know. He came up the long stairway at the back to my little place built the same year he was born, 1914. When I opened the door, he came in rubbing his hands, pursing his lips as he looked over my preparations.

"You mean all you're putting on the spaghetti is garlic?" He was truly pleased, for this was a taste he had to temper in company other than mine. I chopped a good handful of the cloves, heated the olive oil, and soon the air in the room was thick. While I puttered my father sat at the makeshift table I had made and gazed out at the garden.

"Mmmm," he said. "I see your tomatoes are getting bushy. Remember, not too much water as the summer wears on."

"Shall I invite you again when they ripen?"

"I can eat any given number of tomatoes," he said. "Good idea."

It was as it almost always was with him—a buoyant sense of well-being, of good company, boundless talk. Our sense of harmony had been typified in an odd way several summers before, when my father had volunteered to help me construct a writing studio in my yard. I had the walls up, the ceiling joists in, the roof rafters braced, and the floor to the loft nailed down, with a hole about two by three feet where a ladder went through to the sky. Although my father had to attend a wedding in the afternoon, he showed up in his coveralls early that morning, and we got busy hoisting sheets of ¾-inch plywood up into the loft for the roof. They were heavy. We struggled, staggered, then learned about balance all over again, and it got easier. Then we both got up in the open loft to enjoy the scene: the new garden, my blackberry hedge that gave me an inordinate pride of privacy, the cherry tree I had planted, and beyond the hazel clump that funky house of mine that neighbors had recently said was built originally as a soldiers' clubhouse in the Great War, called the "Black Bell Driving Club"—no one knew why.

When we picked up a sheet of plywood to slide it up onto the rafters, I made the classic error that could have my father laughing helplessly during his favorite Laurel and Hardy films. Carrying my end of the plywood I stepped back into the hole in the floor, dropped five feet until the back of my head caught the edge and I grabbed the ladder to stop my fall. There was a lot of blood, pain, and I looked up at my father's face: ashen and afraid. Somehow I climbed back up, wanting to be with him, and lay on the floor of the loft, pressing my bandanna onto the wound and looking past my father's face to the rafters, the summer clouds, the leaves of the maple tree. But my life didn't flash before my eyes. Instead, my first thought was, "Now Daddy won't have to go to that wedding." I knew I would live.

That's how it was with him: even with pain, I felt harmony. Whatever happened when he was around would be all right.

I set two steaming platters of garlic pasta down, and we dug in. I remembered my parents' joke about me when I was small, how I ate with relish whatever was set before me. My father shared that virtue. I remembered his toast with a hump of jam on the corner that so impressed me as a child.

"Daddy," we would say, "you're having a big bite."

"I'll just have my share of jam with the first bite," he would say.

In his later years, he declined dessert—unless my mother made it. Then he would partake with gusto. He was a great bread maker, grinding his own flours by hand from various grains, always trying to get the mix just right. And so this day he ate with relish, wiping the plate utterly clean with the last of his bread. I saw the zesty legacy of the Great Depression there. He held up his plate.

"You can put that back in the cupboard for my next visit." He was leaning forward, the signal he had decided I needed to get back to work, and he wouldn't overstay.

"Can I ask you some things I've always wondered?" I said.

"Ask me," he said.

"Whatever happened to your father? He died during the war—something about a car and a bridge. . . ?"

"That's how it happened in my poem," he said, "but really it was simpler, or more mysterious. I was away at the war, off in CO camp in California, and apparently he was on the road, in a hotel room when he died. I never got the full story myself."

"But what were the stories you heard?"

"There was some talk he was with a woman . . . "

"A woman?" I had never heard this part.

" . . . and alcohol. Some people said it that way."

"Did that fit with your father as you knew him?"

"Not at all. I didn't know what to believe. I never could get to the bottom of it. There were even rumors he was a German spy, but that was probably just the kind of exaggerations that come for a man with a CO for a son." My father looked out to the yard. He had that mild, faraway look that came at such times, the look of a soul buffeted by what he could not change, but steady nonetheless. As his poem "A Catechism" has it: "Who grew up and saw all this and recorded it and / kept wondering how to solve it but couldn't? / Guess who."

"And Ruby," I said—"what happened to your mother? I know she was alive when I was small, but I don't really remember. . . ."

"I was away at the war," he said, "shortly after my father died, and I had a letter from sister Peg: 'Mother's in the hospital again.' *Again?* She had a breakdown when Pop died, but I didn't know about this second thing. I don't remember how I got back to Kansas. I didn't have any money, I just got some time away and somehow got home. Went to Peg's. 'Where's mother?' 'Oh,' Peg said, 'she's at the Poor Farm.' I asked how she was. Peg said she didn't know."

My father stopped talking. He sat with his hands folded on the table looking far away. I remembered the phrase the "Poor Farm" as a kind of dark joke from the Kansas past—"We'll all end up at the Poor Farm"—as if there were a final landmark for defeat.

My father gathered steam again. "I hitchhiked the last hundred miles," he said, "and when I got there, she was sitting on her bed at the institution, dressed, waiting. The man in charge said she had been a mess when she arrived, but she had pulled herself together, and waited for the family to come get her. She had been waiting for some time.

" 'Billy,' she said to me, 'you've got to get me out of here.' I wanted to say, 'Don't worry. I'll get you out.' But I couldn't say that. I didn't have any money; I had to get back to California. I didn't have a way to take her with me. The war. . . . So I said, 'I don't know if I can.'

"Then she looked at me. 'Billy,' she said, 'I'm afraid.' And I wanted to say to her, 'Don't worry. Everything will be fine.' But I couldn't say that, because I didn't know if it would be. So I said, 'I'm afraid, too.' The look she gave me then I will always remember. I could tell she was thinking, 'Billy is telling me the truth.' "

My father stopped talking. His body was stone still, his big hands closed on each other. Tears came down his face. I had never seen that in all my forty-four years. I put my hand on his hands, but he stared straight ahead.

"Daddy."

He slowly softened, wiped his eyes with his napkin, said he had to be going. But he didn't get up. He looked out at the yard again.

"One time in high school," he said, "we were home in the evening, and we heard the tires screech and a thump in the dark outside. We all went out on the porch, and there came Buster, our dog, lurching toward the house. Maybe the way the porch light shone, it looked like half of Buster's head was gone. I turned to see who was going to do something, but no one moved. I realized it was me."

He stopped talking, and I saw in that little story all his years of being "the mule," the one quietly in charge, the one who takes a stand, the one who does the right thing, says it for others, feels and suffers and tells as he has to, alone. He had tears on his face again. He wiped them away. Stood up. Straightened.

"Daddy," I said, "can we do this again? Garlic. . . ."

"Sure," he said, "anytime. But I'll get out of your way today. I know you're a busy man." He carried his plate to the sink and rinsed it off. Normally he would have stayed and insisted on doing all the dishes.

As I stood on the back porch and watched him go down the stair outside, he was unsteady. There was no rail. He was hobbling, reaching out against the wall of the house to steady himself. He's old, I thought. How can that be?

The next day, I went to see him at home. We had a good talk with mother, catching up on all the news. Then he followed me out to the car.

"Those stories yesterday caught me by surprise," he said. "It's a strange thing. I guess I was waiting for someone to ask. Well, so long my friend." We promised to have another day like that soon, and I drove away.

My father wrote every morning for fifty years, telling and telling and telling, sifting through his life for resonant darkness and for fragile light. And yet there were stories from the precious past he carried quietly until I asked for them by name. Some he brought halfway to the light, but then kept secret. I did find later in the archive that he had written for himself an account of the injured dog—the day he became irrevocably the activist in his family. Written in March 1971, he called this passage "When the Years Turn Around," and perhaps it is the social equivalent of his connecting and isolating moment with nature on the banks of the Cimarron:

I was in high school. One night our dog, howling in terror, in pain, fell against the front door. We grouped around, and he lay threshing, a great, dark part of his head as if crushed, gone. The others— my father, mother, sister, brother—waited, all hurt but helpless and afraid. I glanced for my father's move, and when he stood like the others I fell to my knees and reached for the dog, to help. It turned out that there was mud on his head. A car had struck him, but he recovered and licked my hand. My father touched me. He looked at me a new way. At our house that was the time.

He writes that this moment "is not the father turning his possessions over to his son, or the mother willing property." Rather, "it is something more important than that, a real instant that counts, but without a name." My father touched the dog, and his father touched him, and then he knew his place in the world. A painful, difficult, but somehow inevitable place.

As I sat with my father, he touched me, and I knew his place and mine. I felt lucky to have been so eager, asking, so mean.

The story of his mother, too, appears in his writing, in miniature, at the close of a poem called "Ruby Was Her Name":

> At the end she turned to me, helplessly
> honest still: "Oh, Bill, I'm afraid,"
> and the whole of her life went back to her heart
> from me in a look for the look she gave.

Later, in Kansas, I asked around. My cousin Pat—Peg's boy—remembers Ruby's fate in very different terms. "Peg didn't abandon her," he said, "far from it. Poor Farm? Oh no. It was nothing like that."

Who knows? One story was true for Pat. The other story, the one my father told me with tears on his face and his body rock still, was true for him. I am reminded of his poem "Bi-Focal," which ends with a compact claim:

> So, the world happens twice—
> once what we see it as;
> second it legends itself
> deep, the way it is.

He once explained about that poem, "Actually, the world happens three times: once what I superficially see, second what I do my best to see, and third what I suspect I'll never be able to see."

I look back to my father's tears, his stillness, his psychic grip to hold those stories in his body all those years, and then his surrender to tell me a few threads from his deepest times. Tragedies happened. At some cost he survived and prevailed in many ways. Yet there were things he could not solve. Whatever happened in those early days, my father came to see himself as the wanderer, the peace warrior, finally alone.

What was the truth of it all? Was his father cruel, as an early poem has it? "Well," my father said once, "that poem needed my father to be cruel, but that wasn't really how it was." Was his mother the slightly deaf, ineffective, but utterly honest woman his poems claim? Yes, and no, and more. Both his parents were advocates for him, as were mine for me. They were a source of clarity about what is important, even if their teaching was not without contradiction. I have this undated glimpse of my father's father, the traveler, in a letter he sent home from the road:

Dear Folks . . .
      Last Sunday I saw something that impressed me. Here in the hotel you see hard faced discontented looking women with their fur coats, jewelry, dogs etc. When I was parked on the street of Horlan last Sunday a young couple came by with two little kids. The man & woman were not very well dressed, the kids were all bundled up with galoshes and their bloomers showing below their coats but were they happy one kid ahold of Dads hand the other holding onto Mom and laughing and talking their heads off. Certainly looked happier than those fur bedecked ultra-madams who are doing their damndest to enjoy life.

Pop's insight into what constitutes happiness shows great affinity with the stories and the customs that raised me: a boisterous, plucky family stumbles happily through the world.

That feast of garlic was the last meal I shared with my father. I had been asking myself why I shied away from my own writing, why I had reams of beginnings I did not resolve through the sustained work of what I called my vocation. So I decided in August to take two weeks and go to the house in central Oregon—the house my father and I had long ago begun together—and pull the multiple fragments of my novel "Affinities" into a book. All I needed, I told myself, was uninterrupted time alone. I wanted my own story to catch me by surprise, as my father's had caught him.

I would never see him again.

# VI.

## Don't Ever Let Go

# Millions of Intricate Moves

IF A SENSE OF JUSTICE begins in childhood, how does it begin? Behind the playground scuffles and betrayals that teach the honey of justice by the salt of injustice, what does a parent's own vision provide? What language does a parent use to teach a sense of justice, what stories and what silences? In my childhood, there was a fabled thread that linked universal justice to our daily habits at home. Actions large and small, and events distant and close were not distinguished in the realm of ethics in our house. "Do right" applied everywhere. Now the years have brought me to this: with my father gone, and a five-year-old boy at home, I want to know:

How do I follow the thread? How did my father teach me to let go of him, but not the thread? How might my wife and I teach our child? How can elements of my father's philosophy save me, my family, my country, the world?

I hear my father's voice: "Oh, is that all?"

There are always things you wish you had asked. Too late, you discover the questions you never spoke aloud. In writing class, when we get to talking about the mysterious treasury of family heritage, someone always utters our common lament: "I wish I had taped my grandmother's stories. . . ."

"You did," I say. "The mind holds all you heard, somehow. Now you can turn your regret to a plan: it is time to write down now what you *can* remember—resonant scraps of the voice that is gone. And while you're at it, better write your own stories, too, so no one will have to regret you got away without a trace." We all look at one another. "End of sermon," I say.

But my students are too smart for me. They don't bow their heads in prayer; they talk back: "Are you?"

"Am I what?"

"Are you writing down your father's stories, and your brother's, and your own?"

"Touché."

That's the trouble with teaching. Eventually you have to follow your own invitations. That day we began to write in response to the prompt, "Retrieve a moment from childhood that survives for some strange reason encrusted with detail." As if by magic, I felt a tug of the thread and started a story that day that I continued later. In it, I found myself at the source of justice. . . .

One day in the late 1950s we were driving on a Sunday into the foothills of the Cascade Mountains. We were going to find the place called Butte Creek Falls. The man who knew the way, Jim Stauffer, a biology professor at our college, was in the car ahead. As always, my father was driving, mother sat in the front seat with him and baby Barbara between them, and in the back, right to left, Bret, Kit, and me. As we found our way through the forest on a gravel road, there came that feeling that all was right. Sword ferns splayed their whorls in the shade of tall Douglas firs, the sun spangled coins of gold across the green world that now belonged to us. It was morning. We had seen our mother pack the big Hershey bar. And we were going to find a cave. Jim said so.

We tramped down from the road where no trail led, swishing through the ferns, losing our footing and tumbling into the safe, soft duff of Oregon, hearing ahead the whisper of the falls, and then coming upon the grand, sudden thunder off a lip of basalt. And then the cave behind the falls, where we all went into the earth.

One of the strange things about having a writer for a father is the matching up of my impressionistic memory with my father's poem from that day:

### Behind the Falls

First the falls, then the cave:
then sheets of sound around us fell
while earth fled inward, where we went.
We traced it back, cigarette lighter high—
lost the roof, then the wall,
found abruptly in that space
only the flame and ourselves.

. . . . . . . . . . . . . . . . . . . .

When men and women meet that way
the curtain of the earth descends and they

find how faint the light has been, how far
mere honesty or justice is from all they need.

I remember that darkness. But what is so strange about the overlay of the
poem on my own memory is the way the word "justice" brings me back to
the ride home. This time my mother and the baby were in Jim's car, my feet
were wet where I sat behind my father as he drove, and this time a man was
in the front seat beside my father. I didn't know that man, and he said to
my father an idea I had never heard: "When a black person handles my
food, I can't tell whether it is clean, because you can't see how clean the
hands are."

The car went electric. I had so rarely heard my father scold anyone, even
us kids. I don't remember the words, but there was no question the passen-
ger was being straightened out, quietly but without compromise. Silence
followed. Words hung in the air. All around us the green of Oregon was an
arena for a major readjustment in the gears of human kinship.

Where did this thread begin for my father, his clarity about prejudice?
In 1943, while he was stationed in his California CO camp , he wrote to his
brother Bob, the U.S. Army Air Force pilot stationed in Texas:

> The swinging, singing French pilots, with their verve and colorful
> background, should give a good flavor to the place. Your report,
> Bob, of their feeling against the Italians and Germans checks,
> poignantly, with echoes we outsiders get through the papers, maga-
> zines, and radio. It seems there will be no oversupply of under-
> standing for a while. Peg, I understand, became involved in a warm
> bridge club discussion about race problems recently. Well, wise as
> serpents and harmless as doves seems to be indicated, now as in
> bible times!

My father goes on to say he hopes to get acquainted with some soldiers on
the next forest fire, as well as to note his contact with the "Mexicans and
Negroes" he had met on the last. I see my father, like his brother Bob in the
army and his sister Peg back home in Kansas, reaching out to make connec-
tion with everyone.

In our many family moves from place to place, in some ways we lived a
sheltered life. In other ways, we were schooled to the variety of the world.

There is a story in the family about the first time my brother saw a black person. We were in a store, and my mother noticed little Bret staring in fascination at a black child in the aisle. Afraid he might say the wrong thing, she hustled him outside. On the sidewalk, she turned to him.

"Did you notice something about that little boy?"

"Yes, mother! He had gum!"

Gum, one of the great forbiddens.

By then my father had written one of his most compelling poems of dark anguish, "Thinking for Berky":

> In the late night listening from bed
> I have joined the ambulance or the patrol
> screaming toward some drama, the kind of end
> that Berky must have some day, if she isn't dead.
>
> The wildest of all, her father and mother cruel,
> farming out there beyond the old stone quarry
> where highschool lovers parked their lurching cars,
> Berky learned to love in that dark school.

But Berky, the anguish her life brings to his memory, soon has my father looking outward, for he is included in Berky's isolation:

> . . . . . . . . . . . . . . . . . . . . . . . . . . . . .
>
> There are things not solved in our town though tomorrow came:
> there are things time passing can never make come true.
>
> We live in an occupied country, misunderstood;
> justice will take us millions of intricate moves.
> Sirens will hunt down Berky, you survivors in your beds
> listening through the night, so far and good.

I want to know who is "we." Berky and my father? My father's family, the small circle of our clan? Is "we" the few who have met in the essential cave under the earth, or as another poem tells it, those who have experienced "a deathless meeting involving a crust of bread"?

I suspect my father expected the "we" in this occupied country to be

few, but clear-eyed kin. The "occupied country" I take to be America, after
World War II diminished the force of empathy, took something apart that
was elusive and hard to name, but replaced by American patriotism as a
kind of partisan retreat from vast inclusion. The Cold War was not *there* in
a region of air between two superpowers, somewhere over the North Pole.
It was *here,* in the night outside our house where sirens called to one an-
other as they hunted down the quiet of the land.

I can look back now, back to my father's first writing that became
"Thinking for Berky," early on a December morning in 1954, and see him
begin to find his way from clumsy searching toward the final poem:

> We all live in an occupied country;
> freeing will come with many intricate moves.
> Sirens will hunt down Berky from the quiet of our beds,
> in the night things are far that in the day will become good.

His passage from "freeing," to an interim version, "freedom," and finally to
"justice" that will "take us millions of intricate moves"—to my mind this is
the journey he tried to create as a father for his children. Freedom is easy;
any rebel can claim it. Justice is hard, for it requires the cooperation of all
kinds of people joined by negotiated agreement about human dignity. But
the movement *toward* justice—the decision to direct one's life toward a
just society on earth—this, in my father's view, is not hard. The direction is
clear so the life should follow. I believe this was the working assumption
that guided the household where I grew.

There were stories in the family of "witness"—the overt though quiet
declaration of a larger view. My father rarely spoke of such things directly,
but for this very reason the few references were memorable. As a student at
the University of Kansas in the 1930s, he told us, he had taken part in a sit-in
demonstration at the student union to protest the exclusion of black stu-
dents from the central seating area. And shortly after World War II, in the
fall of 1945, my parents were living in Elgin, Illinois, and they invited two
Japanese American men to their apartment for dinner. They had met the
two at the office of the Brethren Church, and extended their habitual hospi-
tality. The morning after that dinner their landlady announced, "I don't
want no Japs in my house. Better find another place yourselves." My parents

gathered their few possessions and moved on. The family lore records the landlady's utterance verbatim—not as a judgment against her, but as an example of how war wrenches people loose from native hospitality.

Over the years there were demonstrations in the news, or locally, and sometimes my father took part:

> We wondered what our walk should mean,
> taking that un-march quietly;
> the sun stared at our signs—"Thou shalt not kill."
>
> Men by a tavern said, "Those foreigners . . . "
> to a woman with a fur, who turned away—
> like an elevator going down, their look at us.
>                                    —*from* "PEACE WALK"

But how do such values, held by adults and articulated in rare conversations, poems, and teaching in the adult world, seep into the child's experience in ways that shape the conscience as it grows? I believe the way we were taught "tolerance" was by a prevailing attitude at home far more extravagant than tolerance. My father enjoyed meeting people alive to experience, honest in sharing what they knew. His was not a tolerant approach, not a studied ethical devotion to justice. His was an appetite for learning that can only happen without restraint. Justice is a matter of yielding to delight in human variety.

Circling back, I seek the roots of the intuitive way of this citizen in my own earliest learning. Our father loved us for how we were different. When I was not yet two years old, my father wrote a poem about me I never knew until it turned up in his papers after he died—a message from far away and long ago:

> The open, easy way of Kim.
> He doesn't worry or hide anything.
> An event drops freely into his eyes
> and is applauded before his conscience
> knows it, by his startled hands.
>
> No proportion is ever old.
> "Is it true?"

Walking into that closed gong sound
the black horses lower their ears.
Whatever strokes their mane was already theirs.

We were living in Iowa then, in the Quonset hut of tin, while my father taught English composition and attended the Iowa Writers' Workshop. When I teach writing, especially with the young, one of the premier assignments is to capture the very first memory in a life—the moment when some indelible event jolted sensation to self-possession.

My own earliest memory is of that winter in Iowa, of my father picking me up and setting me on the counter. I had hurt my knee and he was comforting me, lovingly touching my face. In the album, I see the place in black-and-white—the double sink where my brother and I took our baths side by side, the spare furnishings, the puritan meals. But I remember only the surge of devotion as my father steadied me on the counter's edge.

When I asked my mother about this memory after my father had died, she laughed and told me the "real" story. "Do you know why Bill was so loving then?" she said. "He had been carrying you outside, and when he slipped on the ice, he just threw you up in the air and caught himself from falling. You landed pretty hard, and he carried you inside to see if you were okay."

Why don't I remember falling, hitting hard on icy pavement? Why don't I remember his abandonment, his selfish instinct to save himself? I only remember his big hands on my face, his eyes looking into me.

Both my parents believed world peace began with our life at home. Justice could be achieved long before people were perfect. If justice requires perfection, it can never be. Justice is the big river that carries us along. If I weighed my father's devotion against his shortcomings, I chose the big thing. That's how it would be with anyone.

I'll never sort the millions of intricate moves my father made in his effort to work for a just world, or for clear lessons about justice at home. When I try for clarity, I find consistent devotion on his part, but mysterious outcomes. There is the matter, for example, of that strange recapitulation in my childhood of my father's odyssey during the war. I only learned how this happened after he died.

The archive holds an odd classic, the "Letter to Coach Musselman." In this letter, my father purports to ask his colleague in the Physical Education

Department for special consideration: please put "Paul Spindles," a feeble English major, onto the football squad, in order to advance Paul's bid for a Rhodes scholarship.

> Paul has the academic record for this award, but we find that the -
> aspirant is also required to have other excellences, and ideally
> should have a good record in athletics. Paul is a weakling. . . . We
> realize that Paul will be a problem on the field, but—as you have
> often said—cooperation between our department and yours is a
> highly desirable thing; we do expect Paul to try hard, of course. . . .

The letter goes on to say Paul won't be able to attend practice until late in the season, but he will "show entire good will in his work for you." My father's letter, originally signed "Benjamin Plotinus," ultimately found a place in sports folklore, appearing in places like the halftime program for the Harvard team, and eventually in *Sports Illustrated,* where several alert readers wrote to identify William Stafford as the author.

After my father died, I learned the letter was based on a real incident, a violent one. The football coach at Lewis & Clark College physically beat up an education professor—publicly, during a faculty meeting—for failing several favored players. (They were flunked because they stole copies of the exam from the professor's office.) When my father and several others tried to stop him, the coach went for the smallest of them (the religion professor named Hideo Hashimoto), and chased him across the campus. Hideo had to take refuge in the Manor House that served as the college's administration building. Was the coach fired? No. Punished? No. He was the *Coach*— not a lowly education, religion, or English teacher. He had institutional cachet.

Disturbed by this injustice, my father did not confront the coach, nor the president of the college. Instead, he wrote his letter to Coach Musselman as quiet protest, and gave it to friends. Then he left the college, and took his family back to the Midwest. No shouting. No accusations. Just the personal action of a conscientious objector.

For a year we lived in North Manchester, Indiana, and my father taught at Manchester College, a Brethren institution in a pacifist community where he had gone through training during World War II for medical service overseas at the war's end. (This service never transpired, but we have a photograph of my father attending medical training in Manchester.) In North Manchester, I attended first grade, and I remember a comfortable congruence between the Midwest lore of family stories and the daily experience of our life there—the covered bridge, the turtle my father caught in the lazy river below campus, the school "field trip" that consisted of walking hand in hand through town in spring to listen for bird calls. That year was an idyll, the time my father told me later, "I outflanked all of Dorothy's relatives by joining the Brethren Church."

The following year we moved to California, where my father taught at San Jose State College, thus repeating in the 1950s his epic of the 1940s: from Midwest to Far West. Only then did we move back to Oregon, and my father returned to Lewis & Clark.

My father's one-page letter to Coach Musselman exemplifies the humor, ethics, and free expression of the wanderer, of the "plain, unmarked envelope passing through the world." His writing that seems to be about football is actually about violence, hierarchy, and injustice. Like his poem "The Star in the Hills," this document makes a bold statement with a light touch.

Somewhere Eleanor Roosevelt is said to have answered her critics: "You cannot level any accusation at me that I have not already leveled at myself." My father was like that. He was more aware of his faults, more interested in them, than anyone. In his poem "Judgments," he begins by accusing his high-school friends of becoming successful, confident, even generous. But he keeps the last accusation for himself:

> Last I accuse—
>> Myself: my terrible poise, knowing
>> even this, knowing that then we
>> sprawled in the world
>> and were ourselves part of it; now
>> we hold it firmly away with gracious
>> gestures (like this of mine!) we've achieved.
>
> I see it all too well—
>> And I am accused, and I accuse.

My father saw the dangers of achievement, maturity, talent, and even generosity cutting a person off from others. In his view, devotion to justice has to begin with empathy based on a hard look in the mirror. Finally, his lessons to me about justice were not about other people, what they need, what they deserve. His lessons were about the work a writer does to see the self, and to find there the power to see and embrace others as they are.

That's one thing justice means, behind all the fine distinctions: we are here together. Things happen, and we get hurt sometimes. Helplessly, we enter into millions of intricate human moves; we offer each other what we can. And then we go on.

❦

# Our Ways

RECENTLY I STOOD BY A MALL'S parking lot to make a phone call, and I remembered something whole that time has taken apart. Heat waves shimmered from acres of blacktop. Children trudged with their purchases. Men and women squinted to find their cars. The place, the life felt foreign to me as if I had stumbled into another country simply by standing still. And what was I doing? I was calling my wife somewhere on her cell phone to learn our plans for the evening.

It was then I remembered the days of *The Happy Reporter,* the Stafford family newspaper that lasted one issue sometime in the 1950s. As I recall, my sister Kit was editor, we all contributed our news items, our father typed it up, and our mother ran off an edition for the neighbors on her school's ditto machine. I haven't seen a copy for years, but my mind can fill the void with stories of our unusual ways. The Staffords had a code.

We moved so often the four of us children became our best and sometimes our only friends. At birthday parties, there were no guests outside the family. Our parents, recognizing a gap in each year's holidays, created "Brothers and Sisters Day" sometime each spring—an arbitrary day for little presents and a cake for all four, a celebration of who we were together. At Halloween, the Stafford children didn't go from door-to-door with a bag for candy; we carried a plate of cookies our mother had made and offered them to each neighbor in turn. Later, when we were older, I remember "Trick or Treat for UNICEF," whereby the Staffords went door-to-door to hold out a can for donations of small change.

When we traveled, our parents told us, "Don't forget to talk to strangers." Without approaching a stranger, how could a child get help or find a friend? And at home one night a week, we convened "Sacrifice Meal." The menu was always cornbread and milk. In the center of the table was a bowl where we put our pennies and nickels for charity to strangers far away.

When our parents went to a party, they took us along, and while they hobnobbed with their friends inside we played quietly in the car where it was parked—looking at books if a streetlight were convenient, or whispering in the dark until we fell asleep. When the party ended, our parents returned to gently drive us home.

That one issue of *The Happy Reporter,* as I remember, included an account of a neighbor kid telling her mother, "The kids at the Staffords don't have to just watch TV—they get to go camping, and shoot bows and arrows, and all kinds of other neat stuff." When our family finally did buy a TV, it was placed in the attic. If you really wanted to watch, you went up a shaky folding stair to hunch in the cold on an old couch frequented by spiders.

In daily life, especially in the early days, we didn't buy things. Instead, we found things, made things, borrowed things, or imagined. My parents' dream of "The Stafford Ranch" was our future kingdom all through childhood. As Thoreau reported he had bought many a farm in mind and left the labor to the owner, so we found pleasure in our imagined rural life— someday, maybe. Out on a drive, my father would gesture toward a farm with a barn and pasture. "Let's take that one," he would say. "That'll do."

Our parents were teachers, and there was a resonance of learning in the house, but the approach was offered opportunity rather than direct instruction. Violin, clarinet, flute, piano. Hammer, saw, drill, plane. Flour, sugar, salt, yeast. George Eliot, Emily Dickinson, Ernest Thompson Seton, Jack London. Longing, Memory, Resolve, Truth.

Our mother had the use of her left hand only, from childhood, which lent her an unusual beauty and a unique grace. I had friends who spent a year as students in her fourth-grade class without noticing her right hand always in her pocket. She was there, at the periphery of their attention, guiding them as if by their own intuition. Other mothers seemed ungainly monsters to me—with two good hands they could reach out and grab you, make you do their will. Our mother worked by invitation, beckoning toward the good. We absorbed her advice, hint, or silence. You would figure out her wish, and do right. Our father's worldview was forged in Kansas, and the modern world, when it strayed from that code, was distant. You would learn the good, internalize it, and obey your own rules.

One night years later I watched my parents baby-sit my sister's children. When the young ones sensed their chance with their own parents away, they clamored for ice cream before bed. My father announced his approval. "What a great idea," he said. But then he confessed reluctantly he had better check to see if this might be allowed. They followed him into the living room where he reached for the biggest random book on the shelf and leafed eagerly through its pages until he came to one that made him stand straight and scowl. He read aloud, "No ice cream shall be served to children after 6 P.M." They looked up at him. "Too bad, kids," he said. Then he led them, uncomplaining, to bed.

When faced with a choice of modern delights—whether food or toys or activities—my father had a proverb: "Nothing's too bad for the kiddies." This meant that the parents were in charge, and through privation the kids grew strong for a difficult world. Tough love from Kansas.

It was a sheltered life, I suppose—stable, peaceful, and mysterious. Wherever we went, we lived in another time. For as we moved, in addition to the Midwest presences of our mother and father, two resident muses accompanied us: my mother's mother, the one we called Boppums, and my mother's sister, Helen. They lived with us, or near us, and provided a continuous tone of being from my mother's Nebraska heritage. For our lunch, Boppums might make the farm recipe "rivil soup," an elemental pudding of flour and milk. For birthdays, Helen would make amazing gifts spun from her intensity and thrift. Their belief system was like religion without mention of God; life was guided by a sweet but sturdy doctrine of devotion to family, to calm, to a practiced happiness and its mirror, silence about dark things.

After she died, I found in Helen's kitchen a list of resolutions she had adopted for her ninetieth year. Among them, "Polish my convictions." Throughout my childhood, other families had possessions to polish—silver, cars, mansions, and other toys. We had convictions.

At night in our room, my brother and I would do what we called "whisper and sing" until we fell asleep. As a family, we would sing "We Are Climbing Jacob's Ladder" as we drove home from visiting friends. We would sing "My Home's in Montana" as we crossed the mountains from camping at our sacred places: the Wallowas, or Cove, the Metolius, Steens Mountain, Fly Lake, Devil's Garden, the Deschutes. The natural world was more familiar, in many ways, than any of the houses where we lived for a year or less: the moon over wheat stubble, a river in dry country, the call of a meadowlark or redwing blackbird.

I remember standing with my brother as our father tended burning leaves with a pitchfork one fall afternoon. I was three, my brother four. Our father was telling us about his college, what some faculty characters were like. The college was small, and the faculty members were essentially our relatives, fair game for gossip. He mentioned someone bickering about salary, but we thought he said "celery," and it made sense at the time. The world was such a simple place to us, one might work for vegetables.

We lived in the modern world—the 1950s in America—but we were of another. After my father died, I met a colleague who gave me one example of this double life.

"Your father," he said, "did things no one else would do. I remember once when we agreed to go to a literary conference together. I offered to drive, but he insisted on doing his part by riding his bike to a certain place by the freeway. He would hide the bike behind a tree, he said, climb over the fence and wait in the shadow of a certain overpass. When I came along at 6 A.M., there he was in the dark."

There was the time the family lived in Washington, D.C., while my father was Consultant in Poetry at the Library of Congress. Preparing for a journey, my father asked around the office if it would be possible to walk to the airport from downtown. Everyone said no—you would have to cross too many freeways, then somehow get past the Pentagon. "And just think of the distance," they said.

He walked anyway. One world, two ways of being.

Or I think of my mother, the teacher, writing an open letter to the PTA at her school to point out how Walt Disney offered a severely restricted version of the world's literature. "We can do better," she said. The last season of her career, I realized one day I had never watched her teach. When I came in the front door of her grade school, I followed the distant hum of a spiritual to her classroom: "Who built the ark? Noah! Noah! . . ."

Actually, our mother and father built the ark, and we four children were carried safely through a difficult world.

That's how we were taught. I look back through the lens of my father's death, and my brother's death, to that early morning of our family's world. Since then, something precious, innocent, and perhaps too simple about us has been torn away. We are stronger, if no better. For what accomplishment is more heroic, more difficult in detail and stamina, more important toward world order than the creation of a good childhood for the young? Many around us display in senseless acts their lack of this one thing. If much of the energy in a civilization is dissipated in entropy—"things fall apart"—then childhood must be the place where human destiny is most effectively repaired.

In the last month of his life, my father's writing harkened to such a time and place "where dreamers go forth looking for selfhood." Maybe a pacifist is naïve, in a different way from a soldier's naïve belief in a gun as a tool for resolution. We had our own beliefs, and our own limits.

> When we scattered along through the forest eating
> and chattering, often we'd stop in a clearing
> where sunlight poured through, and we'd sing
> for a while before going on. One would
> begin with a tune till the rest couldn't help it—
> they'd have to join, often beating on a log
> or stamping their feet on the ground in unison.
>
> Often away off other groups would hear.
> We'd know by their faint sounds imitating
> ours. There were times when the wind
> would carry that music while branches waved
> high in the trees. Birds would join in
> while our young ones danced back and forth,
> Heaven there in the woods those days.
> —*from* "OUR WAY THOSE DAYS BEFORE THESE DAYS"

My brother's death broke the spell, and woke us to a different world. But I think the change began earlier. I remember when I told my brother I was getting married, at age twenty, in 1971. "You're getting married before me?" was his abrupt reply. I had betrayed the order of all things. Later, my mother reminded me of a letter I sent home the week after my honeymoon. I reported on travels with my bride, but said it wasn't at all as I had imagined. There was quiet disappointment. Then I accused my parents, "You made home too good."

As I stood at the phone in the maze of the mall, listening to the ringing of my wife's cell phone somewhere far away, I watched my countrymen stalk across shimmering blacktop from car to store, and back to their cars again. What did they seek? What do I seek? What can we give our child, if not, "Heaven there in the woods those days"? To give all, I need my parents' great gifts, together with my own translation of their silences.

☙

# The Bond

WE HAD OUR FAMILY CREATION MYTH, and like most around us it was about the war. According to the family story, told often, William Stafford the wartime pacifist is exiled to the California mountains. The camp is called *Los Prietos* ("The Swarthy Ones" in Spanish), a wild, dry place east from Santa Barbara. He is poor, with limited prospects. In the spring of 1943, Dorothy Hope Frantz, on the day after her date with a soldier, accompanies her preacher father to visit the pacifist boys in camp. The preacher leads the religious meeting, and the pretty daughter performs a skit about a goat—details never divulged. Bill and Dorothy take a walk in the hills at evening, and the sight of dust rising along a distant road causes one of them to begin a sentence from Willa Cather's "Obscure Destinies," a sentence the other completes:

> I suppose there were moonless nights and dark ones with but a silver shaving and pale stars in the sky, but I remember them all as flooded with the rich indolence of a full moon.

I try to imagine the connection they sensed at that moment—their common Midwest background, their passion for reading, their fluid convergence of insight against the whole backdrop of the war. After a handful of visits, according to the story, my father said to her, "Isn't this the way it should always be?" And she said, "But you don't even know if I can *cook*." And he replied, "You don't even know if I can bring something home *to* cook."

They were married in the spring of 1944. My father had to borrow a suit for the wedding. After a short honeymoon, he went back to camp, and the war went on. Later, they lived together in a mountain cabin on Mount Baldy, east from L.A. An idyll: the car that had to ford a stream to get to the outside world; the mailbox under the pine tree. And from those early years the classic photo of the two of them looking out from a pup tent in the forest on their first trip to Oregon.

In much of my childhood I had the feeling my parents flowed along as a river that carried me. I never needed to worry about the river, just how to steer my own craft. There were mysteries, though. After the kids had grown and left home, sometimes my father took to mocking my mother in public, saying cutting things to which she laughed, helplessly. When asked if he wanted to take part in a social event, for example, he might say, "Dorothy won't let me," or "Better ask Dorothy. She'll say no. I'm used to it." He implied his life was a series of disappointments, joys dashed by his wife.

By her report, he was sweet to her in private, but somehow felt the need to mark his distance in public. Trying to seek conciliation between them, I took her side, and tried to talk to him about this, but got nowhere. The two of them were loving and unified in many ways, and this public distance was a mystery. My girlfriend once told me she found this sweet.

"They've been together so long," she said, "and yet they still care deeply what the other says or does. That's a mark of a living relationship." This seemed an odd view to me. I believe my father's essential habit to follow his "own way of seeing things"—and hers to follow her own—led to their problems.

My father once said to the wife of a fellow writer, "It isn't easy being married to a poet, is it?" He recognized his own contradictions. In contrast to his intuitive approach as a writer, once he decided on a course of action in his life, that was it. No amount of talk, or "dithering" as he called it, could change his mind.

During this hard period both confided in me a pair of stories about their impasse. They each told me both stories as if these were landmark mysteries. First, on their honeymoon, as they were driving along in joy, my mother began to sing an old song, something like, *You go where you need to go, you do what you need to do—I'll be by the fireside, waiting for you.* . . .

"Don't sing that," my father said. So Dorothy stopped. No explanation. No discussion. Just an end. In my childhood, I remember her singing beautifully. But there must have been songs, or ways of singing, that we never heard. In her dream after he died he had said to everyone, "Don't silence Dorothy." But on their honeymoon, he did.

The second story was about a time early in their life together when my mother looked over his writing drafts and noted certain subjects or ways of writing my father should not pursue. I don't remember any specific mention of what these subjects were—his assessment of people they both knew? Of her? Of himself? I don't know. His response, though, was definite.

"Don't ever tell me what to write," he said. End of discussion. He had served notice his writing realm was to be utterly private. She might read the finished poems, but at the making place he would be alone.

I suggested to my parents, individually, that they try a counselor. "You think talk will solve it all," my father said, dismissing the idea. I might have replied, "Will silence?"

The magnetic affection working against these resistances, however, was powerful. Is all long love like this, a combination of attraction and resistance? They had ways to stay close, to reach out to each other and celebrate who they were together. I remember, often, my father wrapping his arms around my mother and bringing his face against hers, saying, "Dorothy, us mammals have got to stick together." She would laugh like a girl.

I remember his heroic drives from far places to get home to my mother, or to meet her at some agreed-upon place. And after he died, I learned from a friend what my father had said—typically—to a stranger far from home, rather than directly to his wife of forty-nine years, or in our presence.

"What would it be like for you," the friend had asked him, "if something happened to Dorothy?"

"I would be like a planet spinning by itself," my father said, "growing colder and colder."

What witness for connection could be more absolute than that? And he felt tender, years later, for the miscarriage my mother suffered early in their marriage:

> while the thunder shakes the world
> and the graceful dance and the powerful win,
> still faithful, still in thought, I bow,
>    little one.
>
> —*from* "STILLBORN"

In private, then, the bond was absolute. In public, it could be strange. My father would often read a certain poem, for example, when my mother was in the audience:

### Passing Remark

In scenery I like flat country.
In life I don't like much to happen.

In personalities I like mild colorless people.
And in colors I prefer gray and brown.

My wife, a vivid girl from the mountains,
Says, "Then why did you choose me?"

Mildly I lower my brown eyes—
there are so many things admirable people do not understand.

It seemed a mildly insulting poem. One night, after a reading, a woman in the audience quietly explained it to me: "Your father's in love with her, that's all. That's how life is. Against everything he says and thinks and believes, he loves your mother. Finally, those other claims go right out the window."

If this were true, he did not say so directly, at least not often. I remember the scene in the hospital room, before my mother was to undergo an operation. She was afraid, and he could not comfort her. He stood back from the bed, leaning away as if something corrosive were touching him. He didn't have his usual aura of confident connection to everyone in the room. Maybe he was afraid, needing her too much. Maybe he had to move into the shadows, keep to the periphery where the hard truth lay: mortality.

It fell to me to be directly tender to my mother then.

Several nights after my father died, I watched my mother hold up bravely through a meal we all shared, we survivors. I thought her heroic. We got up to leave, and she was graceful in her good-byes. Then, as often happened, there was some kind of delay. We stayed a few moments longer than planned, and I realized she had disappeared from the room. I found her by the back door crying in the dark.

She had not calculated quite right her ability to keep grief to herself, to protect us from what she could not. She was afraid. She needed him. She was like my father then.

In that moment, though he was gone, I saw their bond.

# Birth of Tragedy

I keep veering off into a look by the universe at people.
Hence the writing of poetry.

— DAILY WRITING, 19 SEPTEMBER 1955

I F YOU SIT AT MY FATHER'S DESK and look straight ahead, just at the altitude of the top of your head you will see a row of tattered books—the favorites. They are not his own, of course, not literature, not books about Kansas or Oregon. These books are more local to his soul than anything—more intimate in the fabric of his daily experience: Nietzsche, Pascal, Kierkegaard, Owen Barfield, John Henry Newman, Wittgenstein. If you open these books to the last page, the one left blank by the binder, you will find he has jotted page numbers of his favorite passages. In his copy of Nietzsche's *Daybreak: Thoughts on Prejudices of Morality,* for example, I find "p. 137 the eye & the artist . . . p. 162 cheerfulness . . . p. 255 music. . . ." In the margin at the listed pages there will often be a check mark beside some trenchant sentence or evocative idea. And sometimes he has jotted a note about his experience in the realm of this thinker:

> Most people are like pools of heavy oil: it takes extreme, wild, loud
> messages, gross signals to stir any patterns. Nietzsche is a pool of
> light, responsive material: any slight, nuancy, potential signal and
> he is all action and response.

Above his desk, and beside these books, you will find a shelf where he kept pages of all kinds for reference, and sometimes in multiple copies for sending along to friends. This stack of papers speaks to the spectrum of my father's interests and appetites:

Flyer for Ray Hunt's horsemanship clinics
Three poems by Jimmy Carter from the *South Dakota Review*
Typed passage from a biography of Gandhi
Flyer detailing the U.S. government's interventions abroad
Passage from WS daily writing about justice and diversity
Typed passage from the life of Saint Teresa
List of changes experienced by "all those born before 1945"
Passage from a biography of Mozart
Passage from a book on surgery: "the exact location of the soul"
Oct. 1983 directive to physicians: "No heroic measures . . ."
Multiple copies of farewell: "I have been forced by the sheer
     weight of fatigue . . ."
Typed passage from the *Aeneid,* Book IV, with a parallel passage
     from Saint Augustine, on a time of stillness in nature

A friend remarked to me that "for William Stafford, his religion was think-ing." I find this true. In a world where, as he said, "the trivial twins of suc-cess and failure may clutter up our days," he had "a tropism toward truth." But this truth could only be earned by the individual in a search my father carried out by writing, by reading, and by wrestling with hard things in his own mind. Was he a writer with philosophical interests, or was he a philosopher whose "findings" are disguised as poems?

> If you don't know the kind of person I am
> and I don't know the kind of person you are
> a pattern that others made may prevail in the world
> and following the wrong god home we may miss our star.
> —*from* "A RITUAL TO READ TO EACH OTHER"

Was he a writer inquiring into the ethics of daily life?

> I do not want to become good in any way but my own way.
> —DAILY WRITING, 15 DECEMBER 1955

My father embedded deep issues in the quiet language of his poems. This led Sylvia Plath to select Stafford poems like "The Well Rising" for a

*Critical Quarterly* anthology of new American poems that was widely read in England in the 1960s:

> The swallow heart from wing beat to wing beat
> counseling decision, decision:
> thunderous examples. I place my feet
> with care in such a world.

In such a world, I see my father as a kind of porcupine turned inside out: outwardly personable, congenial, hospitable, a good and easy friend; but inwardly bristling with pointed questions. He exemplified better than anyone Sir Philip Sydney's idea that one should *think* like a philosopher, but *speak* in the common idiom (in contrast to the false professor who speaks like a philosopher, but thinks like a bumpkin). In a world of conventions, he sought a voice so untamed it could be harsh, as in his original version of the closing lines of his poem "Faux Pas":

> In the jungle where you live wild animals will snarl at night,
> and you will love that sound, its definite "Here I am."

If you wanted to know my father, how would you get past the congenial exterior and enter that bristling mind? I can best experience my father's thorny, philosophical practice by drawing on quotations of all kinds from his reading, his writing, and our conversations. He had the courage to ricochet eagerly from one hard question to the next, and the fearless affection, sometimes, to invite me along. Over the years, my father's letters to me were often accompanied by passages from his favorite philosophers. In some cases, all I found when I slit open the envelope was the quotation, sometimes with a note suggesting why he thought I might need the words of Kierkegaard or Kafka. But often just the passage. He was including me in the world that for him was interior, intimate, even spiritual. I once opened an envelope to find this passage from an unidentified biography of Galileo, a passage my father had sent to underscore an idea from a recent conversation between us about teaching writing:

> The difference between philosophizing and studying philosophy . . .
> is that which exists between drawing from nature and copying

pictures. . . . [M]en who go on forever copying pictures and never get around to drawing from nature can never become perfect artists, or even good judges of painting. . . . In the same way a man will never become a philosopher by worrying forever about the writings of other men, without ever raising his own eyes to nature's works in the attempt to recognize there the truths already known and to investigate some of the infinite number that remain to be discovered.

I took the point that writing classes need to focus on explorations of each writer's quirky talent, rather than editing drafts to accord with successful literary models. Shortly before he died my father mailed me a passage he had copied from *Thus Spake Zarathustra*. He wanted to emphasize an idea we'd discussed: the responsibility of the artist to embrace the isolating necessity of individual experience.

Aren't we drifting through infinite nothing? Isn't empty space breathing on us? Hasn't it grown colder? Isn't night after night closing in on us? Don't we need lanterns in the morning? Are we still deaf to the noise of gravediggers digging God's Grave . . . ?

Why would my father send me such a passage? Is this advice? A lesson? It is not reassuring, directly. But as was often the case with him, to share a bleak view, honestly, was his way of affection, and was prelude to the most vivid life. "The world is such a zestful place," he said in an interview once, "even in its bleakness." He was not a moody pessimist precisely because he *knew* the cold, the darkness, the isolation of a true seeker's life in a culture drunk on superficial things. To share this view with me was to invite meeting at a deep place, an act of trust.

In 1960, he wrote in his daily writing:

Poets do their work alone. . . . [But] in our lives we sometimes feel the need to know what other lonely workers are thinking, finding, learning. I take my job to be that of representing, thus, a certain lonely sector of our separate but perhaps mysteriously joined experiences. Not for myself alone, then, but for ourselves, I speak; and

often it may seem with an arrogance. For my work is—for an in-
terval here—a work of importance: finder and maker, servant and
leader, adventurer of the widest realm and the greatest voyages ever
to be made.

In an interview with a Kansas friend, Steven Hind, my father ventured
some remarks on how he viewed the "toughness" of other writers, reserving
the harder—but paradoxically more positive—outlook for himself:

> STAFFORD: I think Frost is much more pessimistic than I am. I
> think that he is much softer than I, though. He still seemed to
> believe in fixed things. But I don't.
>
> HIND: Would you say that he is, in some ways, more vulnerable?
>
> STAFFORD: Yes. Sentimental. Vulnerable. He's not . . . he's not
> yielding enough to survive in the world as it is. Oh, I once heard
> someone, I think it was Gerald Heard say, "Only saints are hard
> all the way through." Well, Frost is no saint, and he's crusty, but
> the pie's pretty soft inside. Of course, Frost may be a strange one
> to say that about, but Hemingway was a spectacular example of
> a crusty meringue pie.

The alternative to being an armored softie, in my father's view, was to pry
your way inside the shell of appearance, confront the darkness, acknowl-
edge your isolation, and then reach out to others willing to share this expe-
rience. This was affection. By confronting the dark, you know light for
what it is—a fragile, intermittent blessing.

With his friend and colleague Kenny Johnson, my father kept up a long
conversation about such things. It appears that early they staked out their
territory. Kenny did yeoman's service as the pessimist. My father was not
the optimist, exactly, but reveled in his illuminated darkness. The mature
pleasure of their friendship can be seen in a letter my father sent to Kenny,
22 July 1981, typed on the back of an editor's call for poems about "Death
& Suicide":

Dear Kenny,

The book advertised overleaf never did come out, but I thought of using this page to respond to your nudges about my somewhat unjustified—some say—optimism. . . .

Too many things crowd to mind, but I'll send this brief response to your rich letter just arrived and will hope to defend myself at luxurious length one of these times soon when we converge.

Relevant to my position is a book just sent me by an amazing student in Michigan, who often assigns me readings. His book is about the development of "late antiquity," the 3, 4, and 5th centuries A.D. One chapter in the book is about "The Friends of God," a certain phase in church or religious leaders; and I find myself so much adapted to their views that I thought you might find stimulating cynicism in realizing that I hereby appropriate their label as my own. I'll type out here a poem of mine written just one year ago which seems to put me right into their optimistic, arrogant stance.

### Why I Am Happy

Now has come, an easy time. I let it
roll. There is a lake somewhere
so blue and far nobody owns it.
A wind comes by, and a willow listens
gracefully.

I hear all this, every summer. I laugh
and cry for every turn of the world,
its terribly cold, innocent spin.
That lake stays blue and free; it goes
on and on.

And I know where it is.

So—I offer the other side of this page, and then this side, for our series.

Adios—
Bill

My father could treat the "terribly cold, innocent spin" of the world with humor when he was in the company of friends. In the privacy of his own thoughts, in the citadel of himself, this cold could hold a darker tone, especially when he felt that those around him preferred to pretend life is a smooth, uncomplicated story. At such times, he was in the habit of typing out a private bargain with his life:

> Part of my care each day is to respond correctly. For instance, a question asked is not for the discovery of my opinion or feeling but for discovering the adequacy of my adjustment to a situation implied by the question. . . . Like a horse getting acquainted with an electric fence, I learn to recognize those little almost invisible wires. . . . I have to change from simple immersion in living to a much more confusing ritual of making sure events pass without upsetting a participant. And that makes progress through time a succession of congratulation or regret, rather than a parade of wonder. Now becomes only anticipated history.
>
> So sometimes I go outdoors.

The "parade of wonder" that happens "outdoors" is for my father the realm of nature, and of private writing, and of thought outside any given boundary. The only comfort comes in hard truth, and that can be lonesome. There were times when even the consolation of philosophy was not enough to redeem the day: "It's heavy to drag, this big sack of what / you should have done. And finally / you can't lift it any more" (a poem in the Daily Writing, 2 June 1993). In the last days of his life, he typed another such admonishment:

> Every day people around me reveal that they live in
> a country that shocks my soul. Words that they
> speak suddenly open infinity between us.
> Books or friends or conduct that they embrace
> recede to a pinpoint on my screen and go out.
>
> It is my habit never to hurt these people
> around me. Their offenses against my taste, my moral
> sense—my religion—can't be allowed to darken

their lives or our joint residence in our time.
In separate rooms we are traversing our lives.

I recognize I was probably one of the people around him with shocking, inferior ideas. He was alone from me, even as he sent me messages inviting me to waken, join him in the cold, and so achieve honesty, and thus be happy—"happy" in the original sense of the word, in keeping with "hap," what happens. To be congruent with the way things are is to release the strain of all pretense. Thus this handwritten passage he sent me:

17 Nov 91

Kim, my typewriter is ailing—but here's the Nietzsche passage I mentioned . . . "All supposed absolutes—including the notion of an 'absolute truth'—must be doubted and put to the experimental test: 'The right eye must not trust the left, and light for some time to come will have to be called darkness.' In an age when everything is in flux, involved in a process of dissolution and liquefaction, the will to systematize is an indication of 'a lack of intellectual integrity.' . . . The aphorism . . . 'expresses our thoughts, our values, our yeas and nays and ifs with the same necessity with which a tree bears its fruit. . . .'"

My office is filled with such passages my father sent me over the years, each orbiting in some way around this idea of truth, isolation, courage—the strange exuberance of the thinker loose from the grid of the civilized:

Kafka's fundamental outlook may be summarized in some such formula as this: almost everything is uncertain, but once one has a certain degree of understanding, one never loses the way anymore.

I do not believe life was ultimately about other people for my father, nor his connection with them. It was about the inescapable value of the compact self, a self that could be active in remembering, writing, helping others, witnessing for peace and reconciliation. This self could act from the inner source, but did not consist of that action. The source, the essence was something to which those human impulses appealed. All external effort was "easy." The source was hard but inevitable for the true seeker, ever available, the thread of life coiled intense as DNA inside the seed.

As I try to describe what the source was for my father, am I actually describing what it is for me? Did I inherit his way of ultimate reliance on the source? Keats called this world the "realm of soul-making." Maybe the work my father taught me is the continual process of soul-making, the creation of self. My father's busy life with others was the house, but the work itself was at the hearth deep inside, something fundamentally different than structure. The work at the source is endlessly in process.

In this light, my father always found Kierkegaard a worthy companion, as in another passage he sent me:

> As soon as a man appears who brings something of the primitive
> along with him, so that he doesn't say, 'You must take the world as
> you find it,' but rather 'Let the world be what it likes, I take my
> stand on a primitiveness which I have no intention of changing to
> meet with the approval of the world,' at that moment, as these
> words are heard, a metamorphosis takes place in the whole of nature. Just as in a fairy story, when the right word is pronounced, the
> castle that has been lying under a spell for a hundred years opens
> and everything comes to life.

I think of my own belief about the best kind of absentminded professor—the one who may forget where the keys are, but avoids the general epidemic of being absentminded about matters of soul. My father was privately obsessed by matters that most people around him—often including me—seemed to avoid. Unable to convey these perspectives to us directly in family life, he pondered them alone, wrote poems from that pondering, and sometimes mailed out landmark utterances. I find two passages he quoted to me often, and sent me several times:

> KIERKEGAARD: It happened that a fire broke out backstage in a
> theater. The clown came out to inform the public. They thought
> it was just a jest and applauded. He repeated his warning, they
> shouted even louder. So I think the world will come to an end amid
> general applause from all the wits, who believe that it is a joke.

KIERKEGAARD: What is a poet? An unhappy man who in his heart harbors a deep anguish, but whose lips are so fashioned that the moans and cries which pass over them are transformed into ravishing music.

Sometimes my father found a way to share these perspectives with all of us. At the dinner table when I was a child, suddenly there would be another guest. It would be Kierkegaard, or John Henry Newman, or Pascal. My father would pull a sentence or idea out of the air from his reading, and weave it into the flow of our conversation. He would respond to ideas we might have with the observation that "Milton had the same idea. . . ." This would be followed by lines from Milton quoted to us, or from Shakespeare, Wordsworth, George Eliot, Thomas Hardy. He often had a quotation with tremendous literary resonance for daily use in the family. For example, if there were a question about who should get the first drink of water on a hot day, he might say as he stepped back, "Thy need is greater than mine. . . " (Sir Philip Sydney's dying words on the battlefield, as he offered water from his own canteen to a wounded enemy soldier). Or after dinner, if I stood at the sink with him doing the dishes, he would pause with a plate held aloft, the towel trailing down from it, and remember a delicious idea or story or text. I had an appetite for this talk, even though it often caused discomfort: Pascal's wager, perhaps. Hobson's choice. Gandhi's challenge to the *Satyagrahi.*

One evening in his last year, when we had gathered at home, I remember my father launching into an idea from the writer Erik Erikson. "Toward the end of a long life," he said, "you can look back and say one of two things. Either you say, 'No! I should have . . . ! If only I could have . . . ! If only they would have let me . . . !' And all seems lost. But if you have lived in another way," my father said, "then you may say, 'Yes, that was my story. That is what I did, and what I did not do." He paused. "Then," he said, "you may be an elder, helping the young to understand a few things." At the sink he was inviting us all into the exhilarating darkness of his truth.

Poetry was a matter of survival for my father. He wrote in his daily writing in the 1950s about a kind of Mexican song he favored, *Canción Ranchera*: "I don't like it; I *need* it." I don't think he would have said he needed any particular poem he wrote, but he did need the practice of writing, his form of music, of contemplation, finding his compass in the dark. Behind his affection for us, his generosity to many, behind his lifelong work for human reconciliation there was this core state of mind:

> At least at night, a streetlight
> is better than a star.
> And better good shoes on a
> long walk, than a good friend.
> —*from* "So Long"

On one occasion, after hearing him read that poem, my mother asked, "But Bill, what about me?" And my father's distant reply: "Just keep walking, Dorothy. You'll understand."

A cruel remark to her; a tough assessment of his own life.

With his philosophers my father felt most accompanied as a writer, more than by the rest of us. For my father, the way the mind actually worked was infinitely fascinating:

> To think, I hold my head and roll it
> back and forth. What's inside
> wakes up. "Listen—it's time for another
> one of those brilliant sparks you've got."
> —*from* "The Way I Do It"

Or, more domestically, "My formula for writing is to make a brown waffle and sit there eating it and thinking" (Daily Writing, 6 August 1960). I can see my father now, holding his tilted head with his hands, pondering in some distant way, and then letting his hands slide down to rest on his cheeks, as he says, "Well, you could say it's like this. . . ." And then he would say something utterly surprising and strangely inevitable. He let himself go in talk, as in writing. "Each poem is a miracle that has been invited to happen," he said, and "I must be willingly fallible in order to deserve a place in the realm where miracles happen." Under the sometimes unstable conditions of life, for my father, thought and writing were the one sustaining endeavor. "Keep a journal," he once told a group of students, "and don't assume that your work has to accomplish anything worthy:

artists and peace-workers are in it for the long haul, and not to be judged by immediate results."

I remember when he told me he had titled his 1977 poetry collection *Stories That Could Be True,* I wanted him to change it to *Stories That Are True.*

"That's not the way it is," he said. "You try, you make your hunch as good as you can, and then see if the world can catch up to what you have imagined."

One of the last things my father wrote he called "Sometimes, Reading," and he sent it to the *Ohio Review* where it appeared after his death. Alternating between poetry and prose, it is an unusual testimonial about how reading can crystallize a change in life, and how that change can result in a different kind of honesty in writing. He reports what happened when he first opened a copy of Nietzsche's *Birth of Tragedy,* on the eve of World War II, in the library reading room at the University of Kansas. When he looked up from the book, he says, he found "a changed world, deeper but full of wonder and excitement, not to be trusted, but infinitely ready for revelation. Why hadn't my professors told me about this new hemisphere? They had cheated me. Or didn't they know. . . ?" He reports that his world began to unravel: "What held it together / through all those years of my childhood / separated into hundreds of little pieces / . . . I couldn't hold on anymore." But this loss came with a great gift which accompanied him for the rest of his life:

> a new expanse became mine, wild, reckless (so reckless it could
> be conservative too), a rampage of gusto: Galileo (thought experi-
> ments), John Henry Newman (two and two only self-evident beings,
> myself and my creator), Pascal (the awful silence of those infinite
> spaces), Kierkegaard (drink from your own well, purity of heart is to
> will one thing), George Eliot (in death they were not divided),
> Tolstoy, Gandhi, Saint Teresa (let mine eyes see thee, sweet Jesus of
> Nazareth), Goethe (man is a creature for a limited condition),
> Wittgenstein (we must unlearn what educated people know). . . .

He concludes with consolation, as if to a younger companion on a dark road:

. . . and my world now reels on, the world of literature, of super-
fact. But ok, big and scary as it is.
    It feels ok.
    Cross my heart.

At the heart of my father's best-known poem, I find the shadow of that
moment he had experienced in the library before the war. As the speaker in
"Traveling through the Dark" kneels on the road beside the dead doe, her
side warm with her unborn fawn, my father, a good man alone, speaks his
gift, and his isolation:

    I thought hard for us all. . . .

Is that the only way—to think, alone, for others? In my father's stern ac-
counting for his own actions, solitude is often the context. As often with
his daily writing, however, the prose speculations that immediately precede
the first draft of "Traveling through the Dark" offer a more-inclusive if
less-focused view:

    Self justifying acts. Automatic reason attitudes. For instance: a) We
    oppose another group because it opposes us: it will. b) We ridicule
    someone for "not being able" to have an attitude or feeling we have:
    the truth of our remark hinges on the congruency of our percep-
    tion, not on any weakness in the person. . . .
                                        —DAILY WRITING, 17 JUNE 1956

I see my father puzzling out the place of intelligence, and its liability—a su-
perior attitude—in human behavior. This philosophic context shadows the
poem to follow. In his writing that day, my father traveled from the ethics
of prejudice to the story of the deer, from thought to event, from prose to
poetry, with his customary thread of self-judgment linking the two.
    In his prose here, the emphasis is not on one person thinking for us all,
but on what "we" may think or do. Again I ask, who is this "we"? Is it the
wartime CO community? His fellow philosophers? All thinkers and ac-
tivists? Or is it everyone? How can we meet, he asks, and be honest about
what we don't know? In the face of this, I am forced to ask: What work of

connection did my father fit me for? How do his poems accompany me, and accompany us, even as he goes his own distant way?

Even as I ask these questions, I can see my father's level gaze directed toward me. "That's just how it is," he might say. Or, as he did one day in that last year, he might slip me a poem:

*Cliff Dweller*

You could say I live on Acoma, steep
drop all around. Sometimes my foot
slips, and I feel that giddy height.

Often my words drop into nothing:
no answer comes back; a pale
whisper reaches up from the blue distance.

Relatives, friends who walked beside me—
I look around and they're gone. They don't
live on this rock any more.

Stories tell of a place where the land goes on,
firm all around. Your steps can be sure.
In my dreams I parachute into that land.

I wake up. A breeze is blowing the curtain.
I send out a few words toward the edge. Sometimes
they bring back a friend. Sometimes—the blue whisper.

I have been to the library high on the hill at Lawrence, Kansas, where I tracked down *The Birth of Tragedy*, hoping to hold in my hands the very copy my father might have read. But the volume on the shelf carries a curious label at the flyleaf. It is a copy produced "to replace the irreparably deteriorated original." Was it my father who read that book to tatters?

And I have been to Acoma, that oldest village high on the cliff in New Mexico, with its empty streets in the afternoon, and quiet lives unseen. I remember the grooves in the rock by the pool, where centuries ago the people sharpened bone tools. I remember the last surviving window of mica—with its shine that made Coronado believe in distant gold. I wish I could have walked those streets with my father. I had his "Acoma" poem in my pocket. Our guide showed the opening in the cemetery wall—on the south side, toward Mexico. "That's so the spirits of the children the Padres took can find their way back to us," she said. I thought of my father, out there somewhere in the dry country, picking his way lightly along toward where he needed to be.

# VII.

# *The Thread*

# Not in the Presence of Witnesses

A FEW DAYS AFTER MY FATHER'S DEATH, I stood at the copy machine in my office at the college, preparing to make my own set from his daily writing box, the last three dozen pages marked by his pen. It was in the evening; the campus was empty. Outside, autumn—the maples turning gold, the giant cottonwood beginning to let fall its coins. My mother waited in the car there, reading a book about writers and their mothers. I looked out the window where salal reached green toward the sky, feeling my father's departure in the office that once was his, and then I turned to the sheaf of last things in my hand. The last poem, yes, I made a careful copy. The poem he wrote the day before he died, yes, a copy. But then I stopped as I read the next sheet. One glance told me it was private, a blend of philosophical musing and accusation. Was it my place to copy it? I remembered the will: "My literary executor will be my son Kim." He trusted me to do the right thing, and yet I was stalled.

I replaced the poems in their box, locked the office, and went out to the car. My mother was eager to read me what Flaubert said of his mother. Then I told her I had reconsidered and felt I needed to work through the box more slowly, when I could find the time.

That was the beginning of the hardest work, and the best: the gradual exploration of the archive. Here I would find our lost words exactly as he recorded them; here I would be questioned and mysteriously instructed again as I sorted, discovered things, and gradually, judiciously, made them known. Especially in the first weeks and months following my father's death, the pages that most caught me were the private ones. They felt whispered to the sky.

My father used to say that poems are not made of words, but of contexts: the speaker's intensity of need, and the power of the unsaid. In this light, I want to look at a set of things from the William Stafford Archive that are not poems, not letters, not stories or articles. They are acts of witness my father made, but then kept mostly to himself. This series of farewells, statements of belief, and in some cases accusations against himself and others form an elite puzzle within the larger collection of his papers.

What is this archive? I remember maybe ten years before my father's death when a rare book and manuscript dealer called from New York City and asked if he might visit to talk with my father about his work. Since my father rarely said no to requests, even from strangers, the dealer was on the next plane west, and soon we were picking him up at the airport and driving him to the house at Sisters, where much of my father's library was stored. On that drive, the dealer began to enjoy himself, and he began to brag. He told of his great conquests as a manuscript shark, building his way up to the greatest deal of all.

"I almost got the form Marilyn Monroe signed when she became Jewish to marry Arthur Miller," he said. "I had this rabbi way short of cash, and hungry. But at the last minute, the deal fell through. Hell, I could have recouped the purchase price on media-excerpt rights alone, and the eventual sale would have been clear profit."

We knew we had a high roller on our hands, but like the dealer, we didn't know yet what comparative treasure we might hold. By the time we got to the house, our visitor's stories had whetted his appetite for new discoveries. While we tried to stay out of his way, the dealer made a sweep of the library and emerged with a box of books. He brashly offered several thousand dollars for the contents of the box. My father looked at me, but said nothing. It was a telling moment. He didn't know what to do, but I did—or thought I did. By taking action that moment, I sealed my doom: I started taking books out of the box I didn't think should go to the dealer: a copy of Richard Hugo's *A Run of Jacks,* signed to my father, and a half dozen similar treasures. I spread these on the table and looked at my father.

"It seems to me," I said, "we should reserve these, if we decide to sell the others." My father said nothing, but the dealer bristled. The writer's child was getting in the way. "By chance," he said, "you have removed the items that formed the basis of my offer."

I knew it wasn't by chance, but held my peace. No deal.

We had lunch, and gazed at the mountains, the dealer recovered his good humor because we let him tell us stories, and in the afternoon he moved on to the manuscripts and correspondence. My father brought down a box at random—a cardboard grocery box with the top folded shut and bound with sisal cord—and opened it to reveal his humble but consistent system: letters received and carbons of his responses were bound monthly in manila folders. He had brought us a year from the early 1960s, and was muttering about how most of the letters said merely "Meet you at the fence at four . . . "—simple logistics of the writer's life. The dealer was undeterred. He opened a folder, marked the place with his hand, pulled out a letter at random, and began to read aloud—another tactical error. It turned out to be an effusive letter from W. S. Merwin, who had seen my father's early poems in the *New Yorker,* and wanted to get acquainted.

"I think we have something here," the dealer said. He looked a little further and then closed the box. He did not tie it shut but made his pitch on the spot: he would like to be my father's representative for the sale of the whole collection of books, manuscripts, correspondence—the works.

Again, my father looked at me. This time I was silent but we conversed in silence—an eyebrow raised, a shrug, a glance at the dusty box.

"No," my father said with a sigh. "I guess we'll leave it all in the attic. Sorry. We'll let you know if we change our minds." The dealer's shoulders sagged. My father continued, apparently to soften things. "I just wonder, though," he said, "why clutter the lives of generations of graduate students with all this? I don't know why I saved it. It's my compost pile."

"You never know." The dealer looked at my father, at me, at my mother. Shrugged. "Well," he said, "I got to see Oregon. And maybe you *will* change your mind. Things happen."

Things did happen. Years went by, and then my father was gone, and I carried the first of many boxes of his words to the rented office space above the Fat City Cafe, the smell of oily cinnamon rolls following me up the carpeted stair. In the car outside, more boxes. In the attic at home, more. And in the house at Sisters, more again. As I sat down to open the first box, I thought of that encounter with the dealer, who had contributed in his own way to my sense of what it meant to be a literary executor. My father deferred a decision and, in effect, made a decision: leave it all in Kim's hands.

As I first began to enter my father's papers, I was simply overwhelmed. It was a burden, all right, but not the kind one wants to set down or live without. Years earlier I had learned an important distinction from one of my students, a Quaker prayer that joins "things it is easy to be thankful for, and things it is hard to be thankful for." Sitting in the presence of my father's life work, it felt like this: it is easy to receive the gift of his poetry, for there are many treasures here, and I am thankful. It is hard, sometimes, to accept the care of his legacy, for there are many complex tasks to perform and tough decisions to make—but I am thankful, all the same. I would be poorer without this work.

Early in this process I had a dream that gave me an exact phrase: "the specific gravity of treasure." According to the dream, some treasure is simply too heavy to carry. It pulls you down. Other forms of treasure, though, have buoyancy. They help to carry their own weight. Money, power, fame could be too heavy. Children, music, poetry, and the life of a seeker could be buoyant. Difficult, buoyant, essential.

The magnitude of the collection—some sixty cartons of manuscripts and an equal trove of publications, photography archives, audio recordings, and other resources—did not deter me; that could be managed. As a friend said, a local professional I asked to give me a first assessment of what we had, "Your father had a few habits, and incredible consistency." The daily writing, correspondence, manuscripts, publications, and teaching materials were for the most part in good order already. That was a blessing. But it was the decisions that made it hard to breathe as I sat in the midst of it all. Should we ship the whole collection to some library and let others take it from there—professionally? No, we'd keep it for a while. Should we consider this archive the record of a long and active life of writing and publishing now completed, or was the collection an interim resource for a continuing process of publication? If the latter, what should be published? What should not? What kinds of shaping for publication might be appropriate? For example, what kinds of anthologies of my father's unpublished materials should we create? And perhaps most troubling of all, for it would require the goodwill of some editors I did not know, which of his many books should I strive to keep in print?

I contacted HarperCollins, the publisher that had been my father's mainstay from 1962 with *Traveling through the Dark* to *Passwords,* twenty-nine years and eight books later. Robert Bly had edited a selection of William Stafford poems, *The Darkness Around Us Is Deep,* which HarperCollins was due to bring out in a few months. I knew their commitment, at least to that book, was solid. But when I flew to New York two months after my father's death, and met with his editor there, the encounter was brief and I was in for a surprise.

"When your father was alive," she said, "his books did fairly well. But now that he's . . . well, poetry is always a tough sell." She did not foresee publishing my father's work beyond the Bly volume, and certainly not a major project like his selected poems. The other books would not be in print for long. And that was that.

I left her office and went out into the streets of New York, wandered for hours in a daze. Had I failed, so soon, as literary executor? How could I keep his work alive—work that spoke to me with a living voice? I felt helpless, homesick for him. I would have to get used to this feeling.

Back in Portland, I took stock. I did have help, and that was a blessing. It was clear that access to the archive would need to be limited, at least in the short term. Literary pilgrims had already approached us, wanting to see the papers. What if an eager visitor made off with original manuscripts— the first draft of the poem "Traveling through the Dark," for example, or his early letters home about his aspiration to become a poet? For now the archive would have to be private.

Sometimes I was paralyzed when many overlapping decisions had to be made at once. In the archive office above Fat City Cafe, where we first stored my father's papers, I was in pharaoh's tomb, and in the wake of his passing I had to start with the secrets. Personally, I needed his quietest voice, so I began my work by seeking the private, the informal, the reflective pieces shuffled into the whole mix. These are a series of statements that lie behind my father's more public work. I turned first to the farewell messages, several little manifestoes about right living, notes for teaching and broader witness, and the box he labeled "Abandoned Poems."

First among this treasury are the variations on a kind of form letter I found, as if he had prepared to send out copies to decline invitations of all kinds. The longer I searched through the archive, the more examples I found. It was an exercise I had urged my father to adopt. Instead of a personal letter of apology in response to every inquiry from the world—or worse, surrender, and taking on an invitation he should decline—I had urged my father to print a set of cards gently but firmly saying no. "Think of that dress Kit made," I had said, "with the word NO painted in bold strokes. She wore it for certain meetings when she knew people would ask her to do their work for them."

Perhaps in response to these proddings, and perhaps in keeping with his own reluctance, my father had several texts at hand. One was a hand-written note in shaky script titled "Notice to all Patrons." I don't know where he got this, but it started appearing on his office door at the college toward the end of his career there. The text is accompanied by a rugged drawing of a mouse-like creature staggering upright along a road:

> I have been obliged by the
> sheer weight of Fatigue
> to quit my Post & repair
> to My Dwelling-house,
> until I have fully recovered My
> Usual composure. All Patrons will
> find Me of a cheerful Demeanor,
> and in Readiness for Business or
> Consultation, upon a return.

Later, he used a slightly more forceful NO:

### Mentioned in Passing

Now that William Stafford's life has entered the stage of *Moksha*, friends will welcome his withdrawal from those literary engage-ments that for so long filled the calendar. *Moksha* allows continued interest in friends and their projects, but from the sidelines while new people take over the workshops, readings, lectures, critiques and such that have provided much good interchange over the years. Old writers must yield to the young their place, their turn, and say to literary invitations: *Ta-ta, so long, adios, be seeing you.*

He had sent this last one to me with a note: "Thought I might print up & use something like this." I don't know whether he did. I do know he would write often to patrons on the literary scene and urge them to invite others in his place, sometimes specifying replacements by name. My father sent the following, for example, to a friend in Iowa:

> When you mentioned briefly the idea of getting Kim and me together for some sessions in Iowa, I leaned into the thought, but even at the time I knew that I should at my age be turning over such activities to people like you and Kim. Maybe I can cultivate my garden, tease out my writings day by day here at home.

My father's most refined effort in this line is the sheet I found on a shelf above his desk after he died—a dozen copies ready for use:

> Time has caught up with me, and I find myself unable to take part as before in those literary activities that the young are taking over. My traveling, reading, lecturing, ms critiquing have come to a halt—and I am trying to assume gracefully the role of the elderly.
>
> As Wordsworth describes his "Recluse," I have become an elderly person living in retirement.
>
> "Gracefully," I say, gracefully I am trying to accept what time has dealt me; and that means I must turn away from invitations. I hope that this response of mine will lead you to seek out the young, the competent, the ambitious. And I willingly accept life on the shelf.
>
> Sincerely,
> William E. Stafford

On the last day of his life, my father wrote to organizers of the Associated Writing Programs conference, promising to take part if they could not find better speakers. He then recommended a number of people—with complimentary words—known to disagree with his own approach to teaching writing.

In these letters and statements of farewell he tried to be graceful, accepting, resigned as he bowed out, but I don't think his heart was in it. He tried to talk himself into "gracefully" accepting "life on the shelf." He offered the ongoing work to "the young . . . , the ambitious." Was he Lao Tzu riding off into the desert? When he was younger, a farewell in his poems could have a kind of swagger:

> At the last when you come
> I am a track in the dust.
> —*from* "EXISTENCES"

But in age, his claims are lingering: he can't quite let go.

Reading through this series of increasingly winsome farewells, I don't understand his hesitation at decisive departure. He clearly knew, as he said in yet another statement contained in his daily writing box the day he died,

> It is more graceful to assume a private, and finally a reclusive, place.
> After a certain age, you need time to consider, to make decisions,
> even just to take care of yourself. You need time.

He needed time, and rest, but he liked company. So he kept teaching when he was asked. As I puzzle over his hesitation to end this, I find myself inventing a true translation for the common accusation leveled against teachers. The cynical proverb says, "If you can't do, teach; and if you can't teach, teach teachers." But through my father's appetite for meetings with learners, I think I know how it really was for him:

> Those who can't do all their learning and writing alone, because
> they so enjoy the company of fellow human beings, will practice
> their learning in company with others, and will let us call them
> "teacher."

When my father retired from Lewis & Clark College, someone in the dean's office asked if he would like to continue in emeritus status, teaching for no compensation. He declined, they gave him a parting gift of a used typewriter, and that was that. Later, he confided to me, "I enjoyed my years of teaching, but at the thought of doing it some more, and not for money, my gorge rose!" I put with this, however, the fact that my father *did* continue to teach and often for quite limited compensation—or none. He traveled, offered workshops, and attended conferences to the end. When I went to his bank following his death, the banker said to me, "Your father said something to me that I have never heard in all my years in banking: 'I don't understand it—I keep doing exactly what I want, and the money just rolls in.'" This was a man schooled in the Great Depression, not expecting to be paid for the work of his heart and soul.

Of all his farewells, the most mysterious I have found is the one my father sent forth in August 1964. In his fiftieth year, he typed what he called "An Informal Will," and sent it to his friend and colleague at Lewis & Clark College, Kenny Johnson. I never saw this unusual document until after my father's death, when Kenny's son sent it to me. (Later, we found a first version in the Daily Writing, 18 August 1964.) It had apparently served as part of an ongoing conversation between Bill and Kenny about last things, for Kenny has written several comments in the margin: "Die without being noticed . . . No memorial service, no wake? . . . to blot out all physical evidence of one's existence. . . ."

It's odd that this informal will was not in my father's file with other final things, the file labeled, "If we should ever die. . . . " But maybe this one was so personal, he didn't feel the need to leave it with his papers, and sent it forth to a friend instead to find its own way back. Because this document is so unusual, and because it gives an inside view of my father's thinking in a way even the poems, for all their insights, do not, I need to share long passages from it. It begins with my parents' home address in the upper right—including USA—as for a letter, and the date, 20 August 1964. In the first section, my father announces that if there is catastrophic need, he hopes we will understand his desire to disappear. If this should happen, he says, he hopes the family would accept that "any disappearance would mean I had willingly just gone." He would like to be allowed "to sneak out of the world." He then begins a catalogue of his particular relations with us all:

> I take account seriously of those who have suffered in any way
> from my presence in the world, and I ask them to relinquish, in
> light of their own serious thought, any heavy blame:
> Those whom my limitations, inattention, forgetfulness made
> endure a waste of their time, and those who suffered my repeated
> banalities—I ask that they forgive me.
> Also those I have hurt in going my own way, or in doing a job,
> or as an inept part of a group.

He asks forgiveness of those hurt by his life—his writing, his beliefs, his standards.

> And those I helped, too—for it was always true that by full use
> of certain qualities luck gave me I might have done better, and
> done more, for all around me—may they forgive me, all of them
> often terribly dear in my sight, but sometimes, too, simply neg-
> lected, or swimming deep in my inattention, like a dream. All of
> you: we were somewhat alike, remember; and for my part, that is all
> right, I say. And so, goodbye.

I feel I am reading something like Chaucer's "Retraction" here—that mys-
terious passage at the end of *The Canterbury Tales* which purports to be
Chaucer's apology for offensive elements in his work. Read closely, how-
ever, both Chaucer and my father do not say exactly that they are sorry for
what they have done. They are sorry that what they have done—what they
had to do in a life of creation—may have hurt others.

My father then goes on to discuss material possessions, but he appeals
for common sense, without detail. His attention is not on objects but on
relations:

> I look with great hope and goodwill toward my family and friends
> and I think with a tide of gratitude about all they have meant to
> me: may their lives be rich and varied; may they realize in their own
> ways their dearest aims; and may no one carry lasting hurt or con-
> cern or worry because of my way of living, or way of dying.

It is the sign-off that most touches me, for my father addresses everyone
from the absolute center of his life—the inner quiet of his own self:

> Signed this 20th Day of August 1964, not in the presence of wit-
> nesses (for what have witnesses to do with a document meant for
> more than legal significance, and identifiable I hope as typical and
> my own), but in the ease and quiet of my study on this calm sum-
> mer day,
> William Stafford

The genesis of this document must have been a strange time in my father's life. When he first wrote it, on August 18, he had just learned that the principal at the school where my mother taught had bone cancer. Perhaps mortality was in the air. As I said, my father had turned fifty. The year 1964 was the first time he had bought a new car—a white Oldsmobile—for our family trip into Mexico. The year before, in 1963, his *Traveling through the Dark* had won the National Book Award, which began a frenetic series of travels, public readings, and literary notoriety. He may have felt economically stable for the first time in his life, and his early ambition to be a poet had been achieved, publicly. By August, he and my mother had completed the study (also their bedroom) in the garage—perhaps for the first time he had a desk, his work in good order, and seclusion from the family (what my mother called, in a letter to Kansas, a retreat "away from the maelstrom of family life"). All that was done. And about the soul? His brother was in decline, and would die the following spring. Did my father know that? Had he already let his brother go? In July of that summer, we had visited Kansas. Maybe he saw the end.

Both success and mortality have brought him to this point, and he goes into himself, turns away from the world in order to consider death, to accuse himself, ask forgiveness, affirm his affections, and say good-bye. He does not mention his life in poetry, or in teaching. He does not specify family. This is an accounting in more basic terms. He is stern with himself. Against this statement, I read the absolution of the last poem he wrote, in August 1993: "'You don't have to prove anything,' my mother said. . . ." He seems to have found ways to forgive himself in his last thirty years.

In the months after my father died, I would sit in the archive holding such a piece of paper from my father's hand, and begin to cry, or to laugh, to puzzle sometimes in anguish. The storms made me stronger. Here were letters to friends and strangers; the life of art in all stages from first scribble to final text; the practice of the daily writing that continued buoyantly, doggedly, fervently for decades; and the private passages on ethical and philosophical puzzles, the personal statements of account.

I remember the first time I carried from the house the box my father had labeled in a scrawl, "Abandoned Poems," and paused at the tailgate of the car to pull out a sheet and read an abandoned poem at random. "What's wrong with that?" I thought. And then I put it back in its place,

closed the tailgate, and drove away—accompanied by my father, the poet,
our renegade friend:

### Even When You're Sad

Sing hard. Act out that part you have, by
singing when it comes. Invited,
plunge. Places there are where you'll never
be unless the sound is your sound.

Here's a way, for the kind of world
this is, to take before it ends:
Discover a talisman;
hold it; find a road; run.

# Lost Words, Last Words, No Words

T O   A   C H I L D ,   T H E   E C O N O M Y  of the family is a mysterious back-
drop to events that feel inevitable, if inexplicable. I don't remember
questioning why we moved every year until I was eight, sometimes to
another state, or just to another house—Oregon, Iowa, Oregon, Indiana,
California, Oregon—house to house, summer by summer, and always
"Daddy's college," "Dorothy's school," and a place to park the little green
trailer we had pulled into town with our few things, until the next move. I
don't remember explanations, but I do remember the ritual sometime in
early summer, getting our toys into one small suitcase each, helping our fa-
ther hitch up the trailer, saying good-bye to favorite trees, dogs, neighbor
kids, and other companions of the past few seasons, and hitting the road. I
remember the wonders of the country, our thirst across the long stretches
of the heartland. There is a photograph of my brother and me standing by
the road, two stubs in white T-shirts and shorts, each with sunglasses, each
holding a suitcase in which we carried our bowl and spoon—for handouts
from our parents in cafés. And I remember random details of the houses
we came to, the rental with the coal cellar, the chicken house out back, and
the Iowa Quonset hut of tin, its walls rising in a curve like the sky.

Among them all I remember the house that later burned in the little
town of Tualatin, Oregon, maybe because it best displayed the shabby per-
fection of our ways. There was a living room I remember without win-
dows, though it must have had a few. It was long and low, with a woodstove
presiding. You went up two steps to the bedrooms on one side, or to the
kitchen at the back. That was all we needed: Daddy Bill, Mama Dorothy,
my mother's sister Helen, my older brother Bret, and my baby sister Kit.
The youngest, Barbara, came later—after another four or five expedi-
tionary moves.

Our landlord's name was Manlove, there was a railroad track near
enough to shake things when a freight train went by, and a river. That

winter my father kept a list of the kinds of wood he fed the stove, the many driftwood sticks he pulled from the high-water line along the banks of the lazy Tualatin: holly, walnut, cedar, hazel, maple, alder, locust, hemlock, fir. Years later, he would recite that list as if imparting a recipe for the good life, for honor and happiness attainable.

A man of some ambition as a poet, he yet cherished such a list, for that's where it all began. Language grew out of the earth. Poetry was the stuff of river and fire and the daily chores.

They say my father's own first word was "moon." He would be a poet, but no one knew that in 1914, just before the Great War. There, floating over Kansas, was the moon, and my little father shaped his mouth to say its name. He was in a family that noticed such a moment, and remembered. And they also say, when he was little, his sister Peg was languishing in great danger with diphtheria, and he came running into the room shouting, "Is she dead yet?" Thus, from the beginning, the boundaries of his character included reverence and recklessness.

Both my parents had a devotion to first utterance. As I have mentioned, they kept a book they called *Lost Words* to record what we kids said from the start. When, at the age of five, they overheard my brother Bret telling me about history, they wrote it down: "First there was the cave men, then Jesus, then Davy Crockett." They wrote down the obvious—my sister Kit at three asking, "Now is it today?" They recorded the strange, as when I came out from my nap and asked my father, "What do you do if your teeth catch on fire?" And the puzzlement of my younger sister Barbara, once she arrived among us, complaining that "The garbage man isn't leaving us any garbage!" He had taken it all away.

They first called the book *Lost Words,* but my father later changed the name when typing up a new edition to *Voices Remembered.* I prefer the original, for lost words are the common language gone underground like a river when old ones die, only to rise native in the voices of the very young, as if from nowhere. Like a key event in life, this thread disappears, and then reappears in memory, if we are lucky, when the time is right. My parents could not always answer our puzzlements, so they simply recorded questions as we posed them, along with our own provisional answers. By the time we went off to school, this book at home said to us, *You are thinkers, and your talk is worth remembering.* By the time we began to read books, we had made one. We were participants in the culture of ideas, songs, and stories. And so, inevitably, we measured the texts of the great against our own:

> BRET: "Is anything ever so pretty that robbers won't tear it down?"
>
> Fog this morning. Barbara said, "The sky felled on the school ground."
>
> Kit, about the picture of Jesus called "The Good Shepherd": "There's that Indian holding the bear."
>
> KIM: "The next feller that dies I'm going to hold onto his feet." [to see what heaven is like]

There was insight companioned to ignorance and imagination as we tried to understand how the world worked, at the same time experimenting with language. We got it wrong, or strange. Our mother, the teacher of elementary-school children, had a genius for appreciating our inventions. And our father's devotion to the direct honesty of our utterance was in keeping with his practice as a writer. In a poem from *A Glass Face in the Rain* (1982), he speaks in the voice of a distant star:

> Now I am fading, with this ambition:
> to read with my brights full on,
> to write on a clear glass typewriter,
> to listen with sympathy,
> to speak like a child.
> —*from* "TUNED IN LATE ONE NIGHT"

My father found the spontaneity of his children learning the language congruent with his habits as a writer: what comes to you is yours to say.

The *Lost Words* book itself was the size of a sheet of typing paper folded once over. (My father typed his own poems on a half-sheet this size so he could fit a set of them, folded once, in his back pocket.) On the cover of brown manila, a photograph was held with crimson tape—Bret and Kim eagerly partaking of a meal, supposedly consisting of cold pumpkin sauce straight from the can. (This same photo in the album accompanied by the caption, "Kim not a feeding problem."). Brown manila, a simple feast, lost words. In the library of home, this was our talisman of the good life.

As a writer, my own habits thus began early of constantly taking dictation from the world, and these habits took a confirming refresher at midlife. My childhood and my own children together have taught me to pluck my little notebook from my pocket whenever I hear the language invented in a new way by people around me. Writers are not called upon so much to be smart, as to be alert.

Now that my father is gone, his words rise from memory, coming back in my own voice. "Atta boy," I say to our young son as he manages to struggle into his own jacket. "You've got the right idea." Or when the time feels right, I find myself saying in class, "The greatest ownership of all is to look around and understand—as my daddy used to say . . . When you get stuck, lower your standards and keep going . . . How did this poem start . . . ?"

On that strangely perfect last day of his life, I consider again the last words my father spoke to my mother, as he helped her in the kitchen: "Better get another spatula." He often made domestic chore the stuff of poetry, and he was helpful to the end. But were those, in fact, his last words?

What about the four words we found in his hasty scrawl at his desk: "and all my love"? Were those his last, by way of farewell? With my mother's story about those words, they become an echo from the earliest of their years together. The apple, the knife, and four words.

There is also his last poem: "'You don't have to prove anything,' my mother said. . . . It was all easy." The finality of that poem haunts me. The last poem in the life of a poet, when it is this good, takes on a mysterious authority.

But what about the informal will my father wrote in the 1960s? This text, appearing after my father's death, has unusual resonance: "We were somewhat alike, remember?" My father clearly wrote this set of words with careful consideration and an ultimate point of view. Should I read them as his final words for departure?

As my memory travels back through time, my father's last words seem to multiply from a never-ending source. I come to that afternoon when I stopped to see him following our lunch of garlic pasta and before I went off on my own to write. He addressed me with an unusually winsome look:

"Those stories," he said, "I guess I was waiting for someone to ask. Well, so long, my friend."

Last words, and good words.

His poem "Ask Me" seems to lie behind that scene: "ask me / mistakes I have made. Ask me whether / what I have done is my life. . . ." In our last meeting, I did begin to ask. After his death, this process has not stopped. I ask, consider, puzzle, and sometimes recognize a signal I have carried far and finally understood. Our conversations do not seem to be ending.

How about his last words of direct advice to me, as we sat in the car in Bozeman: "Be of good heart, my friend." There is a kind of gold light around that moment. Final? Well. . . .

In dreams, my father comes to me, often as a silent witness. Even in the midst of the dream I realize this is my chance to ask him anything. But the dream will fade before I speak. Or I will ask, and my father will simply look at me without a word, sending the question back into my keeping. Only lately has he begun to speak in these dreams, often a compact, enigmatic message that lingers to puzzle me for some days. In one recent dream, for example, my father appears at a college faculty meeting, sitting off to my left, holding a brown paper bag where a child has copied four of my father's words in a confident scrawl. My father announces he thinks it's wonderful the child is writing before he can read—and copying from the master! Since the faculty meeting is in progress, I try to make my father lower his voice, but he takes no notice. The faculty talk among themselves, occasionally glancing in our direction; my father has something for me to know. He holds up the paper bag for me to see.

Only when I wake do I note the words the child has written: "Chains are our own." Perhaps a reference to one's freedom to live a creative life within an institution? Our restraints are our own either to forge or to dissolve. A child in my care has learned what my father has to teach. Or has the child taken on the role of teaching me?

In another dream I am walking through a city carrying my son, and my father walks beside me in the rain. We have to get back to the park where I have left our childhood dog, the Airedale "Bo," always frightened of storms. No words this time, just the hurrying to take care of my childhood dog and my father and my child all at once.

Then came the dream when I learned how to ask for more, and my father explained the thread he was following beyond this life. This dream, recorded in my notebook when I woke, creates a narrative as compelling to me as any:

> The phone rings. "It's for you," my mother says. "It's Bill." We agree to meet, and abruptly I find myself at his tomb, an arched doorway like a Roman ruin. The tomb is open, and my father stands before me. His clothes are rags, and his face is gray with death.
>
> "I'm teaching," he says. "All the men who didn't learn when they were alive—now they want everything I have." Suddenly he is gone, and I find myself inside his tomb, but the arched doorway behind me has been closed. I go deeper inside, emerging into a sunlit grove I recognize as the Elysian Fields. In my hand, I open my father's billfold, and out springs the sky.

As I woke from this dream, I remembered a poem my father wrote a year after his own father died, which ended, "My life is his dream / the way rain falls" ("The Way Rain Falls," 10 October 1943). I also remembered the beginning of a late poem, "Sky":

> I like you with nothing. Are you
> what I was? What I will be?

The call, the tomb, the account of his continuing life as a teacher, and his unfolding gift to me of the sky—this encounter with my father is another in a series of parting hints: "they want everything I have."

By now, I've given up predicting which words will be my father's last for me. I take up a poem, speak to our children, teach, dream, write, and sometimes as I speak I hear him say what I am saying.

Even now I travel with my father. One journey came about because the last writing project he completed was a series of "poetry road signs" in response to an invitation from a couple of forest rangers who liked his work. They arranged to have seven poems etched onto aluminum and set along the Methow River, east of the Cascades Mountains in Washington State. My father wrote the poems the year before he died; the signs were ready a year after. So in August of 1994, my fiancée Perrin and I left Portland to drive north for the dedication of the signs, and for a memorial gathering for my father in the little town of Twisp. It was to be an emotional trip.

We were in fine spirits as we set out, but within a few miles I felt unease, and I asked Perrin what it could be. She put her hand on my shoulder. I saw in my mind the kind of place in a forest where a great tree has fallen: suddenly there is plenty of light, and the young trees flourish. I remembered the day Perrin had come to visit for the first time, seven months after my father's death. I was a bachelor then, cleaning house in a frenzy—vacuuming, straightening, discarding, scrubbing, hauling the debris from my various workstations to the basement: stacks of books and papers all over. What would she think of my guitar hanging from a deer antler fixed to the wall? The walking stick whittled with the words "LIVE FREE OR DIE"? The piano out of tune? The desk dominating the living room where that sprawling hazel tree loomed toward the west window?

Dusting, I lifted my father's old felt hat from the piano and out of nowhere a sentence went through my mind: "My daddy got out of the way so this could happen." I was stunned. What could that mean? Surely not. But there were the words in my mind.

Driving with Perrin now, feeling my father's absence in a new way, I realized I had never known my father when his father was alive. Since Grandpa Stafford had died in 1942, and I was born in 1949, my only experience of my father was of a man independent in the world, accountable for everything, without recourse to his father. Now I was in that place and felt its strange mixture—bereft, but free. I was closer to him but I couldn't look into his face and say, "So this is the way it is?"

When we got through Seattle, and east over the crest of the mountains, and down into the Methow Valley, we had to stop and wander into the forest. It was a good world of sun, sage, wildflowers, and a quiet wind that just touched the trees. That evening, we arrived in Twisp: Isabel's House of Spirits (the liquor store); the wall mural of the souped-up car with the big blond woman and big-eyed mechanics (the auto-parts store); and the river whispering along through the trees at the edge of town.

The next morning, several dozen of us gathered upriver at the site of the first poetry road sign, my father's poem "Ask Me." There would be a formal ceremony—a reading, some commentary by the forest rangers, Curtis and Sheila, and then some time to look around. I fell into talk with writer John Straley who moonlights with the public defender's office in

Alaska. I was feeling this big emptiness for my father again, as John began telling me about a custom in the practice of law called open discovery by which the prosecutor and the defense attorney share all evidence. Every clue one discovers is given to the other. With open discovery, John said, once all details are shared, the prosecutor and the defense attorney each then creates a story from this evidence, constructs a possible narrative: maybe it went this way, maybe that.

As John spoke, I glanced beyond his shoulder at my father's words etched on the sign by the guardrail, as my nephew began to read the poem aloud:

> Some time when the river is ice ask me
> mistakes I have made.

I looked beyond the sign, where the river itself meandered through the willows and swung out wide into a riffle:

> Ask me whether
> what I have done is my life.

I thought about the accused in John's account, how evidence might lean against a life—the night in question, a knife, possible motives scattered through years of trouble. I thought about my own life following the channel of its destiny:

> . . . . . . . . . . . . . . . . . . . . .
> some have tried to help
> or to hurt: ask me what difference
> their strongest love or hate has made.

We listened to the river, and to the way pines took the wind and passed it along, to the hiss of cars in migration along the road, to the rattle of aspen gold—and in my nephew's voice, my father's poem in the world.

Later, I talked with Perrin. "Once I asked about this poem," I said. "'Daddy, what *does* the river say?' 'Nothing,' he said. 'The river doesn't say anything at all.'"

"He said that?" Perrin said. "What do *you* think the river says?"

"Oh, I think it says all kinds of things. I had always thought that. His answer bothered me. I thought he had it wrong about his own poem."

Next day, Perrin and I drove the long road home. I began to identify a new dimension of my grief. I was learning so fast I wanted to talk with my father. But all I had was my memory and his writing. That was the moment this conversation with my father began to live as a book.

The next weeks were busy with preparation for the wedding as the year before they had been with the aftermath of my father's death. It was a good full circle. The day before the wedding, Perrin and I sat on the porch above the garden and wrote our wedding vows. One line was key: "the courage to step into silence with words." I thought of "the long sleep of Asia," the silence of George in my father's *Down in My Heart,* the whole spectrum of speaking silences with my father, the silences in the last years of my own first marriage. Schooled, informed—haunted—by those silences, I entered into this writing task with fervor. We wrote a passage together: "I will share my own darkness when I am confused, and step into silence with words, no matter how awkward, when there is confusion between us."

Now it is up to us. I have been told by a literary pilgrim that my father's seven poetry road signs have since disappeared. There is only the river, the forest, the wind. This seems strangely appropriate for a poet whose early meditation "The Farm on the Great Plains" ends:

> the line will be gone
> because both ends will be home:
> no space, no birds, no farm.
>
> My self will be the plain,
> wise as winter is gray,
> pure as cold posts go
> pacing toward what I know.

My father's silences speak what the river says into my life, on and on.

After my wedding with Perrin, I continued to work through my father's papers. And then one day, as I sat at the desk typing up a new song of my own, I thought: "My father's most important work now is my work." My work? My poems, my songs, my essays and stories? What is the right balance between my work and my father's work? I've learned such a question often has an answer soon: a page turned up from my father's writing in the early 1950s. In a passage he identified in the margin as "the first novel" my father wrote: "The Father is the good self of the son" (Daily Writing, 8 April 1957).

It's clear from the context he is writing about his own father—that he, William Stafford, is the "good self" of his late father, Earl. But when I read the sentence now, what does it mean? Is my father the good self of Kim? Is the native good self of Kim that place where the spirit of the father, compact and indelible, lives on?

Earlier in the daily writing I find a poem my father wrote ten years after his own father died.

> the younger part of my face
> waiting for father
> grows more severe.
>
> On the launched earth helpless
> the way the deaf read thunder
> I learn to be homeless
> and self-possessed.
>                    —*from* "IN THE MIRROR"

With this witness from my father, I have to write this book. I am living the life my father described in his private writings as "the 2nd novel": "Dorothy feared Kim's lagging in school. I visioned him at his house, with a low sill, quiet with the summer earth, beside a great calm tree, cool as a green bubble" (Daily Writing, 2 May 1957).

In the spring of 1957, then, when I was struggling through the second grade, when I was caught by my criminal habits, my father imagined a second novel based on my future, just as he had imagined a first novel based on his own past. I would be grown up, at one with the summer earth, and governed by a great tree.

He looked forward. I look back. He never wrote the novel. In this book, in my own way, I did.

Perhaps it has taken all this roving through his papers to bring me to a new consideration of my father's silences. Throughout my life, there have been important moments when he might have spoken, but he refrained.

Sometimes, I see now, he simply did not know what to say, as helpless as anyone. Other times, I suspect he knew what he might say, but he chose to be still. He offered independence instead, letting the puzzle be mine. And finally, there have been times when he had so much to say, he let silence carry it all. This is the silence I have now that he is gone. Now that he is my good self in the world, I can say good-bye to him, and go forth: "A glance, and a world, and a hand." I have it all without a word.

And yet words come. After close to a decade of serving as my father's literary executor, I was exhausted. His work seemed to have taken over my life. How could I be a partner, a father, a writer, and my father's keeper? So one day I asked my mother, "Have I done enough for Daddy?"

"I don't know," she said. "What would Bill say?" I had no idea. But a few days later, as I stood at the wall of the endless remodel my wife and I call our home, with sheetrock trowel in hand, I had my chance. I was about to close the last seam with a swipe of finish mud, when the thought went through my mind: I should take some paper and have that conversation with my father. I should ask him my question, and maybe an answer would come. Before I could put down the trowel, however, the conversation began softly in my mind.

"Daddy, have I done enough for you?"

"Years ago," he said. I could see the sweep of his left hand before me. "Years ago you did enough."

"But how will I know," I persisted, "whether to do your work, or my work?"

"Do the thing that's most alive," he said. "Some days this might be my work; most days it will be your work. And eventually you won't be able to tell the difference."

He was not saying do what you are supposed to do. He was not even saying do what you have always wanted to do. He was saying do the thing that has its own buoyancy, "the next thing" for which my father would trade everything he had ever done.

With one stroke of the sheetrock trowel, I closed the seam.

❧

# It Was All Easy

FOUR YEARS AFTER MY FATHER DIED, Perrin and I had a child, and we gave him two first names: William Guthrie. We call him Guthrie, and we play him Woody Guthrie tunes to start him right. But there is also "William"—the grandfather he never met, a legacy.

One day I put young Guthrie into the backpack, grabbed my hat and stick, and we went for a walk in the woods where I had played as a child. Guthrie was nine months old and just that day learning pleasure in the magnitude of his voice. As we walked the forest path, he deafened me with long-winded croon just behind my ear. He took a breath, and then he sang and sang. But as he paused to take another breath, I heard far down the canyon the winter wren with its own endless trill like water pouring and scattering song through the green of Oregon, a boundless generosity flowing through us. Then it was Guthrie's turn again, and I trudged and trembled, shaken by his glorious voice.

Forty years before, by a campfire in the Three Sisters Wilderness, we were all telling stories, and one that came to my father's mind he later made into a poem, and then into a children's book, illustrated by Debra Frasier: *The Animal That Drank Up Sound*. (This is the poem my father had read in Tehran, where the students were amazed he could so directly criticize the State.) In the story, when a hungry creature swallows all the sounds of the world into itself, the world starves for sound. Who can save us from that silence? It is a cricket who comes out of hiding, and with one little cry restores the world.

> Think how deep the cricket felt, lost there
> in such a silence—the grass, the leaves, the water,
> the stilled animals all depending on such a little
> thing. But softly it tried—"Cricket!"—and back like a river
> from that one act flowed the kind of world we know,

first whisperings, then moves in the grass and leaves.

. . . . . . . . . . . . . . . . . . . . . . . . .

But somewhere a cricket waits.

It listens now, and practices at night.

My father's story came from a night by the campfire, but it also came from deep in his life, where the great darkness of World War II was the animal that drank the quiet life-songs from the world. After the war, after the bomb fell, the little voices of the land and of local human life seemed trivial to many, somehow beside the point. The voices of children—what could they say in a world so wrenched awry? Stories from a hometown isolated on the Kansas plains—what could such a small place offer? What could my father offer as he worked and waited at his isolated camp in the mountains? He could write a poem about the effects of Allied bombing in Europe, a poem hauntingly pertinent to the terrorist attacks of September 11, 2001:

> That is what happens when a city is bombed:
>> Part of that city goes away into the sky,
>> And part of that city goes into the earth.
> And that is what happens to the people when a city is bombed:
>> Part of them goes away into the sky,
>> And part of them goes into the earth.
>
> And what is left, for us, between the sky and the earth
>> is a scar.
>
> —*from* "THESE MORNINGS," 20 JANUARY 1944

Terror in the world could paralyze the heart. And yet—like the cricket in his own story, trying to say some small, essential thing—my father tried. In a world yanked into fire and fear, he kept writing his quiet poems about how to see the terror clearly—and about the bounty of the natural landscape, the clarities of childhood, the internal calm that makes affection possible, the yielding to human variety that invites a stranger to be kin. My father was sometimes criticized for his prolific utterance, his quiet teaching, his welcome of minor inspirations and insights. His words seemed plain to some, his subjects ordinary. His response was to offer as an alternative to the loud and the aggressive a quiet language of reconciliation. As he wrote in his preface to a late book of poems, *Even in Quiet Places,* "another language has grown up within the one others use." This language was the poet's truth-telling when official sources lie:

> This new language tolerates unconventional or "incorrect" talk or writing much more than it tolerates implicit discourtesy or dishonesty. The new language is the native tongue of those who grew up during that period when they found correctness used for deception, the years of official evasions and duplicity, Viet Nam and Watergate and on.
>
> Speakers of the new language are seeking not just freedom of speech but freedom in speech—their own lives embodied in language.

My father was branded a western regional, too plainspoken to match the famous and the proud. The big animal of the modern world demanded more. The war had silenced what was familiar to him, and he put words into that great cold—as the wren, the cricket, as Guthrie riding on my back.

My father's poems told us how it was to be small as a lizard in this dangerous human world—a lizard at the bomb-testing site. He was the wanderer, tapping his walking stick and whispering, poem by poem, at the bars of our cells. Having access to the natural world and to the wilderness of his own ideas through writing daily, he embraced hardship the way a wild animal does, holding to a difficult life as the essence of survival.

This all came to me as I held Guthrie in my arms. He had grown weary of the backpack, so I took him out, and we stepped off the path into the forest. We were spirits already, the leaves and their light penetrating our bodies. The wren called, and Guthrie spoke an endless word. What was better than to try, like the cricket or the wren, to be a human being?

I realize now, with wife and children, I need to go back and sort the past in order to find my way in the present, and then beyond. This was my father's necessity, to get back past World War II in order to find his own way. I have had to push through the thicket of my childhood memories in order to find my father on his own home ground.

The day before he died, my father got that call from the insurance agent who had turned up a life insurance policy, originally taken out in 1934, with the beneficiary listed as a "Mr. William Stafford"—but she had not been able to find that man. If he were the right William Stafford, she said, the policy could be worth a lot. He had never believed in life insurance, pouring all he had into present life. But under the circumstances he climbed onto his bike and went to meet her in town. It turned out he was not the right William Stafford, so he told the agent he would volunteer to be her "William Stafford" if she couldn't find the right one, and then he pedaled up the hill home. The next morning he used her question, "Are you Mr. William Stafford?" to begin the last poem he wrote.

Aside from that poem, the story haunts me. For in 1934 my father was twenty. I don't know where in Kansas he was living, whether he had some kind of toe-hold Depression job, whether he was still at home. The earliest dated letter I have reporting on his life is not until 1937.

So I go back to that last poem he wrote, the morning of the day he died, the one that begins "Are you Mr. William Stafford?" Of the many mysteries in that poem, one of the greatest I find in all his work is a single word there: "easy."

> "You don't have to
> prove anything," my mother said. "Just be ready
> for what God sends." I listened and put my hand
> out in the sun again. It was all easy.
>
> Well, it was yesterday. And the sun came,
> Why
> It came.

I love that strange disintegration at the end, the words free of the customary dress of a sentence, of punctuation: the sun came, / Why / It came." That closing sequence feels to me like the last photograph taken by Edward Weston—the stones at Point Lobos where he had made so many tightly designed images, but in the last they seem to drift apart.

But "It was all easy"—? His life was not *all* easy. He was sent into internal exile by his country, he kept alive a tremendous sense of responsibility, and privately he punished himself for failing to fulfill his sense of right, as in that other poem from his last days:

> It's heavy to drag, this big sack of what
> you should have done. . . .

What can this mean, then—"It was all easy"? There were some things that were not only difficult—for him they were impossible. He kept a hard distance now and then, yet he was as kind a father as I could have wished. He bickered with our mother sometimes, yet when my work as executor sent me through his office, on my knees I found something at the back of the bottom file drawer—the place one might hide a dark secret. What I found instead will always be a landmark for me. There, tied together with cotton string, was a bundle about the size of a pale blue brick. They were the letters from my mother in their earliest years together, the 1940s, which he had carried, secretly, through every move they made. She'd never seen them. Did she have his? Well, no. Things get away.

The last poem sums up for me his sense of the predicament of being human. He was denied certainty, but blessed with a sense of engagement with what comes. In a poem he had written thirty years earlier, about the death of his own father, my father uses similar language:

> He picks up what he thinks is
> a road map, and it is
> his death: he holds it easily, and
> nothing can take it from his firm hand.
> —*from* "MY FATHER: OCTOBER 1942"

This time it is "easily"—the certainty of the ready and the wise. My father was, for all his reading and writing, a man of action accepting the conditions that come when something must be done, must be understood, must be left behind. One translation of "easy" might be *I survived the hardest things—and I stayed true to who I am.* Another might be *I look back at what I did, and didn't do, and can say, yes, that is my story.* Or simply *I have the inescapable independence of a seeker—departing*:

> You want to look at people and then look away. That is such a luxury to me. I first learned it from an old wolf pacing its cage. Just look at someone, then look away. A smooth look. A calm departure. Easy. Flowing on.
>
> —DAILY WRITING, 31 JANUARY 1991

Part of what was easy for my father: the wild engagement of writing. As he said when he received the National Book Award in New York in 1963,

> At the moment of writing, when one of those fortunate strokes of composition takes place, the poet does sometimes feel that he is accomplishing an exhilarating, a wonderful, and stupendous job; he glimpses at such times how it might be to overwhelm the universe by rightness, to do something peculiarly difficult to such a perfect pitch that something like a revelation comes. For that instant, conceiving is knowing; the secret life in language reveals the very self of things.

This work was easy *because* the distances, silences, and times of darkness in my father's life cast a bold light on creation. This light was crucial, even when it shone on something as slight as a poem, as he goes on to say:

> It is awkward for the poet in our time to own up to such a grandiose feeling, and the feeling may not last long, nor make much lasting impression. But it is at the heart of the chore of creating. . . . He has to be willing to stay lost until what he finds—or what finds him—has the validity that the instant (with him as its sole representative) can recognize. At that moment he is transported, not because he wants to be but because he can't help it. Out of the wilderness of possibility comes a vine without a name, and his poem is growing with it.

What thread did my father leave behind? What is that vine for us? In his informal will he asked forgiveness of "those I have hurt in going my own way." Did he succeed in releasing us to go our own ways?

I think of the many readers I have met who report being accompanied by my father's words as by an understanding friend. Architects, lawyers, teachers, peace-workers, musicians, and children write me, or take me aside at programs to tell me how certain poems give them guidance and challenge. His vine is growing with them.

And in the family, how do we go our own ways now? I think of my mother, easily social with a wide variety of friends. She is the life of the party in many settings where my father could not have been so comfortable. I think of my sister Kit, living the country life our father always imagined for himself—with her workshop, her horse, and her husband the trainer of horses, her confident ways in teaching children, and her happy dogs that greet you in our father's own way, welcome without restraint. I think of sister Barbara on a recent journey to Turkey, where she found herself on a hill beside a sun-filled pine, and would not come down no matter how her friends, calling to her from below, might demand or beg. She had to stay there with the tree, and later to paint it, filled with light. Our father would have understood. I think of daughter Rosie away at college, confessing in halting words to me long-distance: "Dad, I never thought this would happen . . . I don't know how to explain . . . It's just that, well, I think I might be an English major." She will accomplish anything she may choose. I think of young Guthrie, when he was three, in a pack on my back in the high wilderness, telling me a story:

> When I was alone and I didn't have friends and didn't have a mama and papa, when I was little I would get down on the ground and get a whole bunch of ferns with a wheelbarrow and sleep really cozy, and in the morning the whole world looked different. And I went home, and my papa said, "He is the one who made the world different." And I went back to the forest and went to sleep and when I woke up, the world was like it was before. Now you think about that.

I think of my brother's spirit, in the high country, listening along in silence for words like those.

When I visited my daughter Rosie, at her college in far-off L.A., she showed me the pine tree that had saved her. It was a rangy "Digger Pine" in front of the library. At a low point, she told me, when all seemed wrong, and her life far from what she wanted, she had come one night to stand beside this tree, and gradually she came back to herself. Her witness to me was like a poem of his: a true account of the darkness, then the companionship of simple things, then the "easy" recovery of the good.

My father taught his family and his readers to "make the world different" in the manner of a poem, but with a life. The first step in the direction of the soul's inclination can be clear, and the rest is "easy," though there may be hardship. Stern hardship, opposition, and even tragedy, but also clear direction. By such a compass, perennially available to the seeker, all our lives have what William Stafford would call "bonus"—a sense of treasure beyond logic or calculation. Strangely, the gift he most wanted to give us was not connection, but independence.

### Father and Son

No sound—a spell—on, on out
where the wind went, our kite sent back
its thrill along the string that
sagged but sang and said, "I'm here!
I'm here!"—till broke somewhere,
gone years ago, but sailed forever clear
of earth. I hold—whatever tugs
the other end—I hold that string.

My father's poems will travel on their own. When friends commiserate with me about my father's passing, I often find myself saying to them, "Well, yes, he's gone, but he *did* leave word." His poems paper the walls of our lives. Like Poe's "purloined letter," they may be overlooked because they are so close. Do we wish to speak with him, to question him about hard things, to ask for guidance, solace, new perspective? The script for any conversation, peppered with rich intervals of silence, is right there, line by line: ". . . don't ever let go of the thread."

His poems will speak to us and travel beyond us. I know this because many stories come back to me—the man so poor his wife typed him a copy of my father's book she had checked out from the library. The woman whose teacher in New York told her, "You like poetry. You should move to Oregon. William Stafford lives there." The backwoods guide of Charles Kuralt setting down his paddle in the boundary waters to take from his wallet my father's poem "At the Un-National Monument along the Canadian Border" and to read it aloud in the wilderness:

This is the field where the battle did not happen,
where the unknown soldier did not die.
This is the field where grass joined hands,
where no monument stands,
and the only heroic thing is the sky.
. . . . . . . . . . . . . . . . . . .

"I always read this poem," the guide said, "when I get to the border." In brass letters set in a sinuous pattern across the floor of a Portland building, my father's poem "Climbing along the River" reminds everyone: "Willows never forget how it feels / to be young." I even heard that Oprah Winfrey read my father's poem "A Ritual to Read to Each Other" to close her special program about our national puzzle and anguish—students killing students in school.

And many strangers have told me, "I only met your father once, but he said something I will never forget. . . ." He had a way of leveling with people he met on the road, and offering the kind of direct advice that was rare at home. In one instance, at a memorial reading in the Bay Area following my father's death, I was told:

> I only met your father once—at a party after his reading. I was a student then, and we had a small child at home. When I got a moment with your father at the party, I wanted to talk to him about my writing, but we started talking about our children instead. And then I had to leave the party, get home early and help. When I turned to go, your father looked at me, raised his finger as if to lecture me, and said, "Remember: a light touch with that little one." He was most definite about it, as if he had known me for a long time. I thought of that sentence probably a thousand times, all through our son's growing up. And we still love each other. I think it's because of what your father said.

My father's poems will go forth. His fierce search for truth, gently taught, will travel among the susceptible. And I will go forth, blessed by his light touch on my shoulder.

# Epilogue

W<small>E HAVE PULLED GUTHRIE'S</small> first bike out of the car—his favorite red, with training wheels. He climbs on. For a moment, he stands tall on the pedals, his fingers tight around the handlebars, and then slowly he leans forward and begins to move. A shout from his cousins, the open road ahead, and he will go forever. As he gathers speed, I take my hand from his shoulder.

"Turn around and come back to mama!" Perrin's voice. He turns sharp left, and the bike goes down. I run to scoop him up. He gives not a whimper, but writhes to get out of my arms and back to the bike. I turn him loose.

I can't remember the last time I picked up Rosie. Her departure from childhood passed when I wasn't looking. In the early days I would carry her, and she would fall asleep in my arms. Then one day she was too big. She grew tall, and now she is far away. When I hold Guthrie, I remember how it was. But his time will come as well. Then I will only have the resonance in my body of my father carrying me. When did that happen for the last time? In the heart of my father, maybe the last time came as he wrote in the early morning two weeks after I married, at twenty, and left home for good. Reticent, often silent at emotional times, and sometimes distant, he yet lived by the kind of deep connection that filled his writing. At last, because he is gone, I know his dream:

> In my dream I carried a baby, the second—I knew—of my two children. He liked to be carried, and I sheltered him with some kind of covering. When I held him up, for fun, he liked it. We kissed, the two of us, and he said, "Who gave," meaning who was the generous one, and I said, "You did—because I value it more."
> —D<small>AILY</small> W<small>RITING</small>, 13 S<small>EPTEMBER</small> 1970

293

# *Acknowledgments*

I HOPE OTHERS WILL WRITE accounts of my father—particularly my mother and my sisters who knew him in ways I never could. Sharing stories we have held in common, and some of my own, I have tried to represent my memory of a mysterious and evocative man. For my errors, I apologize; for the chance to try what I hope others may forgive, I am grateful. And I am grateful for what I learned of our father from the life of my brother.

I have had the fine luck to engage my friend Diane McDevitt to help manage the archive of my father's work, and for help on my journey with this material. And I've had the fortune to work with a gifted scholar and editor, Paul Merchant, who directs the archive. Paul has helped me to track down pertinent texts and has provided detailed help throughout this book's development. As Diane has said to me, "We live in a collaborative time. It takes more than one person to do the best work."

I am grateful to the Graduate School of Lewis & Clark College for a sabbatical that helped me write this book.

In addition, friends and writers from across the country have been generous with their time when we asked for help: Robert Bly, Marvin Bell, Jim Hepworth, Jim Heynen, Fred Marchant, Naomi Shihab Nye, Linda Pastan, Jerry Ramsey, Vincent and Patty Wixon, and many others. In the archive itself, I'm grateful for the work of volunteers Loretta Johnson, Sam Jordan, Abel Kloster, Jill Teasley, and Emily Teitsworth. All this help has allowed me to follow my own obsessions among the papers, to make the connections this book required.

Thanks to the editors of the following publications where some passages from this book first appeared, often in different form: *Hungry Mind Review* (Fall 1993); *A View from the Loft* (Spring 1994); *edge walking the western rim,* edited by Mayami Tsutakawa (Seattle: Sasquatch Books, 1994); *Even in Quiet Places,* by William Stafford (Lewiston, Idaho: Confluence Press, 1996); *Down in My Heart,* by William Stafford (reprinted

Corvallis, Oregon: Oregon State University Press, 1998); *The Quarterly* of the National Writing Project (summer 1998); *Orion* (Summer 1998); *Teaching for Justice in the Social Studies Classroom,* edited by Ruth Hubbard and Andra Makler (Portsmouth, New Hampshire, 2000). Thanks also to Graywolf and other independent presses that first published some of the William Stafford poems quoted in this book.

I am grateful to Fiona McCrae, Jeff Shotts, Anne Czarniecki, and all my friends at Graywolf Press for their devotion to my father's work, and their welcome and help as this book came into being.

Finally, it is my wife Perrin who most encouraged me to stay with this project. She never knew my father; he would have been delighted to know her. That I know.

William Stafford was born in Hutchinson, Kansas, in 1914. During the 1930s, he worked as a laborer in oil refineries, and in the fields. He received a B.A. and an M.A. from the University of Kansas at Lawrence and, in 1954, a Ph.D. from the University of Iowa. During the Second World War, he was a conscientious objector and fought forest fires and planted trees in the Civilian Public Service camps of Arkansas and California, an experience he described in his first book, *Down in My Heart.* In 1944, he married Dorothy Hope Frantz, and they had four children. Stafford published over sixty books of poetry and prose, including *Traveling through the Dark,* which won the National Book Award in 1963. A widely respected teacher, he traveled throughout the world to give readings and conduct writing workshops, and served as Consultant to the Library of Congress in 1970. William Stafford taught at Lewis & Clark College for over thirty years, and died at his home in Lake Oswego, Oregon, on August 28, 1993.

Kim Stafford is the founding director of the Northwest Writing Institute at Lewis & Clark College, where he began teaching in 1979, the summer his father retired. He holds a Ph.D. in medieval literature from the University of Oregon, and is the author of a dozen books of poetry and prose. He has worked as an oral historian, letterpress printer, photographer, teacher, and as the literary executor of the Estate of William Stafford. For his book, *Having Everything Right,* he won a citation for excellence from the Western States Book Awards. He lives in Portland, Oregon, with his wife and children.

The text of this book has been set in Adobe Garamond,
a typeface drawn by Robert Slimbach and based on
type cut by Claude Garamond in the sixteenth century.
Book design by Wendy Holdman.
Composition by Stanton Publication Services, Inc., St. Paul, Minnesota.
Manufactured by Friesens on acid-free paper.

Graywolf Press is a not-for-profit, independent press. The books we publish include poetry, literary fiction, essays, and cultural criticism. We are less interested in best-sellers than in talented writers who display a freshness of voice coupled with a distinct vision. We believe these are the very qualities essential to shape a vital and diverse culture.

Thankfully, many of our readers feel the same way. They have shown this through their desire to buy books by Graywolf writers; they have told us this themselves through their e-mail notes and at author events; and they have reinforced their commitment by contributing financial support, in small amounts and in large amounts, and joining the "Friends of Graywolf."

If you enjoyed this book and wish to learn more about Graywolf Press, we invite you to ask your bookseller or librarian about further Graywolf titles; or to contact us for a free catalog; or to visit our award-winning web site that features information about our forthcoming books.

We would also like to invite you to consider joining the hundreds of individuals who are already "Friends of Graywolf" by contributing to our membership program. Individual donations of any size are significant to us: they tell us that you believe that the kind of publishing we do *matters*. Our web site gives you many more details about the benefits you will enjoy as a "Friend of Graywolf"; but if you do not have online access, we urge you to contact us for a copy of our membership brochure.

## www.graywolfpress.org

Graywolf Press
2402 University Avenue, Suite 203
Saint Paul, MN 55114
Phone: (651) 641-0077
Fax: (651) 641-0036
E-mail: wolves@graywolfpress.org

US $16.00/CAN $26.95

**Winner of the Pacific Northwest Bookseller's Association Award**

**A Book Sense 76 Selection**

"A masterful memoir . . . *Early Morning* would be a rare and exceptional book in any season, any year. Coming as it does in a time of national crisis, it is needed." —*BLOOMSBURY REVIEW*

"*Early Morning* lovingly examines William's life and legacy from multiple perspectives—as poet, teacher, pacifist, and father—with a discernment and honesty equal to the task of bringing such a formidably complex and sometimes contradictory character to life on the page. On one level a treasury of the elder Stafford's reflections and aphorisms enriched by the younger one's insightful recollections, *Early Morning* also unforgettably portrays a complicated father-son relationship."—*RUMINATOR REVIEW*

"[A] remarkable tribute."—*BOOKLIST,* **starred review**

"As a book written by a son warily loving an enigmatic, elusive father, this is a masterpiece."—*ROBERT BLY*

William Stafford was born in Kansas in 1914, and published over fifty books of poetry and prose. In 1963 he received the National Book Award for *Traveling through the Dark.*

Kim Stafford is the director of the Northwest Writing Institute at Lewis & Clark College in Oregon.

Cover design: Christa Schoenbrodt, Studio Haus
Cover photograph of William Stafford: Christopher Ritter

ISBN 1-55597-389-2

51600

9 781555 973896

**GRAYWOLF PRESS**
Saint Paul, Minnesota

www.graywolfpress.org